WATCHSTANDING GUIDE
FOR THE MERCHANT OFFICER

ARRIVAL AT THE PILOT STATION

WATCHSTANDING GUIDE

FOR THE MERCHANT OFFICER

Third Edition

ROBERT J. MEURN
Master Mariner

CORNELL MARITIME PRESS
Centreville, Maryland

Published by Schiffer Publishing, Ltd. 2014

Watchstanding Guide for the Merchant Officer, Third Edition
Copyright © 2014 by Robert J. Meurn

Material from *Watchstanding Guide for the Merchant Officer,* First and Second
Editions were originally published by Cornell Maritime Press, in 1990 and 2008.

Copyright © 1990 and 2008 by Cornell Maritime Press

Library of Congress Control Number: 2014934472

Type set in Times

ISBN: 978-0-87033-631-7
Printed in China
First edition, 1990; Second edition, 2008; Third edition, 2014

Published by Schiffer Publishing, Ltd.
4880 Lower Valley Road
Atglen, PA 19310
Phone: (610) 593-1777; Fax: (610) 593-2002
E-mail: Info@schifferbooks.com

For our complete selection of fine books on this and related subjects, please visit our
website at www.schifferbooks.com. You may also write for a free catalog.

This book may be purchased from the publisher. Please try your bookstore first.

We are always looking for people to write books on new and related subjects. If you
have an idea for a book, please contact us at proposals@schifferbooks.com.

Schiffer Publishing's titles are available at special discounts for bulk purchases for
sales promotions or premiums. Special editions, including personalized covers,
corporate imprints, and excerpts can be created in large quantities for special needs.
For more information, contact the publisher.

Dedicated in affectionate remembrance of Captain Piero Calamai (1898–1972), master of the *Andrea Doria*, and David A. Bright (1957–2006), for his relentless search for the truth and devotion to the *Andrea Doria* legacy.

Robert J. Meurn

Contents

Figures, viii

Tables, xii

Foreword, xiii

Preface, xiv

1 Watchstanding Responsibilities, Preparing for and Standing the Watch, 3

2 Bridge Equipment, 20

3 Voyage Planning and Recordkeeping, 40

4 Compliance with the Rules of the Road, 73

5 Shipboard Emergencies and Special Situations, 91

6 Shiphandling for the Watch Officer, 101

7 Arrivals and Departures, 127

8 Bridge Simulation Training, 149

9 Case Studies, 167

Appendices

A Excerpts from the Standards on Training, Certification and Watchkeeping for Seafarers, 1978, 194

B M/V *Capella* Bridge Standing Orders, 204

Index, 218

About the Author, 222

Figures

1-1. Checking compasses, 6
1-2. Instructing lookout, 7
1-3. Observing sun line or meridian altitude, 9
1-4. Determining celestial fix, 9
2-1. How AIS works (Courtesy of USCG), 22
2-2. Automatic pilot, 23
2-3. Author supervising changeover from auto to hand steering aboard TS *Texas Clipper* during summer cruise of 1978, 24
2-4. Doppler speed log, 26
2-5. ECDIS display on CAORF Bridge Simulator at USMMA, Kings Point, New York, 27
2-6. ECHO sounder with settings for feet, fathoms, or meters, indicated for bow or stern and means for setting a shallow alarm unit, 30
2-7. DB10 radar found aboard APL vessels and on the CAORF Bridge Simulator at USMMA, Kings Point, New York, 32
2-8. Rate of turn indicator, 34
2-9. Rudder angle indicator, 35
2-10. Marine GPS (Courtesy of Johnny Appleseed GPS), 36
2-11. VHF radio-telephone, 38
3-1. Main causes of navigation casualty (Courtesy of Captain Richard Beadon), 41
3-2. Vessel on course 110° (T), 48
3-3. Indexing on twelve-mile range scale, 479
3-4. Parallel index to port; PPI north up, gyro stabilized, radar echo between ship head and PI, 50
3-5. Parallel index to starboard; PPI north up, gyro stabilize, radar echo between ship head and PI, 50
3-6. Parallel index to starboard; PPI north up, gyro stabilize, radar echo outside of PI, 50
3-7. Parallel index to port; PPI north up, gyro stabilized, radar echo outside of PI, 50
3-8. Planned approach to an SBM (Courtesy of the College of Maritime Studies, Warsash, U.K.), 51
3-9. Cross-index range (CIR) of 1.86 miles from Gusong Tower (Courtesy of the College of Maritime Studies, Warsash, U.K.), 52
3-10. CIR of 1.86 miles on reflection plotter (Courtesy of the College of Maritime Studies, Warsash, U.K.), 53
3-11. Gusong Tower radar echo in position A on reflection plotter (Courtesy of the College of Maritime Studies, Warsash, U.K.), 53

3-12. Second parallel index line to 067° (T) track from Gusong Tower of 0.38 mile (Courtesy of the College of Maritime Studies, Warsash, U.K.), 54

3-13. Track of vessel changing course from 009° (T) to 067° (T) (Courtesy of the College of Maritime Studies, Warsash, U.K.), 55

3-14. Plotted positions joined in a smooth curve (Courtesy of the College of Maritime Studies, Warsash, U.K.), 56

3-15. Intended maneuver marked (Courtesy of the College of Maritime Studies, Warsash, U.K.), 56

3-16a, b. Determining course and speed to make good a desired track (Courtesy of Dutton's Navigation and Piloting), 58–59

3-17. Passage plan (Courtesy of EXXON), 61

3-18. Passage plan developed by Captain Richard Beadon for the cadet bridge watchkeeping course on the CAORF simulator at the USMMA, 62

3-19. Passage plan for arrival Limon Bay (Cristóbal), Panama, 63

3-20. Chart extract from DMA (Puerto Cristóbal) with track and notations, 64–65

3-21. Notations in conning or bridge notebook for arrival Limon Bay (Cristóbal), 66

3-22. Navigation Record Log, 68

3-23. Log entry for arrival Limon Bay (Cristóbal), Panama, 72

4-1a. The four states in a collision situation (Courtesy of A. N. Cockroft and J. N. F. Lameijer from *Guide to Collision Regulations*), 80

4-1b. In extremis—action required by both vessels (Courtesy of CAORF), 80

4-2. Violation of rules 16 and 17 (Courtesy of Mariner's Weather Log, Sept. 1978), 82

4-3. Assessment, action, and close-quarters situation sectors of the twelve-mile range scale (Courtesy of A.N. Cockroft and J. N. F. Lameijer from *Guide to Collision Regulations*), 84

4-4. Calling a vessel on your starboard bow, 86

4-5. Calling a vessel on your port bow, 86

4-6. Alidade and Azimuth Circle for taking visual bearings, 88

5-1. Hypothermia survival chart, 96

6-1. Turning circle (Courtesy of U.S. Naval Amphibious School, Little Creek, Virginia), 103

6-2. *Above*. A view from the bridge as a 150,000-ton tanker collides with an oncoming wave. *Below*. Head-on poundings by the sea can cause damage to the vessel that may necessitate reducing rpms (Courtesy of the *San Francisco Examiner*), 106

6-3. Formation of ice on the vessel's superstructure will affect the stability, 107

6-4. Sea state photographs for determining wind speed from the Beaufort Wind Force Scale (Courtesy of NOAA, adapted from their May 1987 chart), 108–111

6-5. Meteorological events by month (Adapted from *Ocean Routes*, March 1985. Used by permission), 112

6-6. Heavy weather report (Courtesy of EXXON), 114

6-7. Convoy operations (Courtesy of MEBA District Two), 117

6-8. Standard grid formation used in convoy exercises for vessels assigned to Maritime Pre-Position Squadron TWO in Diego Garcia (distance between ships is 2,000 yards), 117

6-9. Circular formation (form 70) used in convoy exercises for vessels assigned to Maritime Pre-Position Squadron TWO in Diego Garcia, 118

6-10. Underway replenishment, coast-in method (Courtesy of U. S. Naval Amphibious School, Little Creek, Virginia), 119

7-1. Master/pilot information exchange form, 132

7-2. Arrival checklist, 133

7-3. Pre-departure gear checklist, 142

7-4. Bridge sailing or shifting check off, 145

7-5. MV *President F. D. Roosevelt* Pre-Arrival/Departure Gear Test. (Courtesy of American President Lines), 146–147

7-6. Departure checklist—factors for a watch officer to consider, 147

8-1. Major CAORF subsystems, 152

8-2. *Above*. CAORF bridge (port view) *Below*. CAORF bridge (starboard view), 153

8-3. CAORF chart desk with chart, passage plan navigation record log, conning notebook, change of watch check off, and VHF log. Above the chart desk, from left to right, Navtex, fathometer, LORAN, and GPS, 154

8-4. The debrief, 156

8-5. Cadet watch team grading sheet, 157

8-6. Bird's-eye view of observation/control station, 159

8-7. Monitoring and communications capabilities, 161

8-8. Captain Robert J. Meurn Debrief Room, 163

9-1. MV *Stockholm* ramming into the SS *Andrea Doria* on July 25, 1956 (Courtesy of J.C. Carrothers and U. S. Naval Institute), 170

9-2a, b. MV *Stockholm* / SS *Andrea Doria* (Courtesy of Mariner's Museum, Newport News, VA), 171

9-2c. Approaches of the MV *Stockholm* and the SS *Andrea Doria* (Courtesy of J. C. Carrothers and U.S. Naval Institute), 172

9-3. The *Andrea Doria's* 2,500 mph "S" turn, 173

9-4. The long 3 minute turn, 174

9-5. Collision point in relation to pivotal point of the *Andrea Doria*, 174

9-6. The fatal error made by the watch officer on the MV *Stockholm* (Courtesy of J. C. Carrothers and Titanic Historical Society), 178

9-7. The 5,881-ton *Hellenic Carrier* is sailing toward Norfolk, still in fog, with a large hole in her side after a collision with the 26,406-ton *Lash Atlantico* while about twenty-five miles southeast of Cape Henry (U. S. Coast Guard photo, courtesy of *Mariners Weather Log*, May–June 1981), 180

9-8a. *Ziemia Lodzka* southbound approaching the northeast-bound *Vertigo* three minutes prior to collision. Vessels were 1.5 miles apart (Courtesy of Danish Maritime Authority [DMA] report of 24 April 2006), 188

9-8b. Thirty seconds prior to the collision. The *Ziemia Lodzka's* rudder is full to starboard and the *Vertigo's* rudder is port 30° (Courtesy of DMA report of 24 April 2006), 188

9-9. Visual view of the *Ziemia Lodzka* from *Vertigo* at 00:32:00, four minutes prior to the collision. Note masthead light to right of the range light and green side light showing starboard side of *Ziemia Lodzka* (Courtesy of CAORF Simulator, USMMA, Kings Point, New York), 189

9-10a. Visual view of *Ziemia Lodzka* at 00:33 (three minutes prior to the collision, drifting port to starboard across the *Vertigo's* bow) (Courtesy of CAORF, USMMA, Kings Point, New York), 189

9-10b. Bird's-eye view of both vessels at 00:33:03. CPA is now 0.22 miles in 2.15 minutes if both vessels maintain their course and speed (Courtesy of CAORF, USMMA, Kings Point, New York), 190

9-11. Bird's-eye view of both vessels at 00:34, two minutes prior to the collision. According to DMA Report, page 15, the *Ziemia Lodzka* begins to alter course to starboard at 00:33:55, and the *Vertigo* begins to alter course to port in compliance with Rule 17(a)(ii) (Courtesy of CAORF, USMMA, Kings Point, New York), 190

9-12a. Bird's-eye view of collision at 00:36 at latitude 55°-12.38' north and longitude 11°-05.3' east (Courtesy of CAORF, USMMA, Kings Point, New York), 191

9-12b. *Vertigo* foundered at eleven meters depth of water (Courtesy of DMA Report of 24 April 2006), 191

9-13. Proposed air cushion merchant ship. The 420-foot vessel would have a beam of 140 feet and could cruise at eighty knots (Courtesy of Bell Aero-systems and Thomas C. Gillmer from *Modern Ship Design*, Annapolis, MD: Naval Institute Press), 192

Tables

1-1. Leading Primary Causes of U.S. Ship Collisions from 1970 through 1979, 16
1-2. Changing of watch check off, 18
1-3. Maersk line checklist for change of watch, 19
8-1. USMMA bridge watchstanding course, 155
8-2. Levels of normal manning, 165
9-1. Correlation of testimony from M/V *Stockholm* to its course recorder, 178

Foreword

The turbulent world of nautical education and training heaps academic degrees upon its citizens and prepares them for service not only afloat but ashore. The deck officers of today's merchant fleets are much more educated in matters maritime and trained to a higher level than their counterparts of yesterday.

In this climate of advancement it is easy to lose sight of some fundamental aspects of the honorable profession of those who go down to the sea in ships. One of the more important of these is bridge watchstanding, or keeping a safe navigational watch, as my colleagues across the Atlantic say. With some exceptions, training programs generally do not include a segment that deals specifically with watchkeeping. This guide, dedicated solely to watchstanding at sea, is rare and long overdue.

As a former team member of the Ship Simulation Centre of the College of Maritime Studies at Warsash, Southampton, United Kingdom, I was involved in developing and implementing ship simulator-based bridge watchkeeping preparatory courses for the international maritime community. My interest in, and admiration for, Captain Meurn's book is of a personal nature.

The nine chapters of this book provide all the aspects of watchkeeping, including the requirements and recommendations of the International Maritime Organization. In addition, Captain Meurn has devoted chapters to voyage planning and bridge simulation. The former deals with the requirements of appraisal, planning, monitoring, and executing a navigational passage, and the latter summarizes ship simulation establishments worldwide that provide bridge watchstanding courses.

I also am delighted to see that Captain Meurn has not limited the technical vocabulary of the book to that used in the United States. Where applicable, he has included terms used on both sides of the Atlantic. His book should have an international appeal and be an essential part of any watchkeeper's library—and preferably kept very close at hand.

Richard G. Beadon

Preface

It is easy to lose sight of some fundamental aspects of the honorable profession of those who go down to the sea in ships. One of the most important of these is bridge watchstanding.

This book was written to help transition a cadet's or able-bodied seaman's progression to an officer-in-charge of a watch aboard a merchant vessel. An observer on the bridge of a merchant vessel can critique the performance of a watch officer (OOW) and visualize how much better he or she could stand the watch. It is only upon assuming the first watch at sea, with the license on the line, that the officer realizes the full weight of the responsibility for the safe navigation of the vessel. At the very least, the officer of the watch should be ready to comply with the requirements of the Standards of Training, Certification and Watchkeeping for Seafarers (STCW 1978), found in appendix A of this book.

Upon assuming my first watch aboard a C2 cargo vessel, I quickly achieved the turnover when the course was repeated as the second mate departed the wheelhouse. With aids of navigation flashing and many contacts, I moved to the radar where I had observed many watch officers stand their watch. The vessel was en route from New York to Philadelphia and my 2000-2400 watch commenced with the vessel's position unknown and the status of contacts uncertain. I completed a rapid radar plot on five active contacts and determined two to be on steady bearing and decreasing range. Being unfamiliar with the layout of the bridge, and having forgotten my flashlight, I searched with a cigarette lighter for the sound-powered phone to call the master. By now the helmsman was amused and did not even think of helping the brand-new third mate.

After writing all the contact information on a piece of paper illuminated by the lighter, I placed my call. During my long conversation about unnecessary bearings and ranges, the piece of paper caught fire. My screams of pain convinced the captain he was needed on the bridge. Without looking at the radar or my plots, the captain went directly to the starboard bridge wing and took several visual bearings. He then took the conn and extricated the vessel from a precarious meeting-and-crossing situation.

After the contacts cleared, the captain asked me where was the vessel's position. When I answered, "I don't know," he asked about the relieving process and whether I had read the standing orders or signed the night orders. After another negative answer I received a reprimand, which made quite an impression on me at the tender age of twenty-one. I have stood many watches since then, but that first watch made me realize something was missing in my preparation for standing watch. The solution for a new officer, I feel, is to achieve more experience as an acting watch officer, particularly during arrivals and departures, to spend time on a bridge simulator, and to study the guidelines in this book.

Watchstanding Guide for the Merchant Officer, Third Edition should not only help the new watch officer but refresh experienced mates. The safe navigation of the vessel relies on the ship's "team"—the master, the navigator, and the watch officer. This book provides an understanding of safe navigation so all members and potential members of a ship's team can work as a unit in observing the three Cs of safe navigation: communication, cooperation, and coordination. In addition, the six Ps are stressed: proper prior planning prevents poor performance.

I draw on many mariners experiences at sea for this book. I am extremely grateful for their contributions and to those authors who granted permission to quote passages from their books and symposium papers.

Captain Alexander Barinov read every page of the first edition, and his advice and recommendations were crucial in updating this book. Because of his experience as a master mariner and Director of Simulator Operations in St. Petersburg, Russia, his contribution was invaluable and gratefully acknowledged.

Captain George Sandberg, Master Mariner, Professor, and former head of Marine Transportation at the U.S. Merchant Marine Academy (USMMA) read every page and over the past years provided valuable insight and advice that is incorporated throughout this book.

Mr. Harold M. Kingsley, a maritime attorney in New York, provided vital legal advice in the interpretation of the collision regulations found in chapter four and especially in regard to the *Vertigo/Ziemia Lodzka* collision found in chapter nine.

Organizations providing necessary material for the book include the International Maritime Organization (IMO), International Marine Simulator Forum (IMSF), International Maritime Lecturers Association (IMLA), Department of Trade of the United Kingdom, International Chamber of Shipping, United States Coast Guard (USCG), the Maritime Academy Simulator Committee (MASC), and the Maritime Administration.

The assistance of Marilyn Hetsel, Manager of Computer Aided Operations Research Facility (CAORF) Simulator Operations, USMMA, was instrumental in preparing both the 2nd and this edition and is deeply appreciated. And to my wife, Christine, who typed, edited and made recommendations for the original and revised manuscripts for my four books I am deeply indebted. Her constant support and sacrifice for 36 years went beyond the responsibilities of a wife and for which I will always be eternally grateful.

WATCHSTANDING GUIDE
FOR THE MERCHANT OFFICER
Third Edition

CHAPTER ONE

Watchstanding Responsibilities, Preparing for and Standing the Watch

THE term watch, according to the dictionary, means to "look attentively or carefully." Watch also means a "period of time for guarding." In nautical use, it is the time of duty (usually four hours) of one part (usually a third) of a ship's crew. Synonyms for watch include watchful, vigilant, and alert. Watchful suggests paying close attention and observing carefully or keeping careful guard. Vigilant means constantly and keenly watchful for a definite reason or purpose, especially to see and avoid danger. Alert emphasizes being wide-awake and ready to meet what comes.

The officer of the watch is the master's representative, and the OOW's responsibility is the safe navigation of the ship. The OWW must be familiar with the handling characteristics of the vessel and ensure compliance with all regulations for preventing collisions at sea. In addition, the watch officer must ensure an efficient lookout is maintained. On vessels with a separate chart room, the OOW, before visiting that room in the performance of navigational duties, should make sure that it is safe and an efficient lookout is being maintained. Recent developments in the design of merchant ships have greatly reduced the number of crew members. This means that the role of the watchstander is becoming more one of surveillance and data handling.

WATCHKEEPING

Investigations into casualties involving collisions and groundings frequently reveal that the main contributing factor has been the failure to maintain an adequate navigational watch. Regulations and resolutions agreed upon by representatives to the International Maritime Organization (IMO) are intended to assist seafarers in fulfilling their watchkeeping duties properly. To form a basis for the discussion of watch keeping in this book, extracts from the International Convention on Standards of Training, Certification and Watchkeeping for Seafarers, 1978 (STCW 78), the most authoritative literature on the subject, are provided in appendix A. The extracts include "Basic Principles to Be Observed in Keeping a Safe Navigational Watch," "Recommendations on Operational Guidance for Officers in Charge of a Navigational Watch," and "Recommendation on Principles and Operational Guidance for Deck Officers in Charge of a Watch in Port."

In its first version, STCW 78 had little affect on the U.S. mariner because it just formalized internationally a system nearly identical to the U.S. system. The big change came in 1995, when the U.S. Coast Guard (USCG) approached the IMO and asked them to amend the convention. STCW 95 significantly changed the convention. STCW 95 did not have to be ratified like the original convention because it amended an existing convention. The amendments, however, completely rewrote enforcement related to the convention and, more importantly, created an STCW Code (similar to the USCG licensing regulations) that set stringent standards for mariners.

Unlike the original 1978 Convention, the 1995 Amendments required a separate piece of paper to certify that the mariner met the requirements. The STCW Certificate was the result. Starting February 1, 2003, all mariners had to fully comply with STCW 95.

Some mariners who only operate in U.S. waters have fewer requirements. The mariners who have licenses for 200 gross registered tons (GRT) or less, and U.S. Merchant Marine Document Z-Card holders working on Offshore Supply Vessels of 500 GRT or less have different requirements.

Deck Officers whose first day of sea service was before Aug. 1, 1998 had to take courses in:

- Basic Safety Training (BST). STCW 95 Code requires this five-day course. BST is actually four courses: Basic FireFighting, Personal Survival, Personal Safety and Social Responsibility, and Elementary First Aid. This course has to be renewed every five years or, under certain conditions, you have to prove you had at least one year of service on board vessels of 200 GRT or more within the last five years.
- Bridge Resource Management (BRM). This also is called Bridge Teamwork Management and normally is a three-day course.
- Proficiency in Survival Craft and Rescue Boats (PSC). This course is required only of deck officers who do not have an Able Seaman (AB) Unlimited, AB-Limited, AB-Special (AB-OSV will not do it!), or Lifeboatman endorsement on their Z-Cards. The requirement is really for Lifeboatman, but this endorsement is embedded in all the ABs except AB-OSV. A STCW certificate is a piece of paper that is attached to your license or Z-Card. It is separate and distinct. You can have a license or Z-Card without

getting the STCW certificate, (although you cannot get the certificate without having the license or Z-Card).

The license or Z-Card only allows you to work on inland waters. On the East and West coasts of the U.S. this means you cannot operate in the ocean. In the Gulf of Mexico the boundary line lies twelve miles offshore. Perhaps most importantly, foreign governments only recognize the STCW certificate—not your license or Z-Card.

Mariners already licensed had until February 1, 2003 to comply with the new provisions of STCW 95. If they did not convert their STCW 78 certificates to STCW 95 certificates by that date, they were treated as though they never had a license or Z-Card.

New mariners have to complete a program (not a course) to get a STCW 95 Certificate. Additional requirements exist for the license.

For new mates (Officers-in-Charge of a Navigation Watch) on vessels of GRT (500 GT ITC), as part of a USCG-approved program must:

- have seagoing service of at least one year (365 days), which includes on-board training documented in an approved training record book, or have approved seagoing service of not less than three years;
- have performed, during the seagoing service, bridge watch-keeping duties under the direct supervision (on the bridge with you) of the master, chief mate, or a navigator for a period of no less than six months; and
- complete other specified training and education as part of the USCG-approved program.

New ABs, Lifeboatman, and Ordinary Seaman part of the navigation watch (all ABs and anyone standing helm and lookout watches) on vessels of 200 GRT (500 GT ITC), as part of a USCG-approved program must have completed at least six months training and experience; special training, either pre-sea or on board ship, including an approved period of seagoing service that shall not be less than two months; and the requirements in the regulations for AB.

WATCHSTANDING TASKS

The tasks and checklist items of the watch officer can be divided into those that occur on the open sea and those that are applicable only in restricted waters. While the list that follows is not inclusive, it can be used as a guide for each condition of the watch described.

Open Sea

Changing Watch (Before Relieving)

1. Check standing and night orders and special information; acknowledge by signature.
2. Check vessel's position on chart.
3. Evaluate course line projected for duration of watch.
4. Check vessel's speed.
5. Determine if any hazardous potential exists with traffic.
6. Evaluate weather and sea conditions for danger.
7. Check running lights.
8. Check personnel assigned to watch.
9. Check compasses. (See Fig. 1-1)
10. Determine status of electronic navigational aids.
11. Determine status of very high frequency (VHF) monitoring.
12. Check course recorder.
13. Check chronometers.
14. Receive appropriate watch information and relieve mate of watch after adjusting vision for a night watch.

Fig. 1-1.
Checking compasses.
(Courtesy of
USMMA Midship's
Yearbook.)

Change of Watch (Being Relieved)

1. Verify course steered and track for duration of watch.
2. Check status of all navigational equipment.
3. Verify radar plot of traffic.
4. Verbally transfer information regarding status of vessel to relieving mate.
5. Verify that relieving mate has accepted responsibility for the watch by both mates signing the change of watch check-off sheet. (See tables 1-2 and 1-3.)
6. Enter appropriate information into ship log.

Visual Monitoring Tasks

1. Instruct lookout as to duties. (See Fig. 1-2)
2. Clean and adjust binoculars.
3. Scan horizon to detect traffic or navigational aids and verify with binoculars if necessary.
4. Determine type, aspect, and relative motion of contacts.
5. Use azimuth circle/alidade to take bearings.
6. Maintain watch on the ship's smoke, weather changes, water-tight openings, gear secured, personnel on deck, etc.

Fig. 1-2.
Instructing lookout.
(Courtesy of
USMMA Midship's
Yearbook.)

Collision Avoidance Tasks

1. Adjust and operate radar and Automated Radar Plotting Aid (ARPA).
2. Delete or erase plots of past threat contacts.
3. Monitor radar and Automatic Identification System (AIS) for contacts.
4. Monitor and verify contacts on secondary radar.
5. Receive and verify reports of visual contact (lookout).
6. Communicate with the engineering watch as appropriate.
7. Observe visual bearings of visual contacts.
8. Determine closest point of approach (CPA) and collision avoidance maneuver.
9. Communicate on VHF to threat vessel.
10. Inform master of situation and intentions.
11. Execute collision avoidance maneuver.

Navigation Tasks

1. Observe azimuth of celestial body.
2. Determine gyro error and magnetic deviation.
3. Obtain and verify position by use of satellite navigation system.
4. Compare three with dead reckoning (DR) position.
5. Determine current set and drift. Calculate vessel's speed over the ground.
6. Observe and plot sun line. Obtain altitude and intercept and verify with Global Positioning System (GPS). (See Fig. 1-3)
7. Determine time of meridian transit.
8. Observe meridian altitude. (See Fig. 1-3)
9. Determine celestial fix and verify with GPS. (See Fig. 1-4)
10. Calculate and execute appropriate course changes based on navigation fix information.
11. Determine day's run and speed.
12. Monitor radar to detect aids to navigation or other charted positions.
13. Plot radar fix.
14. Determine ETA to pilot station.
15. Use fathometer to check position.
16. Monitor navigational aids: GPS, Electronic Chart Display and Information System (ECDIS), and fathometer.
17. Introduce waypoints in satellite navigator.

Fig. 1-3.
Observing sunline
or meridian altitude.
(Courtesy of
USMMA Midship's
Yearbook.)

Fig. 1-4.
Determine
celestial fix.

Communication Tasks

1. Use sound-powered telephone/walkie talkie, public address (PA) system, etc., to call master, engine room, standby, etc.
2. Monitor channels 16, 13, and Vessel Traffic Service (VTS) channels (if required) on VHF radio-telephone.
3. Use VHF radio-telephone to initiate a safety, urgency, or distress message.
4. Receive and record broadcasts from weather forecast, USCG security, etc.
5. Interpret and reply to flag signals of other vessels.
6. Receive, record, and send flashing light message.
7. Sound ship's whistle as appropriate for maneuvers, emergency, etc.

Ship Control Tasks

1. Change steering mode from auto to manual.
2. Maneuver vessel to clear other vessels and maintain track.
3. Maneuver vessel as needed and if necessary to clear smoke (blowing tubes).
4. Reduce vessel's speed.
5. Maneuver vessel for man overboard.
6. Maneuver vessel to make lee for small boat (for example, pilot boat).

Safety/Casualty Tasks

1. Respond to man overboard emergency.
2. Respond to engine or steering failure, other emergencies.
3. Monitor vessel for loose gear, watertightness, etc.
4. Participate in lifeboat and emergency drills.
5. Respond to specific equipment alarms (for example, gyrocompass casualty).

Heavy Weather Tasks

1. Check that all movable objects on deck, ports, and deadlights have been secured where necessary.
2. Warn department heads and crew to check and secure objects below decks.
3. Inform engine room.
4. Inform master.
5. Adjust speed and course as necessary. Take on ballast.
6. Warn crew to avoid upper deck areas that are dangerous due to weather; ensure that safety lines and hand ropes have been rigged where necessary.
7. Monitor weather reports more frequently.
8. Transmit weather report.

Ice Navigation Tasks

1. Inform master.
2. Inform engine room. Keep a good lookout.
3. Adjust speed. Skirt to windward, if possible. Maintain headway.
4. Shut watertight doors as appropriate. Drain fire mains on deck.
5. Warn ship's crew to keep ice from accumulating topside.
6. Monitor appropriate broadcasts from an ice advisory service.
7. Transmit danger messages. (See International Convention for Safety of Life at Sea [SOLAS 1974] Chapter V, Regulation 2[a].)
8. Enter ice mass perpendicular to edge at slow speed. If you must collide with large chunks of ice, do it head on.

Tropical Storm Area Navigation Tasks

1. Inform master.
2. Inform engine room.
3. Adjust speed and course as necessary. Take on ballast.
6. See that movable objects on deck are checked and secured.
7. Warn department heads and crew to check and secure objects below decks and rig safety lines on deck.
8. Monitor appropriate meteorological instruments and weather reports.
9. Transmit danger message, if necessary. (See SOLAS 1974 Chapter V, Regulation 2[a].)
10. Transmit weather report.

Miscellaneous

1. Wind and compare chronometers.
2. Observe and record marine weather observations.
3. Prepare weather report.
4. Maintain conning notebook, miscellaneous logs, and records.
5. Obtain appropriate marine weather forecasts and map.

Restricted Waters

Changing Watch (Before and Upon Relief)

The changing of the watch in restricted waters includes the same tasks listed in the open-sea condition. Greater emphasis should be placed on specific information required from radar plotting for detecting traffic or aids to navigation.

Visual Monitoring Tasks

The tasks required in restricted waters for visual monitoring are identical to those for the open sea condition with the addition of the following tasks:

1. Observe and identify specific aids to navigation.
2. Be alert for local traffic.
3. Observe and plot visual lines of position for visual fix.

Collision Avoidance Tasks

Tasks noted in collision avoidance for the open sea are essentially the same as those required for restricted waters, with the addition of the need to identify the line of demarcation specified in the International Regulations for Preventing Collisions at Sea, more commonly referred to as the Collision Regulations (COLREGS).

Navigation Tasks

Tasks described in the open-sea condition also apply to coastwise or harbor approach navigation. Particular items (2, 4, 5, 10, 12, 13, 14, 15, 16, and 17) receive more emphasis in restricted waters depending on circumstances. Other tasks performed at this time are:

1. Predict zone time of sunset or sunrise for ETA at pilot station.
2. Determine ETA at berth.
3. Determine vessel's clearance with bottom at berth.
4. Predict time of sighting specific aids to navigation.

Communication Tasks

These tasks are practically identical to those noted in the open-sea condition. At the approach to a harbor, additional specific communication tasks required are:

1. Inform pilot of vessel condition upon arrival (for example, equipment status).
2. Order proper flags to be hoisted.
3. Notify vessel personnel of arrival information.
4. Place or receive calls via coast stations.

Miscellaneous Tasks

Preparing for harbor entry.

Anchoring/Docking /Undocking

1. Monitor navigation process. Assist master and pilot as required.
2. Check appropriate equipment before entering or getting underway.
3. Stand anchor watch.

PREPARING FOR AND STANDING THE WATCH

The "International Chamber of Shipping (ICS) Navigation Casualty Report No. 15" of January 1976 summarized the results of many international investigations. The report stated that two factors seem to be the main causes of collisions and groundings: failure to keep a good lookout and weaknesses in bridge organization.

An extract from the "Chamber of Shipping of the United Kingdom Casualty Analysis No. 2" includes the following about keeping a good lookout:

> The maintenance of a continuous and alert lookout by the officer of the watch is the single and most important consideration in the avoidance of navigational casualties. The keeping of an efficient lookout requires to be interpreted in its fullest sense, which includes the following items:
>
> (a) A constant alert all-round visual lookout to enable a full grasp of the current situation, including ships and landmarks in the vicinity, to be maintained;
> (b) The need to observe changes in the weather, including especially the visibility;
> (c) The need to observe closely the movements and compass bearing of approaching vessels;
> (d) The need to identify ship and shore lights with precision;
> (e) The need to observe the radar and echo sounder displays;
> (f) The need to ensure that the course is steered accurately and that helm orders are correctly executed.

Weaknesses in bridge organization were addressed in the "Chamber of Shipping of the United Kingdom Casualty Analysis No. 1":

> Weaknesses in bridge organization have also been a common failure in many casualties. This term includes such matters as the following:
> (a) Setting double watches in appropriate circumstances;
> (b) Ensuring sufficient personnel are available in special circumstances, e.g., heavy traffic;
> (c) Precise instructions for calling the master;
> (d) Posting lookouts;
> (e) Manning the wheel;
> (f) An established drill for changing over from automatic to manual steering; and
> (g) Precise instructions regarding reducing speed in the event of reduced visibility.

Masters may issue standing instructions covering the foregoing, supplemented by a night order book, but in any case there is a clear requirement that officers of the watch should be in no doubt of what action masters expect them to take.

According to "Special Study-Major Marine Collisions and Effects of Preventive Recommendations," a report by the National Transportation Safety Board dated September 9, 1981, the leading cause of marine collisions from 1970 through 1979 was human error. (See table 1-1.) These percentages remain approximately the same for each year since 1979.

In 1982, 236 ships (totaling 1,460,000 GRT) were lost through various causes. Five years later 1.56 ships (totaling 1,207,400 GRT) were lost. [1] (Records are not available for accidents that did not result in the loss of a ship.) The reason for this reduced casualty rate is difficult to determine, but what is known is that human error plays a major role then and today in shipping casualties and accidents.[2]

The following extract is from the "United Kingdom Department of Trade Merchant Shipping Notice No. M.854, Navigation Safety." Its annex can be found in chapter 3.

U.K. Dept. of Trade Merchant Shipping Notice No. M.854

NAVIGATION SAFETY

Notice to Shipowners, Masters and Deck Officers in the Merchant Navy and Skippers and Second Hands of Fishing Vessels

1. Research into recent accidents occurring to ships has shown that by far the most important contributory cause of navigational accidents is human error, and in many cases information which would have prevented the accident was available to those responsible for the navigation of the ships concerned.
2. There is no evidence to show serious deficiency on the part of deck officers with respect to either basic training in navigation skills or ability to use navigational instruments and equipment; but accidents happen because one person makes the sort of

---

1. Institute of Shipping Economics and Logistics. *Shipping Statistics Yearbook,* 1987. Bremen, West Germany, 1987.

2. R. D. Vardon. "Lessons That May Be Learned from Casualty Investigations for Teaching of Shipboard Personnel." Paper presented to Fifth International Conference of the international Maritime Lecturers Association, Sydney, Nova Scotia, September 1988.

mistake to which all human beings are prone in a situation where there is no navigational regime constantly in use which might enable the mistake to be detected before an accident occurs.

3.   To assist masters and deck officers to appreciate the risks to which they are exposed and to provide help in reducing these risks it is recommended that steps are taken to:

(a) Ensure that all the ship's navigation is planned in adequate detail with contingency plans where appropriate;

(b) Ensure that there is a systematic bridge organization that provides for:

   (1) comprehensive briefing of all concerned with the navigation of the ship;

   (2) close and continuous monitoring of the ship's position ensuring as far as possible that different means of determining position are used to check against error in any one system;

   (3) cross checking of individual human decisions so that errors can be detected and corrected as early as possible;

   (4) Information available from plots of other traffic to be used carefully to ensure against overconfidence, bearing in mind that other ships may alter course and speed.

(c) Ensure that optimum and systematic use is made of all information that becomes available to the navigational staff;

(d) Ensure that the intentions of a pilot are fully understood and acceptable to the ship's navigational staff.

4.   The Annex to this Notice provides information on the planning and conduct of passages which may prove useful to mariners. (This annex can be found in chapter 3.)

PREPARATION

In accordance with STCW, the watch system should be such that the efficiency of watchkeeping officers is not impaired by fatigue. Duties should be organized so that the first watch of a voyage and the subsequent relieving watches are rested sufficiently and otherwise fit for duty. In accordance with the United States *Code of Federal Regulations*, Title 46, Parts 157.20-5(b) and 157.20-10(a), the three-watch system extends to all licensed officers, who shall not be required to be on duty more than eight hours in one day except under extraordinary conditions. On today's merchant vessel fatigue can be a problem, especially for the chief mate who stands a watch on three-mate vessels.

TABLE 1-1

Leading Primary Causes of U.S. Ship Collisions from 1970 through 1979

National Transportation Safety Board, Washington, D.C., Special Study on "Major Marine Collisions and Effects of Preventive Recommendations" (9 Sept. 1981)

Primary Cause	Yearly Percentage (%)										Composite Percentage
Human Error—Total	66	68	73	64	67	70	61	69	74	61	67.3
Licensed Officers/Documented Seamen	14	14	14	13	39	49	42	49	50	41	32.5
Unlicensed/Undocumented Seamen	36	31	32	38	18	10	9	11	12	10	20.7
Pilot State and Federal	10	15	15	8	5	4	5	4	7	6	7.9
Other Persons	6	8	12	5	5	7	5	5	5	4	6.2
Equipment Failure	5	7	7	4	5	10	11	8	9	8	7.4
Floating Debris/Object	12	11	9	9	9	3	6	8	6	4	7.7
Adverse Weather—Storm	6	8	8	7	6	6	6	4	4	3	5.8
Unknown-Insufficient Data	2	1	1	7	7	5	4	3	4	5	3.9
Other Causes	9	5	2	9	6	6	12	8	3	19	7.9
Yearly Collision Totals	1093	1119	1086	1264	1213	1465	1539	1263	1528	1621	—
Fiscal Year	1970	1971	1972	1973	1974	1975	1976*	1977	1978	1979	

*1976 is a 15-month period including the transition quarter. (Source U.S. Coast Guard, courtesy National Transportation Safety Board)

The watch officer must prepare himself for the watch, keeping in mind that *proper prior preparation prevents poor performance*. Relieving the watch and standing the watch are closely linked. Relieving time is a time to rehearse, and the better transition allows more time for the looking out, which is a primary task. The watch officer should, prior to relieving the watch, go out on each bridge wing to visually sweep the horizon. This enables the OOW to determine weather, relative wind, and the visible vessels and navigation aids. In the evening, the watch officer's night vision can adjust. Upon entering the wheelhouse, a glance at the rpm indicators, speed over the ground, course (gyro and magnetic), rudder angle indicator, engine order, telegraph, and automatic or manual steering aids the relieving process. This should be accomplished prior to discussions with the watch officer being relieved. Before relieving, determine the vessel's position and compare with a previous position taken by the watch officer on duty. If the watch officer to be relieved is involved with a course or speed change or a rules-of-the-road situation, wait until the situation is resolved before relieving. If there is any doubt, the master must be called to the bridge.

The relieving officer must be familiar with the passage plan and chart that will be used during the four-hour watch. The watch officer should annotate the conning notebook with key navigational and ship events that will occur during the watch. (see Fig. 3-21.) The OOW must read and sign the standing orders prior to his first watch, be in the chart room at least twenty minutes before the watch, and become familiar with the chart that will be used. If the watch is at night, the OOW should read and sign the night orders and allow time for vision adjustment. The changeover should be thorough before the course is repeated. This officially transfers the watch. Ongoing and relieving watch officers should sign a check-off list similar to table 1-2. (Another type of check-off list used by the Maersk Line is shown in table 1-3.)

STANDING THE WATCH

For standing or keeping the watch, the OWW must comply with the vessel's standing orders. Appendix B was compiled using many of the standing orders in the experience of the author and Captain Richard Beadon. These orders can be used as a quick guide for any type of vessel and provide guidance for standing the watch.

TABLE 1-2

Changing of Watch Check off

Changing over the Watch. Note: Changeover should be postponed when the ship is about to be, or is already, engaged in a collision avoidance maneuver or a navigational alteration of course.

Date:	Time:						
1. Standing orders, supplementary master's instructions and navigational warnings.							
2. Position, course, speed, and draft of the ship.							
3. Course plotted on chart in coastal waters for duration of watch.							
4. Prevailing and predicted tides, current and expected weather, visibility.							
5. Operational condition of all navigational and safety equipment on the bridge including radars, electronic navigation aids, course recorder, and VHF							
6. Gyro and magnetic compass errors.							
7. Movement of vessels in vicinity which may affect own ship identified on radar and visually.							
8. Identification of shore lights, buoys, etc.							
9. Conditions and hazards likely to be encountered during watch.							
10. Possible effects of heel, trim, squat, etc., on underkeel clearance.							
11. All members of the watch capable of carrying out duties.							
12. Vision adjustment.							

Signed by: _____   _____

              Relieving Officer   Officer Being Relieved

TABLE 1-3

Maersk Line Checklist for Change of Watch

Time

Date:	00	04	08	12	16	17	1730	20
1. Plotted position and present course								
2. Navigation coming watch								
3. Magnetic/gyro compass								
4. Movements of vessels in vicinity								
5. Master's watch instructions								
6. Expected change of running conditions								
7. Expected change of weather conditions								
8. Lookout								
9. Navigation lights								
10. Smoke detector								
11. Radar and radar plots								
12. Logbook entries								
Officer to be relieved (initial)								
Relieving officer (initial)								

Courtesy Maersk Line

CHAPTER TWO

Bridge Equipment

U NLIKE aircraft cockpits, merchant ship bridges are not standardized. Years ago merchant ship bridges had a lot of brass work, and
the equipment was basic and simple to operate. As a result of the
rapid development of technical equipment, modern merchant bridges are
now highly automated. The objectives of this automation, in addition to
reduced crews, are to reduce workload, display relevant information, and
facilitate automatic controls.

As soon as possible after joining a ship, and before taking over the
first watch, an OOW must become familiar with all bridge and associated chart room equipment, its use, operation, capability, and limitations.
Instructions and manuals issued with the equipment must be studied and
closely followed.

Since models of bridge equipment vary with the manufacturer, the
following operational procedures are general descriptions of the equipment and guidelines.

AUTOMATIC IDENTIFICATION SYSTEM (AIS)

Most of the following description is extracted from the USCG Navigation
Center Web site:

Picture a shipboard radar display, with overlaid electronic chart data
that includes a mark for every significant ship within radio range, each
as desired with a velocity vector (indicating speed and heading). Each
ship "mark" could reflect the actual size of the ship, with position to GPS
or differential GPS accuracy. By "clicking" on a ship mark, you could
learn the ship name, course and speed, classification, call sign, registra-
tion number, MMSI, and other information. Maneuvering information,
closest point of approach (CPA), time to closest point of approach (TCPA)
and other navigation information, more accurate and more timely than
information available from an automatic radar plotting aid, could also
be available. Display information previously available only to modern
Vessel Traffic Service operations centers could now be available to every
AIS-equipped ship.

With this information, you could call any ship over VHF radio-telephone by name, rather than by "ship off my port bow" or some other imprecise means. Or you could dial it up directly using GMDSS equipment. Or you could send to the ship, or receive from it, short safety-related e-mail messages.

The AIS is a shipboard broadcast system that acts like a transponder, operating in the VHF maritime band, that is capable of handling well more than 4,500 reports per minute and updates every two seconds. It uses Self-Organizing Time Division Multiple Access (SOTDMA) technology to meet this high broadcast rate and ensure reliable ship-to-ship operation.

Each AIS system consists of one VHF transmitter, two VHF SOTDMA receivers, one VHF DSC receiver, and standard marine electronic communications links to shipboard display and sensor systems (AIS Schematic). Position and timing information normally is derived from an integral or external global navigation satellite system (e.g., GPS) receiver, including a medium frequency differential GNSS receiver for precise position in coastal and inland waters. Other information broadcast by the AIS, if available, is obtained electronically from shipboard equipment through standard marine data connections. Heading information, and course and speed over ground would normally be provided by all AIS-equipped ships. Other information, such as rate of turn, angle of heel, pitch and roll, and destination and ETA could also be provided.

The AIS transponder normally works in an autonomous and continuous mode, regardless of whether it is operating in the open seas or coastal or inland areas. Each station determines its own transmission schedule (slot), based upon data link traffic history and knowledge of future actions by other stations. A position report from one AIS station fits into one of 2,250 time slots established every 60 seconds. AIS stations continuously synchronize themselves to each other to avoid overlap of slot transmissions. Slot selection by an AIS station is randomized. When a station changes its slot assignment, it pre-announces both the new location and the timeout for that location. In this way, new stations, including those stations that suddenly come within radio range close to other vessels, will always be received by those vessels.

The required ship reporting capacity according to the IMO performance standard amounts to a minimum of 2,000 time slots per minute, though the system provides 4,500 time slots per minute. The SOTDMA broadcast mode allows the system to be overloaded by 400 to 500 percent through sharing of slots, and still provide nearly 100 percent throughput for ships closer than 8 to 10 NM to each other in a ship to ship mode. In the

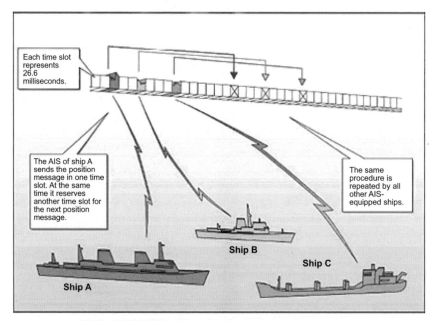

Fig. 2-1. How AIS works. (Courtesy of USCG.)

event of system overload, only targets further away will be subject to drop-out, in order to give preference to nearer targets that are a primary concern to ship operators. In practice, the capacity of the system is nearly unlimited, allowing for a great number of ships to be accommodated at the same time.

The system coverage range is similar to other VHF applications, essentially depending on the height of the antenna. Its propagation is slightly better than that of radar, due to the longer wavelength, so it's possible to "see" around bends and behind islands if the land masses are not too high. A typical value to be expected at sea is nominally twenty nautical miles. With the help of repeater stations, the coverage for both ship and VTS stations can be improved considerably.

The system is backwards compatible with digital selective calling systems, allowing shore-based GMDSS systems to inexpensively establish AIS operating channels and identify and track AIS-equipped vessels, and is intended to fully replace existing DSC-based transponder systems.

AIS provides a great deal of information about threat vessels to the OOW. This information will assist the watch officer in making VHF calls to vessels of concern. Collisions have occurred between AIS-equipped vessels where neither vessel called on VHF to confirm how they would meet or cross (see case five in chapter 9). This is inexcusable and reveals the OOW must use the information technology provides to prevent such collisions.

AUTOMATIC PILOT

Whenever the nature of the surrounding waters and weather conditions allows, the automatic pilot (see Fig. 2-2) should be used. The OOW should bear in mind the necessity to comply at all times with the requirements of Regulation 19, Chapter V of SOLAS 1974. The OOW must supervise changes of steering mode from hand to auto and vice versa (see Fig. 2-3). Such lack of supervision contributed to the grounding of the *Torrey Canyon* on Seven Stones Reef off Land's End in the United Kingdom in 1967. The OOW should adjust weather and rudder settings prior to engaging the auto mode. Once in auto mode, the performance of the steering must be monitored closely to see if the settings are having the desired effect, and then fine-tuned as necessary. During this period the helmsman must stand by the helm and assist in the monitoring. When changing from auto to hand steering, the OOW must take into account the need to station the helmsman and put the steering in manual control in good time to allow any potential situation to be dealt with in a safe manner.

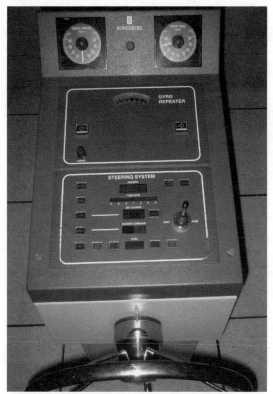

Fig. 2-2. Automatic pilot.

Hand-steering mode should be used during the first thirty minutes of each watch, in confined waters, in restricted visibility, within five miles of closing vessels, navigation aids, obstructions, etc., and when other circumstances deem it prudent.

Helm orders must be loud and clear, and leave the helmsman in no doubt as to what is required (see pp. 101–102). These orders must be repeated in a similar manner by the helmsman. The steering is to be monitored closely at all times to ensure that helm orders are repeated correctly and executed by the helmsman, and the course being steered is correct. Close monitoring of the steering is necessary particularly in pilotage waters. It is the responsibility of the OOW to ensure the course is maintained and helm orders are executed correctly.

BINOCULARS

Although binoculars should be kept handy, it is not necessary, as on Navy ships, for the OOW to strap them about the neck. However, they must be designated for the watchstander's use and should be kept in a designated box. While in use, they should be carefully handled. The proper adjustment for focusing should be made prior to assuming the watch. Binoculars can be individually focused or center focused for both eyes.

Fig. 2-3. Author supervising changeover from auto to hand steering aboard TS *Texas Clipper* during summer cruise of 1978.

The most common marine binoculars are designated 7x50, meaning 7 powers and an objective lens .50 mm in diameter, making them suitable for night use. The bigger the lens, the more light-gathering ability of the binoculars.

To care for your binoculars:

1. Keep the lens covers on the binocular lenses when the binoculars are not in use, thereby keeping the optics free from dust and finger smears.
2. When wiping the lenses, use the lens cloth that comes with the binoculars or a soft, lint-free cloth.
3. To remove any remaining dirt or smudges, add one drop of alcohol to the cloth.
4. Store the binoculars in a moisture-free area.

COMPASSES

Merchant ships are fitted with gyrocompasses. Magnetic compasses, however, are statutory instruments and as often as necessary (and at least once a year) a complete examination of the deviation should be carried out by swinging the ship. The deviation of the compasses should be determined after each alteration of course and at least once every watch when a steady course is steered. The result of the determination should be entered in the ship's logbook and the deviation book. An azimuth should be taken and recorded once a watch to determine gyro error.

COURSE RECORDER

The course recorder should show Greenwich Mean Time (GMT), and when the ship is at sea the position, wind, and weather at noon should be entered on the recording paper. A notation of the date, time, and port should be made every time the course recorder is started and secured. It also is a good practice for OOWs to initial their recorders for their watches. It is important when starting the course recorder and every time it is checked that its time is synchronized as close as possible to GMT.

DOPPLER SPEED LOG

This indicator provides information on lateral motion of the bow and stern and the forward and aft movement in knots, meters, or feet per second. An arrow also should indicate the direction of movement. The Doppler speed log (see Fig. 2-4) is a tremendous aid when anchoring or docking. The OOW should monitor it at sea and compare it to other instruments and speed between fixes for verification purposes. The OOW must be aware of whether the Doppler mode is "water track" or "ground track." Generally, it is better to be in ground track, where actual speed over the ground, incorporating the effects of current and wind, is indicated. Some Doppler logs fitted to ships can change automatically from one mode to another, which can be very confusing and dangerous to the navigator.

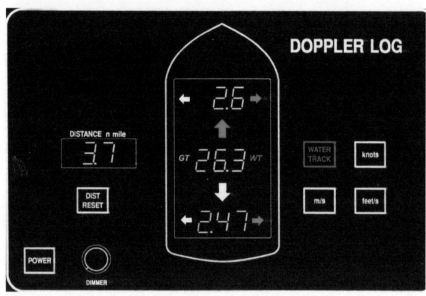

Fig. 2-4. Doppler speed log.

ELECTRONIC CHART DISPLAY AND
INFORMATION SYSTEM (ECDIS)

Electronic Chart Display and Information System (ECDIS) is a computer-based navigation information system capable of continuously determining a vessel's position in relation to land, charted objects, aids-to-navigation, and unseen hazards. When provided with adequate back-up arrangements, it can meet the chart requirements called for in SOLAS 1974. As an automated decision aid, it also assists the mariner in route planning and monitoring, and displays additional navigation and chart-related information (e.g., radar/ARPA, AIS, water levels, current flow, and weather).

ECDIS (see Fig. 2-5) has emerged as a promising navigation aid that will significantly improve maritime safety and commerce. More than simply a graphics display, ECDIS is a real-time geographic information system (GIS) that combines spatial and textual data into a readily useful operational tool. As an automated-decision aid capable of continuously determining a vessel's position in relation to land, charted objects, aids

Fig. 2-5. ECDIS display on CAORF Bridge Simulator at USMMA, Kings Point, New York.

to navigation, and unseen hazards, ECDIS represents a new approach to maritime navigation and piloting. ECDIS is expected to eventually elimi-nate paper charts.

The IMO finalized international performance standards for ECDIS in May 1994. The IMO Performance Standards for ECDIS were formally adopted by the Nineteenth Assembly of IMO on November 23, 1995. IMO was recommending mandatory implementation of ECDIS for oceangoing vessels in 2012.

As specified in the IMO Performance Standards, the primary function of ECDIS is to contribute to safe navigation. ECDIS must be capable of displaying all chart information necessary for safe and efficient navigation organized by, and distributed on, the authority of government-authorized hydrographic offices. With adequate back-up arrangements, ECDIS may be accepted as complying with the up-to-date charts required by regulation V/20 of the SOLAS 1974. In operation, ECDIS should reduce the navigational workload of using the paper chart. It should enable the mariner to execute in a convenient and timely manner all route planning, route monitoring, and positioning performed on paper charts. ECDIS also should facilitate simple and reliable updating of the electronic navigational chart. Similar to the requirements for shipborne radio equipment forming a part of the global maritime distress and safety system (GMDSS), and for electronic navigational aids, ECDIS onboard a SOLAS vessel should be in compliance with the IMO Performance Standard.

For the electronic navigational positioning system to be used with an IMO- compliant ECDIS:

- The vessel's position must be derived from a continuous positioning system of an accuracy consistent with the requirements of safe navigation.
- A second independent positioning method of a different type should be provided and ECDIS should be capable of detecting discrepancies between the primary and secondary positioning systems.

Regulation 19 of the new Chapter V-Carriage Requirements for Shipborne Navigational Systems and Equipment allows an ECDIS to be accepted as meeting the chart carriage requirements of the regulation.

The regulation requires all ships, irrespective of size, to carry nautical charts and nautical publications to plan and display the ship's route for the intended voyage and plot and monitor positions throughout the voyage. The ship also must carry back-up arrangements if electronic charts are used fully or partially.

The MSC, during its seventieth session from December 7–11, 1998, adopted performance standards for Raster Chart Display Systems, through amendments to the performance standards for ECDIS, to allow the systems to be used with raster charts where vector electronic chart systems are not available.

A raster chart is just a visual scan of a paper chart. It is a computer-based system that uses charts issued by, or under the authority of, a national hydrographic office, together with automatic continuous electronic positioning, to provide an integrated navigational tool.

A vector chart is more complex. Each point on the chart is digitally mapped, allowing the information to be used in a more sophisticated way, such as clicking on a feature (for example, a lighthouse) to display the details of that feature.

The international standard for vector charts was finalized by the International Hydrographic Organization (S-57, Version 3), and IMO-adopted performance standards for ECDIS, using vector charts, in 1995 by Assembly Resolution A.817(19).

The amendments to Resolution A.817(19) state that some ECDIS equipment may operate in Raster Chart Display System (RCDS) mode when the relevant chart information is not available in vector mode.

The amendments to the ECDIS performance standards indicate which performance standards for vector charts apply equally to raster charts, and add specific specifications for raster charts, covering such aspects as display requirements, alarms and indicators, provision and updating of chart information and route planning. The amendments state that when used in RCDS mode, ECDIS equipment should be used together with an appropriate folio of up-to-date paper charts.

The MSC during its seventieth session agreed to a Safety of Navigation Circular on Differences between RCDS and ECDIS. This circular is number 207 of January 7, 1999.

The electronic tools the watch officer has available are changing the way of navigation aboard vessels. The Electronic Chart and Information System (ECDIS) is now mandated on most commercial vessels and Integrated Bridge Systems (IBS) are being accepted in the industry. This technology may affect the passage plan but it does not change the basic watchstanding principles and techniques. Approved ECDIS systems have all the capabilities for creating a complete passage plan from berth to berth. All the methods used when preparing a paper chart for a passage are similar when preparing a passage on an electronic chart. What must be stressed is the necessity for bridge teams and pilots to be properly trained in their use. As these systems are now a major resource on the bridge of vessels, Bridge Resource Management (BRM) courses should include the use of this equipment.

Although ECDIS systems are designed to improve safety, reduce maritime casualties, and lighten the work load of the Watch-stander, it must be remembered that the realization of these goals are dependent on using the equipment properly. The old saying "garbage in, garbage out" applies. It is critical that the system is configured and calibrated properly.

ECHO SOUNDER (FATHOMETER)

This instrument produces an underwater sound pulse and measures the elapsed time until return of an echo, which is received by a microphone. The depth, in feet, meters, or fathoms, is interpreted according to an equation (depth = speed x ½ time interval between sound pulse and echo) and displayed on an indicator. Displays include rotary flashing light, electrical meter, digital readout, or bottom profile. Whatever the display, it is essential that the OOW be certain what unit of measure and range is being used (see Fig. 2-6). This instrument should be used whenever the ship navigates in waters where the depths make it serviceable and where the safe navigation of the ship requires it.

Where the ship carries a depth recorder with an alarm, the echo sounder should be used when navigating in narrow waters and in all other circumstances where the depth of water makes it a useful aid that may increase the safe navigation of the ship.

The echo sounder is not used to its maximum capability aboard the bridges of most merchant vessels. It can be very useful in an approach to port or when making a landfall where there are distinct depth contours, such as the one-hundred-fathom curve, can give an OOW an excellent line of position (LOP). This LOP can be used with a celestial LOP, visual

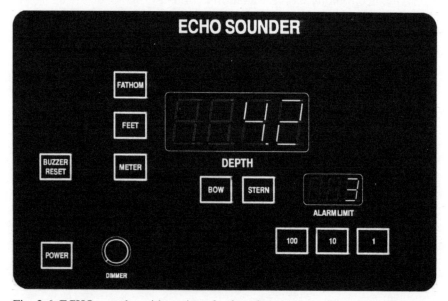

Fig. 2-6. ECHO sounder with settings for feet, fathoms, or meters, indicated for bow or stern and means for setting a shallow alarm limit.

bearing, and radar range to provide an excellent fix. In addition, a line of soundings may be used in determining a vessel's position.

A precaution in taking soundings: these depths on charts are uncorrected for any variation in salinity, density, or temperature. In addition, the quality of the bottom may indicate a different depth than on the chart. If in doubt, the OOW should never hesitate to call the master. Note times in the deck logbook in GMT when the echo sounder is activated and is secured. One fathometer should be run continuously at sea when navigating in depths of less than one hundred fathoms and the depths should be recorded every half hour. Depths should be taken at the time of each fix and the depth shown on the chart alongside the time of the fix for comparison with the charted depth. In addition, with each fix these depths should be noted on the navigation record log and the conning notebook. (see Fig. 3-21.) The shallow water alarm must be set to whatever depth is necessary to give ample warning of the vessel standing into danger. When comparing soundings from the chart with the fathometer, the user must make allowance for the height of the tide and the draft of the ship. If the fathometer transducer is forward and the ship has a trim by the stem the watch officer must be aware that the fathometer is showing more than the true depth below the keel at the deepest part of the vessel.

FLASHLIGHT

A flashlight and a penlight are mandatory for OOWs during night watches. For night vision it is a good idea to equip the flashlight with a red lens. Replace the batteries before each voyage and make sure the flashlight is off before placing it in the back pocket. The penlight, which can be carried in the breast pocket, is extremely valuable and will not need a red lens due to its narrow beam width. At no time should the OOW illuminate anything on the bridge with a cigarette lighter.

MANEUVERING PRINTER

The printer for engine maneuvers should show GMT and keep the same time in minutes as clocks in the engine room. When the ship is at sea, this should be checked at noon each day.

RADAR (RADIO DETECTION AND RANGING)

Radar (Radio Detection and Ranging) is a method to determine distance and direction of objects by sending out a beam of microwave radio energy and detecting the returned reflections. The OOW must keep in mind that radar is more accurate as a ranging device than as a bearing device. Radar is a tremendous advantage both as a navigation aid and as an anti-collision device. It can be used in all conditions of visibility but is particularly useful in poor visibility and at night. Fixes can be obtained rapidly and anti-collision solutions can provide tremendous peace of mind to the OOW. Radar also can locate and track squall lines and other heavy weather. In avoiding collisions the importance of visual bearings cannot be overstressed.

Visual bearings and radar ranges provide the best early assessment of the possibility of a collision threat to a vessel. One radar must be on for early detection. A second radar should be on at a close range scale. Range scales must be appropriate for the circumstances. When a pilot is embarked it is important for the OOW to ensure that one radar is available

Fig. 2-7. DB10 radar found aboard APL vessels and on the CAORF Bridge Simulator, USMMA, Kings Point, New York.

for the pilot and the other available for the master and OOW. The OOW must be aware of the possibility of shadow sectors due to the ship's superstructure. A change of course can unveil these areas for radar detection.

No matter how good a radar is, its value as an aid is entirely dependent upon the person who operates it. The OOW must be fully conversant with the radar's capabilities and limitations to understand and interpret the radar picture correctly. It is important to carry out radar practice in clear weather to obtain the confidence and routine that is necessary for proper use of radar in restricted visibility.

Information obtained from the radar must be used so that early steps can be taken to prevent any risk of collision. Using radar does not relieve the navigator of the obligation to maneuver in a seamanlike manner, according to the provisions of Rules 2 and 19 of the COLREGS.

Instructions in the use of various radars should be formal. After formalized instruction the OOW, using the instruction manual, must become proficient in the operation of radar and its menu so that this vital equipment may be used to its maximum capability. An example of today's menu-driven radar with push button keyboards and trackball is the DB10 radar (see Fig. 2-7). Gone are the days of manual knobs on radars with reflection plotters and grease pencils for rapid radar plotting.

As radars become more automated it is even more important for watch officers to keep abreast by continuing education and experience in professional practice.

REVOLUTION PER MINUTE (RPM) INDICATOR

The revolution per minute (rpm) indicator must be monitored by the OOW, particularly in pilotage waters, to ensure the rpms desired are answered when maneuvering and maintained when at sea.

RATE OF TURN INDICATOR (ROT)

The OOW, in addition to listening to the clicks of a gyrocompass (two clicks for each degree), should observe the rate of turn indicator (ROT) (see Fig. 2-8) during course changes and when applying rudder. Knowing how fast a vessel turns with various angles of rudder is a tremendous aid to a shiphandler, especially when entering a channel. Most indicators show in tenths of a degree to a maximum 2° per second the ROT to port and starboard. The rate of increasing or decreasing can be used to advantage by the OOW and helmsman. Both the bridge and helm should have a ROT indicator. It is important for the OOW to know whether the ROT is calibrated in degrees per minute or degrees per second.

Fig. 2-8. Rate of turn indicator.

RUDDER ANGLE INDICATOR

The rudder angle indicator often is not observed frequently enough. Every time a helm command is given all eyes on the bridge should glance at the rudder angle indicator to verify the rudder is going in the direction intended. Even with the ship in automated steering, the OOW should keep an eye on the indicator to verify how easily the course is maintained or if weather and sea adjustments to the automatic pilot are needed. The rudder angle indicator, as shown in Fig. 2-9, is outstanding in that it can display on three sides (port, starboard, and aft) the angle of the rudder. The OOW must keep in mind that the rudder angle indicator indicates the actual angle of the rudder. When a steering test is conducted, the OOW must wait until the rudder angle indicator matches the helm command before comparing to the rudder angle indicator in after steering. For a pre-departure steering test the rudder angles of 30°, 20°, and 10° port and starboard should be compared on the bridge and after steering on each steering pump. As a

Fig. 2-9. Rudder angle indicator.

final check, the after steering repeater heading should be compared with that on the bridge.

For a pre-arrival steering test the same procedure should be followed if time and searoom permit. At a minimal, the steering pre-arrival test should verify port and starboard 10° rudder angles on each steering pump. When a pilot is aboard and at the conn a helm order (rudder angle and direction) should be verified by the pilot, master, helmsman, and watch officer on the rudder angle indicator.

SATELLITE NAVIGATOR (SATNAV)

The idea of using satellites for navigation began with the launch of *Sputnik 1* on October 4, 1957. Monitoring that satellite, scientists at Johns Hopkins University's Applied Physics Laboratory noticed that when the transmitted radio frequency was plotted on a graph, a curve characteristic of the Doppler shift appeared. By studying this apparent change of radio frequency as the satellite passed overhead, they were able to show that the Doppler shift, when properly used, described the orbit of the satellite.

Most navigation systems use time and distance to calculate location. Early on scientists recognized the principle that, given velocity and the time required for a radio signal to be transmitted between two points, the distance between the two points can be computed. To do this calculation, a precise, synchronized departure time and measured arrival time of the radio signal must be obtained. By synchronizing the signal transmission time between two precise clocks, one in a satellite and one at a ground-based receiver, the transit time could be measured and then multiplied by the speed of light to obtain the distance between the two positions.

This three-dimensional Navigation Satellite Timing and Ranging (NAVSTAR) enables travelers to obtain their positions anywhere on or above the planet. Data transmitted from the satellite provides the user with time, precise orbital position of the satellite, and the position of other satellites in the system. Currently, a full constellation of twenty-four orbiting satellites is devoted to navigation.

Using a commercial GPS (see Fig. 2-10), the user can calculate distance by measuring the time it takes for the satellite's radio transmissions traveling at the speed of light to reach the receiver. Once distance from four satellites is known, position in three dimensions (latitude, longitude, and altitude) can be calculated by triangulation, and velocity in three dimensions can be computed from the Doppler shift in the received signal. The new GPS receivers do all of the work. A traveler simply turns on the unit, makes certain that it is locked onto at least four satellites, and the precise position of the GPS unit is displayed automatically. One innovative application of GPS technology is to determine Earth's ground movement after

Fig. 2-10. Marine GPS. (Courtesy of Johnny Appleseed GPS.)

an earthquake. Referencing a network of these sensitive receivers can lead to a remarkably accurate assessment of plate movement.

There are two available radio signals that GPS receivers can use: the Standard Positioning Service (SPS) for civilians, and the Precise Positioning Service (PPS) for military and other authorized personnel. The most significant cause of errors in positioning is the deliberate effort by the Department of Defense to decrease the accuracy of user systems for national security reasons. Selective Availability (SA) refers to the purposeful degradation of the information broadcast by the satellites. SA affects the accuracy of the SPS, but not PPS. With SA, a GPS system will be accurate 95 percent of the time to within 328 feet (100 meters) horizontally and 512 feet (156 meters) vertically.

For those who require positions with higher accuracy, Differential Global Positioning Systems (DGPS) add a new element to GPS. DGPS places a GPS stationary receiver at a known location on or near the Earth's surface. This reference station receives satellite signals and adjusts for transmission delays and SA, using its own known latitude, longitude, and altitude. The stationary receiver sends out a correction message for any suitably equipped local receiver. A DGPS-compatible receiver adjusts its position calculations using the correction message. DGPS reference stations are constructed, operated, and maintained by the USCG.

Even with its high degree of reliability and accuracy the SATNAV cannot be totally relied upon. Sources of error include ionosphere interference, multipath reflections, interference, and human error. An illustration of this was the grounding of a containership in the Strait of Malacca in 1981. The OOW, while lighted aids were flashing all about his vessel on a dark clear night, was obtaining fixes based on SATNAV readout. These devices are no better or worse than their operators. Whenever possible the vessel's position should be fixed by visual bearings (actual bearings taken from the wing repeaters). Care is needed in transferring SATNAV positions to the chart. British admiralty charts give a caution with correction factors for this purpose. SATNAV receivers give a continually updated readout based on the last fix, updated by courses steered and the ship's log. As the gyro and log can have errors, and no allowance is made for tidal stream, leeway, drift or current, this position must be used with caution and regard to the time interval since the last fix.

VERY HIGH FREQUENCY (VHF)

Frequencies in the very high frequency (VHF) band (30–300 MHz) can be found on the VHF receivers on the bridge (see Fig. 2-11) The two most used frequencies can be found on channel 16 (156.8 MHz), international distress, and channel 13 (156.65 MHz), ship-to-ship or bridge-to-bridge.

Fig. 2-11. VHF radio-telephone.

They are basically line-of-sight frequencies that are limited by the curvature of the earth and height of the antennae.

Officers of the watch must be familiar with VHF procedures and talk on the radio with brevity and clarity. It is a tremendous anti-collision device that can give peace of mind to the officers of the watch on vessels approaching each other. Masters should encourage OOWs, and even cadets, to use VHF in contacting pilot services and arranging for pilot embarkation. The initial "uh-uhs" and jitters will soon be replaced by clear and concise communications.

Uncertainties can arise in verbal communications with other vessels over the identification of vessels and interpretation of messages received. At night in restricted visibility or when more than two vessels are in the vicinity, positive identification of the two vessels is essential but can rarely be guaranteed. Even where positive identification has been achieved a misunderstanding between the parties due to language difficulties still is possible, however fluent they are in the language used. An imprecise or ambiguously expressed message can have serious consequences. A proposed method to reduce the difficulty in identifying the vessel is explained in chapter 4, pages 85–86.

THE FUTURE

The future can best be summarized from a paper entitled, "Electronics in Navigation: Is There a Limit? Should There Be a Limit?" by Dr. Bernhard Berking, Professor, Hamburg Polytechnic of Maritime Studies, to the Fifth International Conference, Maritime Lecturers Association (IMLA) in Sydney, Canada, on September 21, 1988. The conclusion of Professor Berking's paper follows:

"Due to the complexity of the problem and to the steady technical progress, the limits of electronics in navigation cannot precisely be defined for the far future. Electronics and automation will still increase in importance, will perform more and more "decision making" procedures and will solve most tasks (even bad-weather navigation and emergency situations) on a highly automatic level. It is not expected that they will necessarily lead to automatic navigation on an unmanned vessel although technically they will come close to it.

Navigation is not a 100 percent deterministic procedure and depending on ship, cargo, sea in different situations, many unforeseeable events within a sometimes hostile environment may occur.

Clearly, there is an enormous impact of these topics on navigational education and training. The objectives will change. The producing of information, e.g., the construction of LOPs, etc., will be replaced by the extraction of relevant data from complex information systems and particularly by judging the quality of information.

This requires the mariner's understanding of the principles of electronics and data processing, particularly the potentials and limits of computers and programs."

CHAPTER THREE

Voyage Planning and Recordkeeping

PASSAGES should be planned from berth to berth. The number one cause of navigation casualties, as shown in Fig. 3-1, is failure to plan the navigation. Proper prior planning prevents poor performance. These plans should be detailed but not to the level where contingencies would disrupt all the advance planning. Critics could ask why you should plan when contingencies always seem to alter the plan. The answer to this criticism lies in the fact that the prudent mariner can anticipate most of these contingencies. For example, a transatlantic voyage in December or January should include contingency planning for rough seas. Similarly during hurricane season or any other meteorological event (see Fig. 6-5), contingency plans should be made for the peak periods or likely occurrence of these events.

The requirement for planning an intended passage in advance is defined in resolution A-285 (VIII) of the IMO. A comprehensive guide to the planning and conduct of a navigational passage is best summarized in the United Kingdom Department of Trade Notice No. M. 854, "Notice to Shipowners, Masters and Deck Officers in the Merchant Navy and Skippers and Second Hands of Fishing Vessels." The introduction to this notice can be found in chapter 1. The annex to the notice, reproduced below, provides information on the planning and conduct of passages that may prove useful to mariners.

GUIDE TO THE PLANNING AND CONDUCT OF PASSAGES

Pilotage

1. The contribution which pilots make to the safety of navigation in confined waters and port approaches, of which they have up-to-date knowledge, requires no emphasis but it should be stressed that the responsibilities of the ship's navigational team do not transfer to the pilot and the duties of the officer of the watch remain with that officer.

2. After his arrival on board, in addition to being advised by the master of the maneuvering characteristics and basic details of

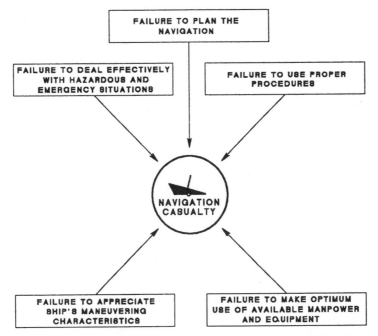

Fig. 3-1. Main causes of navigation casualty. (Courtesy of Captain Richard Beadon.)

the vessel for its present condition of loading, the pilot should be clearly consulted on the passage plan to be followed. The general aim of the master should be to ensure that the expertise of the pilot is fully supported and monitored by the ship's bridge team.

3. Attention is drawn to the following extract from Resolution A-285 (VIII):

Despite the duties and obligations of a pilot, his presence on board does not relieve the officer of the watch from his duties and obligations for the safety of the ship. He should cooperate closely with the pilot and maintain an accurate check on the vessel's position and movements. If he is in any doubt as to the pilot's actions or intentions, he should seek clarification from the pilot and if doubt still exists, he should notify the master immediately and take whatever action is necessary before the master arrives.

Responsibility for Passage Planning

1. In most deep-sea ships it is customary for the master to delegate the initial responsibility for preparing the plan for a passage to

the officer responsible for navigational equipment and publications, usually the second officer. For the purposes of this guide
the officer concerned will be referred to as the navigating officer.

2. It will be evident that in small ships, including fishing vessels,
    the master or skipper may himself need to exercise the responsi-
    bility of the navigating officer for passage planning purposes.

3. The navigating officer has the task of preparing the detailed
    passage plan to the master's requirements prior to departure.
    In those cases when the port of destination is not known or is
    subsequently altered, it will be necessary for the navigating
    officer to extend or amend the original plan as appropriate.

Principles of Passage Planning

There are four distinct stages in the planning and achievement of a
safe passage:

- Appraisal
- Planning
- Execution
- Monitoring

These stages must of necessity follow each other in the order set out above.
An appraisal of information available must be made before detailed plans
can be drawn up and a plan must be in existence before tactics for its
execution can be decided upon. Once the plan and the manner in which
it is to be executed have been decided, monitoring must be carried out to
ensure that the plan is followed.

Appraisal

1. This is the process of gathering together all information relevant
    to the contemplated passage. It will, of course, be concerned
    with navigational information shown on charts and in publica-
    tions such as sailing directions, light lists, current atlas, tidal
    atlas, tide tables, Notices to Mariners, publications detailing
    traffic separation and other routing schemes, and radio aids to
    navigation. Reference also should be made to climatic data and
    other appropriate meteorological information which may have
    a bearing upon the availability for use of navigational aids in
    the area under consideration such as, for example, those areas
    subject to periods of reduced visibility.

2. A check list should be available for the use of the navigating
    officer to assist him to gather all the information necessary for a

full passage appraisal and the circumstances under which it is to be made. It is necessary to recognize that more up-to-date information, for example, radio navigational warnings and meteorological forecasts, may be received after the initial appraisal.

3. In addition to the obvious requirement for charts to cover the area or areas through which the ship will proceed, which should be checked to see that they are corrected and up-to-date in respect of both permanent and temporary Notices to Mariners and existing radio navigational warnings, the information necessary to make an appraisal of the intended passage will include details of:

(a) Currents (direction and rate of set);
(b) Tides (times, heights, and direction of rate of set);
(c) Draft of ship during the various stages of the intended passage;
(d) Advice and recommendations given in sailing directions;
(e) Navigational lights (characteristics, range, arc of visibility, and anticipated raising range);
(f) Navigational marks (anticipating range at which objects will show on radar and will be visible to the eye);
(g) Traffic separation and routing schemes;
(h) Radio aids to navigation (availability and coverage);
(i) Navigational warnings affecting the area;
(j) Climatological data affecting the area;
(k) Ship's maneuvering data.

4. An overall assessment of the intended passage should be made by the master, in consultation with the navigating officer and other deck officers who will be involved, when all relevant information has been gathered. This appraisal will provide the master and his bridge team with a clear and precise indication of all areas of danger, and delineate the areas in which it will be possible to navigate safely taking into account the calculated draft of the ship and planned under-keel clearance. Bearing in mind the condition of the ship, her equipment and any other circumstances, a balanced judgment of the margins of safety which must be allowed in the various sections of the intended passage can now be made, agreed, and understood by all concerned.

Planning

1. Having made the fullest possible appraisal using all the available information on board relating to the intended passage, the navigating officer can now act upon the master's instructions to

prepare a detailed plan of the passage. The detailed plan should embrace the whole passage, from berth to berth, and include all waters where a pilot will be on board.

2. The formulation of the plan will involve completion of the following tasks:

    (a) Plot the intended passage on the appropriate charts and mark clearly, on the largest scale charts applicable, all areas of danger and the intended track taking into account the margins of allowable error. Where appropriate, due regard should be paid to the need for advance warning to be given on one chart of the existence of a navigational hazard immediately on transfer to the next. The planned track should be plotted to clear hazards at as safe a distance as circumstances allow. A longer distance should always be accepted in preference to a shorter, more hazardous route. The possibility of main engine or steering gear breakdown at a critical moment must not be overlooked.

    (b) Indicate clearly in 360-degree notation the true direction of the planned track marked on the charts.

    (c) Mark on the chart those radar conspicuous objects, ramarks or racons, which may be used in position fixing.

    (d) Mark on the charts any transit marks (ranges), clearing bearings, or clearing ranges which may be used to advantage. It is sometimes possible to use two conspicuous clearing marks where a line drawn through them runs clear of natural dangers with the appropriate margin of safety. If the ship proceeds on the safe side of this transit (range) she will be clear of the danger. If no clearing marks are available, a line or lines of bearings from a single object may be drawn at a desired safe distance from the danger; provided the ship remains in the safe segment, she will be clear of the danger. Decide upon the key elements of the navigational plan. These should include but not be limited to:

        (1) safe speed having regard to the maneuvering characteristics of the ship and, in ships restricted by draft, due allowance for reduction of draft due to squat and heel effect when turning;

        (2) speed alterations necessary to achieve desired ETAs en route, e.g. where there may be limitations on night passage, tidal restrictions, etc.;

        (3) positions where a change in machinery status is required;

        (4) course alteration points, with wheel-over positions; where appropriate on large-scale charts taking into

account the ship's turning circle at the planned speed
and the effect of any tidal stream or current on the ship's
movement during the turn;

(5) minimum clearance required under the keel in critical
areas (having allowed for height of tide);

(6) points where accuracy of position fixing is critical, and
the primary and secondary methods by which such positions must be obtained for maximum reliability;

(7) contingency plans for alternative action to place the ship
in deep water or proceed to an anchorage in the event of
any emergency necessitating abandonment of the plan.

3. Depending on circumstances, the main details of the plan
referred to above should be marked in appropriate and promi-
nent places on the charts to be used during the passage. These
main details of the passage plan should in any case be recorded
in a bridge notebook used specially for this purpose to allow
reference to details of the plan at the conning position without
the need to consult the chart. Supporting information relative to
the passage, such as times of high and low water, or of sunrise
or sunset, should also be recorded in this notebook.

4. It is unlikely that every detail of a passage will have been anticipated, particularly in pilotage waters. Much of what will have
been planned may have to be changed after embarking the pilot.
This in no way detracts from the real value of the plan, which
is to mark out in advance where the ship must not go and the
precautions which must be taken to achieve that end, or to give
initial warning that the ship is standing into danger.

Execution

1. Having finalized the passage plan, and as soon as estimated
times of arrival can be made with reasonable accuracy, the
tactics to be used in the execution of the plan should be decided.
The factors to be taken into account will include:

(a) the reliability and condition of the ship's navigational
equipment;

(b) estimated times of arrival at critical points for the tide
heights and flow;

(c) meteorological conditions, particularly in areas known to be
affected by frequent periods of low visibility;

(d) daytime versus night-time passing of danger points, and any
effect this may have upon position fixing accuracy;

(e) traffic conditions, especially at navigational focal points.

2. It will be important for the master to consider whether any particular circumstance, such as the forecast of restricted visibility in an area where position fixing by visual means at a critical point is an essential feature of the navigation plan, introduces an unacceptable hazard to the safe conduct of the passage; and thus whether that section of the passage should be attempted under the conditions prevailing, or likely to prevail. The Master should also consider at which specific points of the passage he/she may need to utilize additional deck or engine room personnel.

Monitoring

1. The close and continuous monitoring of the ship's progress along the pre-planned track is essential for the safe conduct of the passage. If the officer of the watch is ever in any doubt as to the position of the ship or the manner in which the passage is proceeding, he should immediately call the master and, if necessary, take whatever action he may think necessary for the safety of the ship.
2. The performance of navigational equipment should be checked prior to sailing, prior to entering restricted or hazardous waters and at regular and frequent intervals at other times throughout the passage.
3. Advantage should be taken of all the navigational equipment with which the ship is fitted for position monitoring, bearing in mind the following points:
    (a) visual bearings are usually the most accurate means of position fixing;
    (b) every fix should, if possible, be based on at least three position lines;
    (c) transit marks (ranges), clearing bearings and clearing ranges can be of great assistance;
    (d) when checking, use systems which are based on different data;
    (e) positions obtained by navigational aids should be checked where practicable by visual means;
    (f) the value of the echo sounder as a navigational aid;
    (g) buoys should not be used for fixing but may be used for guidance when shore marks are difficult to distinguish visually; in these circumstances their positions should first be checked by other means;
    (h) the functioning and correct reading of the instruments used should be checked;

(i) an informed decision in advance as to the frequency with which the position is to be fixed should be made for each section of the passage.
4. On every occasion when the ship's position is fixed and marked on the chart in use, the estimated position at a convenient interval of time in advance should be projected and plotted.
5. Radar can be used to advantage in monitoring the position of the ship by the use of parallel indexing technique. Parallel indexing, as a simple and most effective way of continuously monitoring a ship's progress in restricted waters, can be used in any situation where a radar-conspicuous navigation mark is available and it is practicable to monitor continuously the ship's position relative to such an object.

PARALLEL INDEXING TECHNIQUES

Parallel indexing has proven to be an instantaneous, effective method to monitor the maintaining of a vessel's track over the ground.

Basic Principle

Whenever a vessel is underway and maintaining her track, any fixed object appears to move in a reciprocal direction at the same speed. This is readily apparent on a radar screen when the radar is operating in relative motion—every fixed object appears to move in the opposite direction at your vessel's speed.

Item Required

The item needed to undertake parallel indexing is radar in relative motion, north up and stabilized. Radar must be well tuned with *no* errors of centering, gyro heading marker bearing, azimuth stabilization, electronic bearing indicator index, or variable range marker index.

Technique

The following discussion is adapted from a parallel indexing teaching method used at the College of Maritime Studies at Warsash, UK, and reprinted with permission.

Fig. 3-2 shows a vessel proceeding from A to C on a course of 110° (T) to pass five miles off a stationary, isolated radar-conspicuous target. The same situation transferred to a PPI display (see Fig. 3-3), would show the target tracking down the imaginary line ABC parallel to the course line if the vessel maintained her course line.

When the ship is at position A in Figure 3-2, the echo will appear at position A in Figure 3-3 and when at position B on the chart the echo will

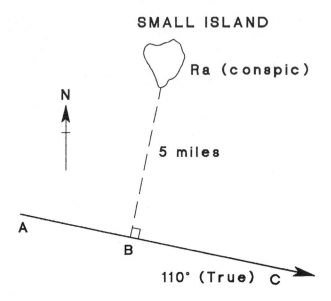

Fig. 3-2. Vessel on course 110° (T).

appear at B on the PPI, and similarly for position C. Having understood this basic principle, it should now be possible to construct the line ABC *prior* to arriving at position A on the chart.

From position A (see Fig. 3-2), obtain a bearing and range of the target. This is found to be 074° (T) 8.8 miles. The bearing and range are now inserted from the center of the PPI giving us position A (see Fig. 3-3). The method of laying off the bearing is by electronic bearing indicator (EBI). The method of laying off the range is by means of the variable range marker (VRM).

Likewise from position B on the chart, a bearing and range of the target are obtained. This is 020° (T) 5.0 miles. Position B can now be constructed as can position C 317° (T) 11.0 miles.

We now have points A, B, and C, and when these points are joined, the direction of the line obtained will be the same as the course line, that is, 110° (T).

We now have a parallel index (PI) line and as previously mentioned, if the ship keeps to her charted track, the echo of the target will keep to the line ABC and we are in a position to continuously monitor the ship's progress along its charted course.

It should be stated at this point that using PI does *not* relieve the watch officer from his obligation of fixing the vessel's position on the chart by other means such as visual fixes and other navigational aids.

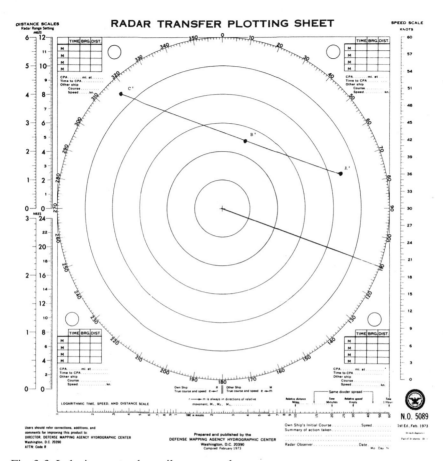

Fig. 3-3. Indexing on twelve-mile range scale.

Echo Deviation from Line

Due to leeway, collision avoidance, or poor steering, the ship will deviate from its track. As a result, the radar echo will depart from its parallel index line. The ship will have to alter course to bring the radar echo back on the PI line and bring the ship back on track. If the radar echo is to port between the PI line and the ship's heading line on the radar, alter course to starboard (see Fig. 3-4). If the radar echo is to starboard between the PI line and the ship's heading line on the radar, alter course to port (see Fig. 3-5). If the PI is between the ship's heading and the radar echo to starboard on the radar, alter course to starboard (see Fig. 3-6). If the PI is between the ship's heading and the radar echo to port on the radar, alter course to port (see Fig. 3-7).

SHIP
HEAD

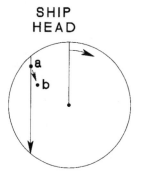

Fig. 3-4. Parallel index to port; PPI north up, gyro stabilized, radar echo between ship head and PI.

SHIP
HEAD

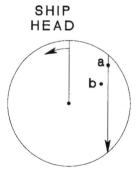

Fig. 3-5. Parallel index to starboard; PPI north up, gyro stabilized, radar echo between ship head and PI.

SHIP
HEAD

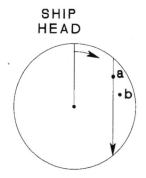

Fig. 3-6. Parallel index to starboard; PPI north up, gyro stabilized, radar echo outside of PI.

SHIP
HEAD

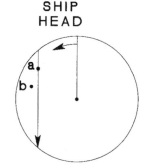

Fig. 3-7. Parallel index to port; PPI north up, gyro stabilized, radar echo outside of PI.

Application

An example from the College of Maritime Studies in their bridge watch-standing course best illustrates the concept of applying PI techniques. This example was developed by Captain David Douglas of the college and Captain Richard Beadon, former principal lecturer at the college.

Fig. 3-8 shows a planned approach to a single buoy mooring (SBM). The initial course of 009° (T) is along a range (transit) with a quick flashing white light in line with an occulting white light.

Course is then altered to 067° (T) along a range (transit) of a flashing yellow light on the SBM with a flashing red light behind. The same planned track can be monitored by using radar. The first essential is to select a radar reference object that is identified easily—in this case Gusong Tower. The perpendicular distance (cross-index range) from Gusong Tower to the 009° (T) track is 1.86 miles (see Fig. 3-9). The planned initial track of 009° (T) can be represented as follow:

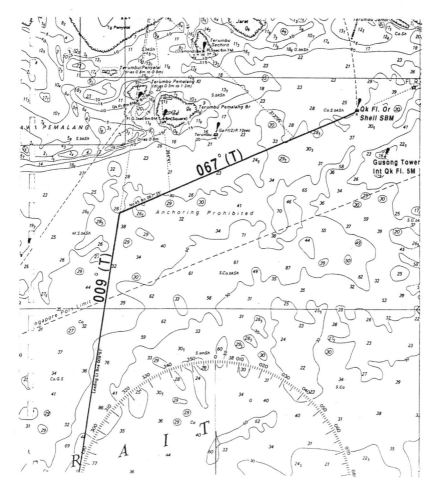

Fig. 3-8. Planned approach to an SBM. (Courtesy of the College of Maritime Studies, Warsash, U.K.)

1. Select the appropriate range scale; in this case three miles.
2. Line up the engraved cursor lines in the direction of the planned track of 009° (T).
3. Set the variable range marker to the cross-index range of 1.86 miles.
4. Select a PI line parallel to the cursor lines and tangential to the variable range marker (see Fig. 3-10).

If the ship remains in the planned track, then the radar echo of Gusong Tower will move along the PI line in a reciprocal direction to the track. However, suppose that the ship is set to the left of the planned track and is in position A (see Fig. 3-9). The radar echo of Gusong Tower will appear

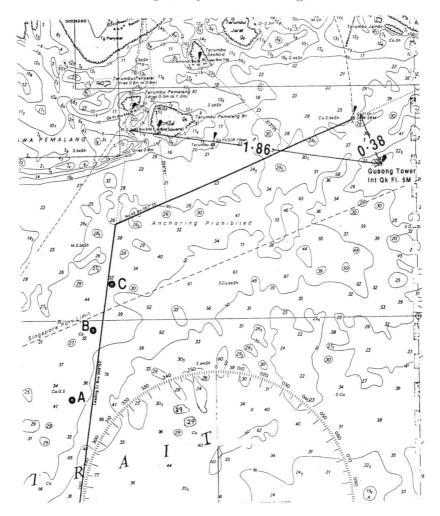

Fig. 3-9. Cross-index range (CIR) of 1.86 miles from Gusong Tower. (Courtesy of the College of Maritime Studies, Warsash, U.K.)

in position A (see Fig. 3-11). It is apparent therefore, that the ship is not on the planned track.

As the radar echo is farther away than anticipated, the ship must be to the left of the 009° (T) track, and an adjustment of course to starboard is necessary. Several minutes later the ship is at position B. The radar picture (see Fig. 3-11) indicates that the ship is still to the left of, but regaining, the planned track and the adjustments made to the course can be reduced. Later at position C the radar echo of Gusong Tower indicates that the ship is very nearly on the planned track, having overshot slightly to the right. Further adjustments of course can be ordered as necessary.

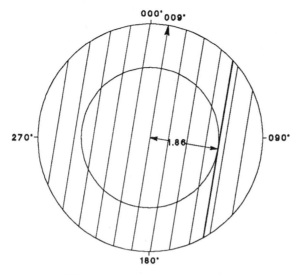

Fig. 3-10. CIR of 1.86 miles on reflection plotter. (Courtesy of the College of Maritime Studies, Warsash, U.K.)

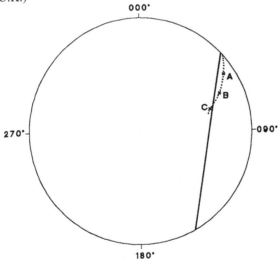

Fig. 3-11. Gusong Tower radar echo in position A on reflection plotter. (Courtesy of the College of Maritime Studies, Warsash, U.K.)

The information from the radar is twofold:

1. By comparing the position of the radar echo of Gusong Tower with the parallel index line drawn, the observer can immediately tell where the ship is, relative to the planned track.

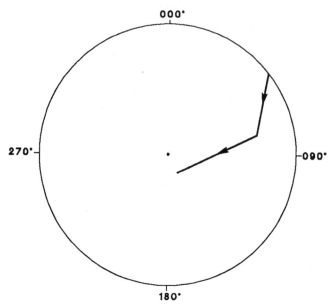

Fig. 3-12. Second parallel index line to 067° (T) track from
Gusong Tower 0.38 mile. (Courtesy of the College of
Maritime Studies Warsash, U.K.)

2.   Frequent checking of the echo of the radar reference object
shows the observer the *tendency* to diverge from or regain the
planned track.

The final planned track to SBM is 067° (T). The cross-index range
form Gusong Tower to the 067° (T) track is 0.38 miles (see Fig. 3-9).

A second parallel index line can now be inserted to join up with the first
parallel index line as shown in Figure 3-12. If the ship follows the planned
track on the chart, then the radar echo of Gusong Tower will move along
the parallel index lines in the direction shown by the arrows.
Note and compare the shapes of the two diagrams:

The chart (see Fig. 3-8) shows the motion of the ship relative to
Gusong Tower.

The reflection plotter (see Fig. 3-12) shows the motion of Gusong Tower
relative to the ship.

In altering course from 009° (T) to 067° (T) the ship will follow a
curved track similar to that shown in Figure 3-13. From the chart the
range and bearing of Gusong Tower from each lettered position are
measured as follows:

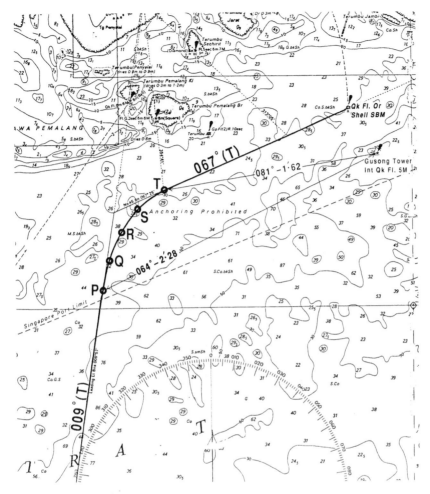

Fig. 3-13. Track of vessel changing course from 009° (T) to 067° (T). (Courtesy of the College of Maritime Studies Warsash, U.K.)

P bearing 064° (T) range 2.28 miles
Q bearing 069° (T) range 2.13 miles
R bearing 074° (T) range 1.99 miles
S bearing 078° (T) range 1.82 miles
T bearing 081° (T) range 1.62 miles

These positions can be joined into a smooth curve (see Fig. 3-14).

The ship's progress now can be monitored continuously during all phases of the approach to the SBM by plotting the movement of the radar echo of Gusong Tower. Corrective helm or engine orders can then be given to maintain the planned track.

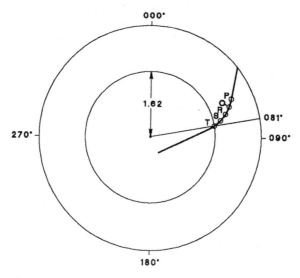

Fig. 3-14. Plotted positions joined in a smooth curve. (Courtesy of the College of Maritime Studies, Warsash, U.K.)

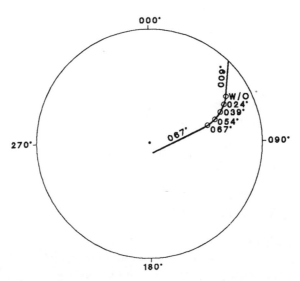

Fig. 3-15. Intended maneuver as marked. (Courtesy of the College of Maritime Studies, Warsash, U.K.)

Increased control of the ship's navigational safety can be achieved if the lettered positions correspond to anticipated headings during the progress of the turn:

P—Wheel-over position, ship's head 009°
Q—Ship's head passing through 024° (T)
R—Ship's head passing through 039° (T)
S—Ship's head passing through 054° (T)
T—Ship's head passing on course 067° (T)

Figure 3-15 shows the intended maneuver. Monitoring of the ship's progress will show the present position of the ship relative to the intended track and the tendency to diverge from or regain the intended track. Comparison of actual and anticipated headings during the turn will allow the rate of turn to be adjusted and the alteration of course to be accurately controlled.

Notes on the Use of Parallel Indexing

1. Parallel indexing is not a complete navigation system on its own. It should be used in conjunction with regular fixing, visual lookout, depth monitoring, and whatever other navigational information is available. At the passage-planning stage the track selected should, wherever possible, be suitable for visual and radar monitoring.
2. Practice makes perfect. There is no substitute for the regular use of parallel indexing whenever opportunities occur. Without regular practice, errors and mistakes easily can be made.
3. With regular practice, straight parallel index lines can be quickly and accurately inserted and new lines drawn as the ship proceeds along her planned route.
4. Parallel indexing is most accurate when the radar reference object is abeam, and least accurate when the radar reference object is near the ship's fore-and-aft line. This is due to the possibility of bearing errors.
5. Accurate identification of the radar reference object is essential. As a precaution against the dangers of misidentification, radar fixes on the chart should not make use of the radar reference object.
6. For a curved clearing line the optimum radar reference object is small, easily identified, and on the inside of the curve.
7. When using parallel indexing, make sure that the range scale in use is the same as that for which the lines were drawn.
8. Accuracy is improved if the shortest range scale possible is used. When using a short range for parallel indexing it is imperative that longer ranges are also monitored.

It is an accepted practice that the track on the chart must be carefully checked to avoid errors on the part of the navigator. It is equally true that parallel index lines should be carefully checked before use.

THE PLAN

The passage plan from berth to berth should be made in detail with all waypoints and columns filled in.

The majority of entries on a voyage plan are obvious, but some explanatory notes are listed below from left to right on Figure 3-19:

1. Way points are major course changes or important positions where fix's should be obtained. The way points can be alphabetical or numerically indicated.
2. Position should be by bearing and distance from a radar conspicuous or geographic navigational reference mark. Offshore latitude and longitude can be indicated to be verified by GPS. Where appropriate, parallel index lines should be indicated left or right to verify the track.
3. The speed shall be the speed expected to make good, taking into account anticipated set and drift.
4. The course to steer is what must be steered to make the track. See Figure 3-16a.

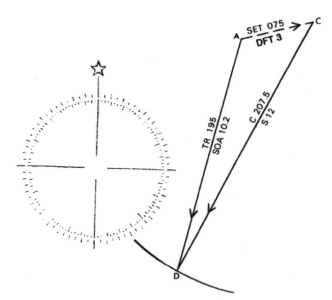

Fig. 3-16 a. Determining course and speed to make good a desired track. (Courtesy of Dutton's Navigation and Piloting.)

In Figure 3-16a from point A, the position of the vessel, lay out the line AD of indefinite length in the direction 195°. Plot the current vector, AC, in the direction of the set, 075°, for a distance equal to the velocity of the drift, 3 knots. With C as a center, swing an arc of radius equal to the vessel's speed through the water, 12 knots, intersecting AD at D. The direction, CD, 207.5°, is the course to order and the length AD, 10.2 knots, is the estimated SOA. Notice that vectors AD and AC, representing the intended track and current respectively, have been plotted with respect to the earth (point A), while vector CD has been plotted with respect to the water.

5.   The track is the course made good as a result of steering a course that takes into account set and drift and speed of advance. The track is what is laid down on the chart. See Figure 3-16b.

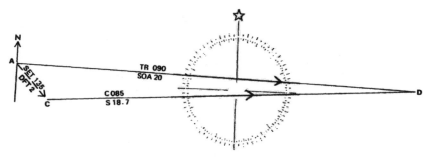

Fig. 3-16 b. (Courtesy of Dutton's Navigation and Piloting.)

Given the set and drift of the estimated current, and the direction of the desired track and the required speed of advance, find the course and speed to be used.

Required: A vessel at 1300 is 100 miles due west of her desired destination. If the ship is to arrive at her destination at 1800, find the course and speed to order if a 2-knot current southeast (135°) is predicted.

Solution: In Figure 3-16b the vessel is located at point A with point D as its destination, 100 miles due east. With five hours to reach this destination, she obviously must maintain a speed of advance of 20 knots. Lay off AD in the direction 090° to represent the intended track and of a length equal to the intended SOA, 20 knots. Lay off the current vector, AC, in the direction of its set, 135°, from Point A and of a length equal to the drift, 2 knots. Complete the current sailing vector diagram by drawing CD. The direction of CD, 085°, is the course to steer, while its length, 18.7 knots, is the speed to order to make the passage. Again, notice that vectors AD and AC, representing intended track and current respectively, have been plotted with respect to the earth, while vector CD has been plotted with respect to the water.

6. The current should be noted by set (direction going to) followed by its speed or drift in knots.

7. Distance to go should be the distance to next way point over total distance to go.

8. Underkeel clearance (UKC) must take into account the vessel's draft and indicated in feet, meters or fathoms, which is determined by the datum on the chart.

9. Posit fix method should be circled and several methods if possible should be utilized.

10. Remarks should be helpful notes or reminders in order to follow the plan. Frequency of fixes are dependent upon how restricted the waters and the margins of safety are. In confined waters fixes may have to be taken once every three minutes, less confined waters may only require fixes once every six minutes. Off shore fixes may only be required once every 20-30 minutes. Generally, how long may the vessel proceed before exceeding the margins of safety will determine the frequency of fixes.

11. Contingency plans are situations which may occur and as a result could result in changes to the plan. If not on the plan they should be listed on the back of the plan as shown in Figure 3-18 (top of plan). They could include for example: safe anchorages, weather concerns or pilot not available, etc.

The information should be noted on the charts to be used for the passage. In addition, all the above information should be noted in the watch officer's conning notebook or bridge notebook for the portions of the passage where he or she will have the watch. Examples of passage plans are found in Figures 3-17 and 3-18.

An actual completed plan for arrival in Limon Bay, Panama, with orders to anchor in anchorage Bravo is shown in Figure 3-19. The chart extract from DMA 26068 (Puerto Cristóbal) with all notations is shown in Figure 3-20. Final notations in the conning or bridge notebook for this portion of the arrival are shown in Figure 3-21 and during the watch a navigation record log (see Fig. 3-22) should be maintained.

RECORDKEEPING

The Deck Log

The deck log is the legal and permanent record of the ship's life and operations. Because of the many ramifications involved, it is essential that an accurate, complete, and proper log be kept. Obviously it is not possible to list here all of the incidents that should be logged.

735-0091

VOYAGE PLAN AND NAVIGATION CHECK LIST SHEET ____ OF ____

VESSEL ____ FROM ____ TO ____ DEPARTURE ____ MASTER ____

TO BE COMPLETED BY NAVIGATING OFFICER				TO BE COMPLETED BY MASTER								TO BE COMPLETED BY WATCH OFFICER						WATCH OFFICER'S COMMENTS	MASTER'S COMMENTS
Departure or A/C Position From Latitude - Longitude	A/C To Latitude - Longitude	True Course	Distance	Est. Speed	Running Time	E.T.A. At Next A/C Position		Time Master To Be Called	If position off course — or not verified, master to be called immediately	Position Fixing Frequency	Position Fixing Methods	Log Distance	Expected Minimum Sounding	Actual Sounding	Course Correction, Compass Error, Currents, etc.	Actual Time A/C	Time New Course Verified	Ie. Defective equipment, reasons for diversion from course, any difference between expected and actual soundings, compass error, currents.	And additional instruction, to include manual or auto steering, doubling up of watches, lookouts and calling master.
						Date	Time												

COURSE CHECKED BY: WATCH OFFICER ____ WATCH OFFICER ____ WATCH OFFICER ____ WATCH OFFICER ____

IMPORTANT – E.T.A. AT A/C POSITION *MUST* BE ENTERED ON CHART BY WATCH OFFICER.

SAILING DRAFT

CHANGES IN DRAFT (Ballast change or cargo shift)

Shore Management Check

____ SIGNATURE

Fig. 3-17. Passage plan. (Courtesy of EXXON.)

PASSAGE PLAN SS CAPELLA	MASTER:	VHF INFORMATION	WEATHER	TIDAL INFORMATION
DATE ARRIVE DEPART TRANSIT	OOW: Nav: Radar: Helm:			

WAY POINT	1. POSITION 2. INDEXING INFO	TIME	ENGINE STATUS	SPEED	TRACK	CURRENT	COURSE TO STEER	DISTANCE (To go)	UKC Fm M	POSN FIX METHOD	REMARKS
										Vis Radar Loran Satnav	
										Vis Radar Loran Satnav	
										Vis Radar Loran Satnav	
										Vis Radar Loran Satnav	
										Vis Radar Loran Satnav	
										Vis Radar Loran Satnav	
										Vis Radar Loran Satnav	

Fig. 3-18. Passage plan developed by Captain Richard Beadon for the cadet bridge watchkeeping course on the CAORF simulator at the USMMA.

It is suggested that all officers responsible for log entries (especially newly assigned officers) review the general instructions below. Masters are responsible for proper log maintenance and should make a concentrated effort to see that these instructions are followed. When top and bottom of the log are referred to in the sections that follow, these terms apply to a standard logsheet found aboard most merchant vessels.

1. Keep all entries legible. Use proper nautical terms.
2. *Do not erase.* Any corrections must be carefully indicated by a line through the original entry and initialed.
3. All times are to be recorded on a twenty-four-hour basis.
4. Officers making single entries must sign their name and rating after each entry and may not use initials. The log must be signed at the end of each watch by the officer standing watch.
5. Enter any accidents, casualties, fires, or unusual happenings that may affect the safety of the ship or cargo, or the welfare of the crew.
6. Log entries regarding casualties are to be made as complete and accurate as possible and confined to statements of fact. Any assistance given to, or received from, an outside party should be recorded in detail.
7. Arrival, departure, SBE (standby engines), FWE (finished with engines), tests, drills, and inspections are commonly entered in *red.*

PASSAGE PLAN (CONTINGENCY PLANS ON REVERSE SIDE)

VESSEL: M/V CAPELLA	FROM: NEW YORK		TO: PANAMA		SHEET NO: 6 OF 6	

DATE: 16 FEB 04	MASTER: MARINER	CHART NO:	WEATHER FORECAST: WIND NW FORCE 2 CLEAR VIS. SUNRISE 0550	TIDAL INFORMATION: HW 0618 .9 FT BASE ON COLON
	OOW: LEE			
DEPART: / ARRIVE: CRISTOBAL / TRANSIT:	NAV: BROWN	VHF: 12 CRIS. SIG STA 13 BRIDGE TO BRIDGE 16 HAIL & DISTRESS		
	RADAR: JONES			
	HELM: BURLEIGH			

WAY POINT	1. POSITION: 2. INDEXING INFO:	TIME	ENGINE STATUS	SPEED	COURSE TO STEER	TRACK	CURRENT	DISTANCE (TO GO) TO NP/TRK / TO CO	UKC FT (M) FM	POSIT FIX METHOD	REMARKS FREQUENCY OF FIXES: 6 MIN
A	L 09°-27.9'N L 079°-55.8'W S'BUOY Ø/83 3.15 MI	0600	UK SEA SPD	14.9 kt	180°	180°	NEC	.85 MI / 6.6 MI	104 M +	VIS RADAR LORAN SATNAV	• PRE ARR TEST • CALL MASTER & C/M • CALL E/R • CALL CRIS SIG STA
B	SEA BUOY Ø 1.0 MI	0606	UK 108 RPM ARRIVAL	14.9 KT	141°	141°	NEC	2.48 / 5.67	10.4	VIS RADAR LORAN SATNAV	• HOIST FLAGS • MAN AFT STG • & READY • ARRIVAL 0606
C	SEA BUOY Ø 1.0 MI PI 0.3 MI P/S ON BKNTR	0612	60 RPM	8.5 KT	180°	180°	NEG.	1.42 / 3.19	8.1	VIS RADAR LORAN SATNAV	• SECURITY CALL • SET UP PI • ENSURE STATIONS MANNED
D	BKWATER	0621	60 RPM	8.5 KT	180°	180°	NEG.	0.7 / 1.77	6.1	VIS RADAR LORAN SATNAV	• SECURITY CALL • WALK OUT PORT & • ENGAGE BOW THRUSTER
E	WEST BRKWATER @ Yd MI H'BUOY Ø228	0630	60 RPM C/S 40 RPM	6 KT	224°	224°	NEG	1.07 / 1.07	6.0	VIS RADAR LORAN SATNAV	• W/O FOR & AGE TO GO • MSS ON TIME & DIST TO 4'M • RIG & BUOY
F	& AGE BRAVO	0650	ASTERN RPM	0	224°	224°	NEG	0 / 0	1.5	VIS RADAR LORAN SATNAV	• LET GO PORT & • & & BUOY WATCHING • CALL CRIS. SIG STA
										VIS RADAR LORAN SATNAV	

Fig. 3-19. Passage plan for arrival Limon Bay (Cristóbal), Panama.

8. Passage summary and port time information are entered on the voyage summary page. It is not necessary to make these entries on the daily log page.

The following items must be logged and underlined or written in red. On U.S. vessels these entries must be logged in red:

- SBE
- FWE
- Arrival or departure—time (to nearest tenth of an hour) and position
- Arrival or departure—fuel, water, and drafts
- Gear test
- Fire and boat drills
- All legal tests of equipment (line-throwing appliance, emergency lighting system, etc.)
- Pratique
- Commence loading and complete loading of fuel and amount loaded
- Breakdowns (not under command)
- Significant weather or sea conditions where reduction of speed is required
- Stowaway, contraband, and narcotic searches
- Any other item as indicated by the master, mate, or watch officer

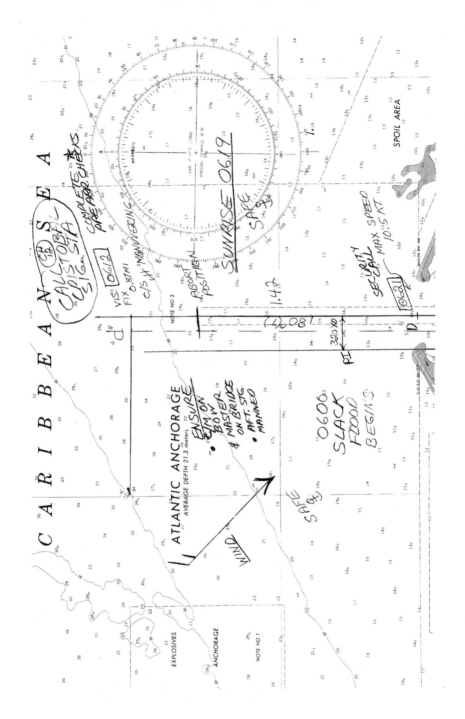

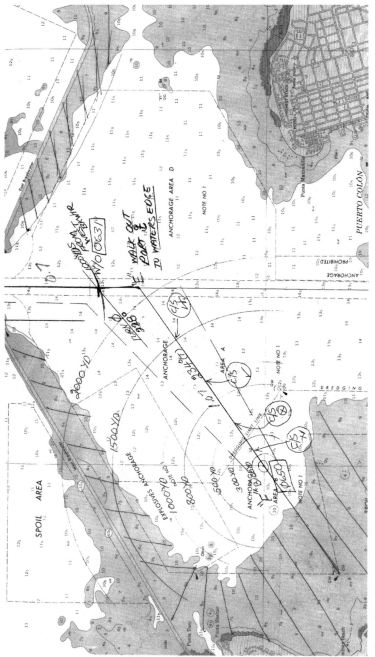

Fig. 3-20. Chart extract from DMA (Puerto Cristóbal) with track and notations.

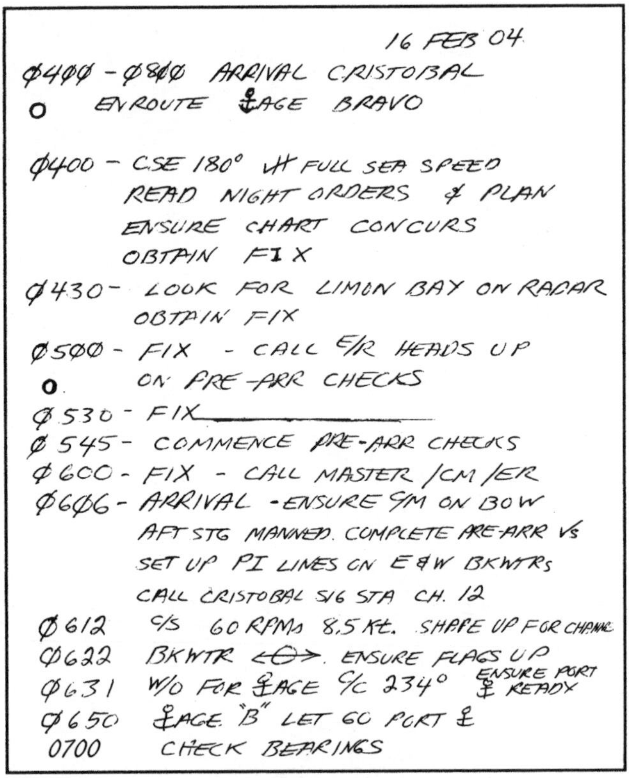
16 FEB 04
Ø4ØØ - Ø8ØØ ARRIVAL CRISTOBAL
O ENROUTE ⚓AGE BRAVO

Ø400 - CSE 180° ↗H FULL SEA SPEED
READ NIGHT ORDERS & PLAN
ENSURE CHART CONCURS
OBTAIN FIX
Ø430 - LOOK FOR LIMON BAY ON RADAR
OBTAIN FIX
Ø5ØØ - FIX - CALL E/R HEADS UP
O ON PRE-ARR CHECKS
Ø530 - FIX
Ø545 - COMMENCE PRE-ARR CHECKS
Ø600 - FIX - CALL MASTER /CM /ER
Ø6Ø6 - ARRIVAL - ENSURE 9M ON BOW
AFT STG MANNED. COMPLETE PRE-ARR Vs
SET UP PI LINES ON E & W BKWTRs
CALL CRISTOBAL S/6 STA CH. 12
Ø612 C/S 60 RPMs 8.5 Kt. SHAPE UP FOR CHANNL
Ø622 BKWTR <⊖>. ENSURE FLAGS UP
Ø631 W/O FOR ⚓AGE C/C 234° ENSURE PORT ⚓ READY
Ø650 ⚓AGE "B" LET GO PORT ⚓
0700 CHECK BEARINGS

Fig. 3-21. Notations in conning or bridge notebook for arrival Limon Bay, (Cristóbal) Panama.

The following items shall be logged by the master or mate. On U.S. vessels they are required to be logged in red:

- Securing of hatches and all hull openings
- Cargo gear test
- Sanitary inspections
- Deaths
- Accidents
- Any casualty on board or to the vessel

The deck log has certain entries for when the vessel is at sea and when it is in port. Wherever the vessel is, it is essential that an accurate, complete, and proper log be kept. The importance of the deck log cannot be sufficiently emphasized. In the case of any proceedings, legal or otherwise, it is the only record that will be accepted as evidence.

Sea Log

The entries that are suggested below customarily commence when the vessel records SBE, last line from a berth, anchor aweigh from an anchorage, or last line from a mooring buoy. The sea portion of the log usually terminates upon first line to berth, anchor set, or first line to a mooring buoy. It can terminate with the entry of FWE and when pilot and tugs depart.

1. Across top of log enter the vessel's name, passage, and date.
2. Lined area of log has two lines for each hour of the day. Only the lines at the end of each watch need be filled out. Make sea watch entries in respective columns. The compass columns are self explanatory. Fill weather columns as follows:
   (a) Wind. Enter wind direction.
   (b) Force. Use Beaufort scale.
   (c) Barometer. Enter corrected reading.
   (d) Air. Enter outside temperature.
   (e) Water. Enter seawater temperature.
   (f) RPM. Enter average rpm for watch.
   (g) Sea. List direction and state.
   (h) Swell. Enter direction and state.
   (i) Weather. State condition of sky—clear, overcast, rain, fog, haze.
   (j) Visibility. Record state of visibility.
   (k) Vessel. Enter vessel movements.
3. Enter exact time of course changes.
4. Enter exact time of any significant weather changes on line to nearest hour.
5. Enter date for end of navigational day at noon, center of page.
6. Sections at bottom of page are self-explanatory. Soundings should be taken at least twice a day, preferably at 0800 and 1700.
7. All navigation data entered must be sufficiently complete and in such form as will facilitate plotting the ship's position (dead reckoning) at sea or at anchor or on pilot passage.
8. The following are required entries:
   (a) Details of ballasting—times, amount, and tanks.
   (b) Fire and boat drills.
   (c) Test of line throwing gun.
   (d) Inspections of steering engine daily.
   (e) Sanitary inspections conducted.
   (f) Inspections of deck cargo lashings daily.
   (g) Ventilation or recirculation of cargo holds daily if cargo holds equipped with a dehumidifier (time on and off).
   (h) Search for contraband prior to arrival.
   (i) Stripping and overhaul of lifeboats.
   (j) Measures taken to ease vessel.

M/V CAPELLA
NAVIGATION RECORD LOG

NAVIGATOR: WATCH TEAM: DATE:

TIME	OBJECT #1 BEARING AND/OR RANGE	OBJECT #2 BEARING AND/OR RANGE	OBJECT #3 BEARING AND/OR RANGE	UKC	ACTUAL DEPTH	CHARTED DEPTH	DISTANCE LEFT OR RIGHT OF TRACK

CHART SOUNDINGS ARE: FEET   FATHOMS   METERS (CIRCLE ONE)   SHIPS DRAFT:

FIX INTERVAL IS   3   OR   6   MINUTES   (CRICLE ONE)   PAGE____ OF____

Fig. 3-22. Navigation Record Log.

(k) Diversions and detentions—reason, time lost, and miles deviated.

(l) Precautions taken during reduced visibility.

(m) Time changes.

(n) Times when radar is not working and repairs are not possible. This entry shall be signed by the master, chief, officer, and second officer.

(o) Changeover of steering gear daily.

(p) Fathometer operation daily.

(q) Test of smoke detection alarm daily.

9. Arrivals, sailings, and shifts
    (a) Time engines tested astern and when anchors ready to let go.
    (b) Time of standby engine—first bell and time and position of arrival.
    (c) Time pilot aboard and name of pilot.
    (d) After pilot is on board make following entry as appropriate, "Various movements (bells and courses) proceeding upriver under pilot's direction."
    (e) Enter names of principal lighthouses, jetties, and landmarks, etc., passed.
    (f) If vessel anchors, enter time let go, port or starboard anchor, amount of chain, fathoms of water, and true bearings of anchorage. Enter time began heaving, anchor aweigh, anchor in sight, clear anchor, and anchor secured for sea.
    (g) Enter names and times tugs alongside and location at ship.
    (h) Enter time entering locks, secure in locks, and clear of locks.
    (i) Enter time first line to dock, time alongside, and time secure.
    (j) Enter time FWE and give conditions, such as, "1706 FWE, vessel secure port side to city dock No 9, berth 2."
    (k) Enter times pilot and tugs away.

The same entries as appropriate will be made for sailing and shifts:

    (a) Enter test of navigation gear.
    (b) Enter time single up, last line, and clear of dock.
    (c) Enter time and place of departure.

Port Log

The suggested entries and format apply to the vessel while it is secured to a berth, mooring, buoy, or anchor.

1. Across the top, fill in the vessel's name, port, dock, and date. On dock line, give vessel's location in port, such as name and number of dock, repair yard, mooring buoy, anchorage, etc.
2. The first remark at the start of each day should state the status of the ship and be entered at the top of the lined area of log page, for example: "Vessel lying idle, as before, at Market Street Wharf, port side to."
3. Enter routine inspections of lights, lines, gangways, etc., and results thereof.
4. Enter summary of weather at sunrise and sunset in the wind force, barometer, air temperature, and weather columns, such as, "0620, Sunrise, ESE 2, 30.39, 57°, partly cloudy." Enter any significant weather changes.
5. Enter drafts at 0800, 1700, and 2400.
6. Enter all watchmen's names, times of duty, and location.

7. Enter times of use of deck, cargo, gangway, and special lights.
8. Enter times lighters or other vessels come alongside and leave. Give names of tugs towing, location alongside, and work performed.
9. When bunkering, observe all regulations, that is, red (bravo) flag or light displayed, scuppers plugged, bilge soundings at least once every hour and one hour after finish, and make appropriate entries.
10. Enter bilge soundings as required.
11. Enter injuries to all personnel other than crew members. Limit entries to simple statements of fact.
12. Enter the times and names of any officials, surveyors, or inspectors aboard, and purpose and result of visit, for instance:
    (a) Government inspectors
    (b) Classification society surveyors
    (c) Board underwriter inspector
    (d) Customs, immigration, quarantine officers
    (e) Police
    (f) Cargo surveyors
    (g) Others
13. Drydock entries should be made as follows:
    (a) Time enter lock (cross sill).
    (b) Time lock gates shut.
    (c) Time commenced pumping.
    (d) Time rest on keel blocks.
    (e) Time dock is dry.
    (f) General condition, cleaning, and painting bottom.
    (g) Time began flooding.
    (h) Time vessel afloat.
    (i) Time lock gates opened.
    (j) Time clear drydock.
14. The following are required entries:
    (a) Search for stowaways prior to sailing.
    (b) Inspections of shell plate and wheel after dock and shifts.
    (c) Start and finish of government inspections.
    (d) Vessel secure for sea prior to sailing.
    (e) When radar is not working and repairs are not possible. This entry to be signed by the master, chief office, and second officer.
    (f) Time posted notice to crew, such as sailing, shift, call back, and restrictions and quote notice.

Movement (Bell) Book

Recommended engine telegraph signals and symbols used on the bridge and in the engine room are as follows:

Order	Symbol	How Indicated
Stand by engines	SBE	Telegraph position
Dead slow ahead	⤴	Telegraph position or ring slow ahead twice
Slow ahead	⤴	Telegraph position
Half ahead	⤴	Telegraph position
Full ahead	⤴	Telegraph position
Emergency full ahead	⤴	Ring full ahead two or more times in succession
Stop	X	Telegraph position
Dead slow astern	⤵D	Telegraph position or ring slow astern twice
Slow astern	⤵	Telegraph position
Half astern	⤵	Telegraph position
Full astern	⤵	Telegraph position
Emergency full astern	⤵	Ring full astern two or more times in succession
Finished with engines	FWE	Telegraph position

No erasures are made in either the logbook or bell book. Incorrect entries must be rectified by drawing a single line through them, initialing, and rewriting the entry.

Entries

The log entries on many merchant vessels are extremely poor. Entries are too brief and most voyages could not be reconstructed accurately if need be. In addition, admiralty lawyers in many maritime cases cannot substantiate arguments of the shipowners due to poor or nonexistent log entries. The shipowner requires many records but none is as important as a well-documented logbook. Many times a shipowner will require too many records to be kept during the watch, which interferes with the keeping of a proper lookout. Notations during the watch should be made in the watch officer's conning notebook and after being relieved the OOW should not leave the chart room until a well-documented log entry of the watch is written and signed. An example of such an entry for arriving in Limon Bay in accordance with the previous passage plan (see Fig. 3-19) is found in Fig. 3-23.

VIA __PANAMA CANAL__   DATE __16 FEB 2004__

> 00-04   VESSEL enroute Singapore via Panama Canal. Steering 180° T, 180 rpm @ 14.9 kTs. Vessel riding easy in a long low NWly swell. Calm Sea. Excellent visibility
>   Shipwreck O'Malley C/m
>
> 04-08   ENROUTE as before 0401 Limon Bay BkwTr on radar Ø 172°T @ 30.5 NM. 0505 Punta Toro LT brok Ø 201°T @ 18.5 NM. 0545 commenced pre-arrival checks. 0606 Arrival Christobal with "S" bouy Ø 136°T @ 1.0 NM. A/c 141°T. 0612 Sea Buoy Ø @ 0.84 NM. A/c 180° T & gyro. Reduce speed to 60 RPM. Completed arrival checks - all in apparent good order 0621 Breakwater @. Various courses as per bell book. 0650 Let go port @. 0656 To set in 39 feet of water with Two shots on deck and Punta Toro LT Ø288.5°T, West Breakwater Ø 028°T, mid buoy "H" Ø 034°T. 0700 Port officials aboard. Stores Barge alongside stbd. Start Loading stores. 0730 Port officials ashore, vsl cleared. Anchor Ø checked frequently - continue loading stores.
>   Sally O'Hara 3/m
>
> 08-12   Vessel anchored as before continue Taking stores. 0945 Finish Taking stores, stores barge away.

CHIEF OFFICER_____   MASTER __J. M. Mariner__

Fig. 3-23. Log entry for arrival Limon Bay (Cristóbal), Panama.

CHAPTER FOUR

Compliance with the Rules of the Road

T HE International Rules (commonly called 72 COLREGS), developed by the Inter-Governmental Maritime Consultative Organization (IMCO), became effective on July 15, 1977. In May 1982, IMCO was renamed the International Maritime Organization (IMO). These rules are applicable on waters outside of established navigational lines of demarcation and are referred to in this chapter. In particular "Part B-Steering and Sailing Rules" is examined to make the OOW aware of how to comply practically with these regulations. Radio-telephone procedures will be detailed, along with how to use the VHF as an anti-collision aid. Finally, a recommendation on how to inform the captain will be discussed.

STEERING AND SAILING RULES

Rules 4, 5, 7, 8, 11, 14, 15, 16, and 17 are reprinted below. The portions of most concern to the OOW appear in italics. A comment follows each rule. The author gratefully acknowledges permission from A. N. Cockroft to paraphrase his comments from the book he co-authored with J. N. F. Lameijer, *A Guide to Collision Avoidance Rules.*

Section I
Conduct of Vessels in Any Condition of Visibility

Rule 4

Application

Rules in this section apply to any condition of visibility.

Comment:
OOWs should bear in mind that this section applies in any condition of visibility, restricted or unrestricted.

Rule 5

Lookout

Every vessel shall at all times maintain a proper lookout by sight and hearing as well as by all available means appropriate in the prevailing circumstances and conditions so as to make a full appraisal of the situation and of the risk of collision.

Comment:

The lookout must give full attention to keeping a proper lookout and no other duties should be undertaken or assigned that could interfere with that task.

The duties of the lookout and helmsman are separate, and the helmsman should not be considered the lookout while steering, except in small ships where the steering position provides an unobstructed all-round view and there is no impairment of night vision or other impediment to keeping a proper lookout. The OOW may be the sole lookout in daylight, provided that on each such occasion:

1. The situation is carefully assessed and established without doubt that the arrangement is safe.
2. Full account is taken of all relevant factors, including, but not limited, to state of weather, visibility, traffic density, proximity of danger to navigation, the attention necessary when navigating in or near traffic separation schemes.
3. Assistance can be immediately summoned to the bridge when any change in the situation requires.
4. Ship owners and managers should mandate, by instructions, posting a lookout on their vessels when and where they are most effective. In the author's opinion, a lookout is most effective when posted as far forward and as low down as possible, and that position is on the bow. On many occasions, the lookout is the first to detect a threat. It could be a vessel that was not detected by the bridge's radar, OOW, or Master.

Rule 7

Risk of Collision

    (a) Every vessel shall use all available means appropriate to the prevailing circumstances and conditions to determine if risk of collision exists. If there is any doubt such risk shall be deemed to exist.

    (b) Proper use shall be made of radar equipment if fitted and operational, including long-range scanning to obtain early warning of risk of collision and radar plotting or equivalent systematic observation of detected objects.

(c) Assumptions shall not be made on the basis of scanty information, especially scanty radar information.

(d) In determining if risk of collision exists, the following considerations shall be among those taken into account:

(i) Such risk shall be deemed to exist if the compass bearing of an approaching vessel does not appreciably change;

(ii) Such risk may sometimes exist even when an appreciable bearing change is evident, particularly when approaching a very large vessel or a tow or when approaching a vessel at close range.

Comment:

The importance of visual bearings cannot be stressed enough. OOWs often are glued to the radar scope and seem reluctant to go out on the windy bridge wings to take visual bearings. Many bridge wings are long and in adverse weather OOWs may be reluctant to make the trek, uncover the repeater cover, and trek back. This may no longer be a problem with centerline repeaters now being installed on most bridges.

Visual bearings will drift right or left or become steady. With a steady bearing there is a risk of collision in a meeting or crossing situation. The OOW also can use the bridge window and a grease pencil to determine bearing drift. Of course the OOW's point of observation cannot change during this observation of bearing drift. This bearing drift also can be observed by staying in the same position and noting the drift relative to a bridge window frame. Radar should be used as an aid to verify the type of situation. The use of binoculars to determine aspect along with visual bearings to determine drift should be foremost in the OOW's mind. Radar should be used for long-range scanning and later to verify the closest point of approach (CPA).

Rule 8

Action to Avoid Collision

(a) Any action taken to avoid collision shall, if the circumstances of the case admit, be positive, made in ample time and with due regard to the observance of good seamanship.

(b) Any alteration of course and/or speed to avoid collision shall, if the circumstances of the case admit, be large enough to be readily apparent to another vessel observing visually or

by radar; a succession of small alterations of course and/or
speed should be avoided.

(c) If there is sufficient sea room, alteration of course alone may
be the most effective action to avoid a close-quarters situation provided that it is made in good time, is substantial and
does not result in another close-quarters situation.

(d) Action taken to avoid collision with another vessel shall be
such as to result in passing at a safe distance. The effective-
-ness of the action shall be carefully checked until the other
vessel is finally past and clear.

(e) If necessary to avoid collision or allow more time to assess
the situation, a vessel shall slacken her speed or take all way
off by stopping or reversing her means of propulsion.

Comment:

A large tanker proceeding at normal passage speed probably would need
a distance of about two miles and a time of fifteen minutes to complete a
crash stop. The same vessel at the same speed could carry out a 90° turn
in three minutes and probably need a distance of only a half-mile to make
the turn.

Suppose you are the OOW of such a ship steaming at full speed. You
sight another vessel broad on your starboard bow, approaching you at a
fast speed. The compass bearing is steady. You decide (wisely) to take
action at a range of five miles. If you operate full-astern propulsion, the
range may be only one mile when you stop. If, however, you alter course
60° to starboard, the range will still be about four miles by the time you
steady on the new course. The foregoing may be constrained by sea room
due to restricted waters and/or depth of water.

Whatever giving-way action you take it must be positive enough and
early enough to *be certain of avoiding a collision.*

Section II
Conduct of Vessels in Sight of One Another

Rule 11

Application

Rules in this Section apply to vessels in sight of one another.

Comment:

The OOW should realize that each vessel must see the other for these rules
to apply. If vessels are in restricted visibility Rule 19 applies. Once the
visibility improves or they clear a fog bank and can see each other, then
the rules in this section apply.

Rule 14

Head-on Situation

(a) When two power-driven vessels are meeting on reciprocal or nearly reciprocal courses so as to involve risk of collision each *shall alter her course to starboard* so that each shall pass on the port side of the other.

(b) Such a situation shall be deemed to exist when a vessel sees the other ahead or nearly ahead and by night she could see the masthead lights of the other in a line or nearly in a line and/or both sidelights and by day she observes the corresponding aspect of the other vessel.

(c) When a vessel is in *any doubt* as to whether such a situation exists she shall *assume that it does exist and act accordingly.*

Comment:

To avoid possible dark lanes immediately ahead of a ship the sidelights are screened to show approximately 2° across the bow. The effect of yawing also must be taken into account. This will vary with the steering arrangements and steering qualities of the ship. The direction of the ship's head, and not the course made good, must be used to determine whether vessels are meeting end on or crossing. This may be important in conditions of strong wind or tide, where one vessel is drifting more rapidly than another, so that one vessel may see another end on fine on the bow and the bearing may remain constant.

It must be noted that Rule 14 generally will be superseded in the following situations:

1. Each vessel already is clear of the other port to port or starboard to starboard.
2. By night, both sidelights of the other vessel are seen anywhere but ahead.

Whether power-driven vessels are meeting on reciprocal courses or crossing at a fine angle, it is important that neither vessel alter course to port. If there appears to be a need to increase the distance of passing starboard to starboard this implies risk of collision. Several collisions have resulted because one vessel altered course to port to increase the passing distance and the other vessel turned to starboard. Several collisions also have been caused when it was a clear starboard to starboard meeting and one vessel altered course to starboard. In these situations, and in case of any doubt, early VHF communication between the vessels is paramount.

Sometimes it is not easy to say with any degree of accuracy whether vessels are in a head-on situation governed by Rule 14, or a crossing situation subject to Rule 15. A rule of thumb that may help is to add 180° to the course of the other vessel. If this figure is not within 6° of your course (allowing 3° on each bow) you may assume the other vessel is crossing. When a vessel is in any doubt as to whether she is meeting another vessel on a nearly reciprocal course or is crossing within the meaning of the rules of this section, she shall *assume that she is meeting* at a nearly reciprocal course.

Rule 15

Crossing Situation

When two power-driven vessels are crossing so as to involve risk of collision, the vessel which has the other on her own starboard side shall keep out of the way and shall, if the circumstances of the case admit, avoid crossing ahead of the other vessel.

Comment:

A vessel required to keep out of the way shall make a substantial alteration (at least 30°) of course to starboard. By showing your port sidelight (if at night) to the standon vessel, you are clearly indicating your compliance with Rule 15.

Rule 16

Action by Give-way Vessel

Every vessel that is directed to keep out of the way of another vessel shall, so far as possible, take early and substantial action to keep well clear.

Comment:

Rules 8(a), 15, and 16 clearly indicate that your action should be positive, early, and substantial, and you should avoid crossing ahead of the other vessel. The OOW has to decide what positive, early, and substantial means in each individual case. A good rule of thumb is to make an initial altera-tion of course of 30° at a range of five miles.

What early action means will depend upon the types of vessels involved and the speeds at which they are going, but generally the OOW should take action as soon as the officer has determined his or her vessel is the give-way vessel. Again, avoiding action must be positive enough and early enough to be *certain* of avoiding a collision.

The give-way vessel should take positive action in ample time so that the stand-on vessel can maintain her course and speed. If the stand-on vessel takes action in accordance with Rule 17(a)(ii), the give-way vessel still is obliged to take action to ensure that a safe passing distance is achieved, as required by Rule 8(d).

Rule 17

Action by Stand-on Vessel

(a) (i) Where one of two vessels is to keep out of the way the other shall keep her course and speed.

 (ii) The latter vessel may however take action to avoid collision by her maneuver alone, as soon as it becomes apparent to her that the vessel required to keep out of the way is not taking appropriate action in compliance with these rules.

(b) When, from any cause, the vessel required to keep her course and speed finds herself so close that collision cannot be avoided by the action of the give-way vessel alone, she shall take such action as will best aid to avoid collision.

(c) A power-driven vessel which takes action in a crossing situation in accordance with subparagraph (a) (ii) of this rule to avoid collision with another power-driven vessel shall, if the circumstances of the case admit, not alter course to port for a vessel on her own port side.

(d) This rule does not relieve the give-way vessel of her obligation to keep out of the way.

Comment:

When two vessels in sight of each other are approaching with no change in compass bearing, so that there is risk of collision, one of them is required to keep out of the way. There may be four stages relating to the permitted or required action for each vessel (Fig. 4-1a):

1. At long range, before risk of collision exists, both vessels are free to take any action.

2. When risk of collision first begins to apply the give-way vessel is required to take early and substantial action to achieve a safe passing distance and the other vessel must keep her course and speed.

3. When it becomes apparent that the give-way vessel is not taking appropriate action in compliance with the rules the stand-on vessel is required to give the whistle signal prescribed in Rule 34(d) and is permitted to take action to avoid collision by her maneuver alone, but a power-driven vessel must not alter course to port to avoid another power-driven vessel crossing from her

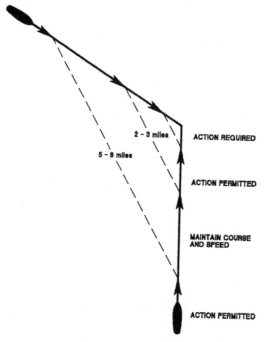

Fig. 4-1a. The four states in a collision situation. (Courtesy of A. N. Cockroft and J. N. F. Lameijer from Guide to Collision Regulations.)

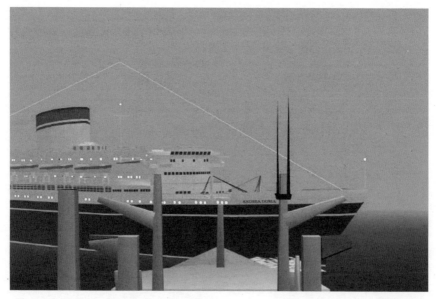

Fig. 4-1b. In extremis: Action required by both vessels. (Courtesy of CAORF.)

own port side. The give-way vessel is not relieved of her obligation to keep out of the way.

4.   When collision cannot be avoided by the give-way vessel alone the stand-on vessel is required to take such action as will best aid to avoid collision. (See Fig. 4-1b)

The collision in Figure 4-2 occurred in clear visibility, during the day, and is inexcusable. Early on in the situation (beyond five miles), the stand-on vessel should have called the give-way vessel on VHF and requested when the give-way vessel planned to alter course to starboard in order to cross astern of the stand-on vessel. The stand-on vessel should not waste time by asking about intentions. This watch officer should take charge of the situation and request compliance with the Rules of the Road. The stand-on watch officer should then take constant visual bearings to verify a left bearing drift which indicates that the give-way vessel has altered course to starboard. The Master must be advised and kept informed on the developing situation. By two miles between vessels the Master should be on the port bridge wing. You can determine instant compliance visually with the rules by a left bearing drift, change in aspect and/or change in the running lights. At night you will be looking for the green starboard side light to disappear and the red (port) side light to become visible. Compliance with the rules will become apparent visually earlier than by radar.

No bearing drift to the left necessitates more VHF calls and within two miles the sounding of the danger signal (at least five short blasts on the whistle and on the VHF by pressing the talk switch during the blasts). Finally, with no alteration of course by the give-way vessel the stand-on vessel may take action in accordance with Rule 17(a)(ii). At this point it is recommended that the stand-on vessel order hard left rudder to avoid a port side impact and in the hopes that the give-way vessel is altering course to starboard with a hard right rudder. Both vessels would then counter their swings with opposite rudder to avoid a stern collision. By altering course to port the stand-on vessel is presenting the strongest part of the vessel (the bow) for possible impact and not by exposing its more vulnerable port side.

The two vessels should never get into this circumstance if they comply early on with Rules 16 and 17.

The distances at which the various stages begin to apply will vary considerably. They will be much greater for high-speed vessels. For a crossing situation involving two power-driven vessels in the open sea is suggested that the outer limit of the second stage might be of the order of five to eight miles and that the outer limit for the third stage would be about two to three miles.

A disadvantage of permitting the stand-on vessel to take action to avoid collision by her maneuver alone is that the give-way vessel may be tempted to wait in the hope that the stand-on vessel will keep out of the way. The purpose of Rule 17(d) is to emphasize that the give-way vessel is not relieved of her obligation to take early and substantial action to achieve a safe passing distance. By the provisions of Rule 17(a)(ii), a stand-on vessel is not permitted to maneuver until it becomes apparent that the give-way vessel is not taking appropriate action in compliance with the rules.

Fig. 4-2. Violation of Rules 16 and 17. (Courtesy of Mariner's Weather Log, September 1978.)

Section III
Conduct of Vessels in Restricted Visibility

Rule 19

Conduct of Vessels in Restricted Visibility

(a) This rule applies to vessels not in sight of one another when navigating in or near an area of restricted visibility.

(b) Every vessel shall proceed at a safe speed adapted to the prevailing circumstances and conditions of restricted visibility. A power-driven vessel shall have her engines ready for immediate maneuver.

(c) Every vessel shall have due regard to the prevailing circumstances and conditions of restricted visibility when complying with the rules of Section I of this part.

(d) A vessel which detects by radar alone the presence of another vessel shall determine if a close-quarters situation is developing and/or risk of collision exists. If so, she shall take avoiding action in ample time, provided that when such action consists of an alteration of course, so far as possible the following shall be avoided:

    (i) an alteration of course to port for a vessel forward of the beam, other than for a vessel being overtaken;

    (ii) an alteration of course towards a vessel abeam or abaft the beam.

(e) Except where it has been determined that a risk of collision does not exist, every vessel which hears apparently forward of her beam the fog signal of another vessel, or which cannot avoid a close-quarters situation with another vessel forward of her beam, shall reduce her speed to the minimum at which she can be kept on her course. She shall, if necessary, take all her way off and in any event navigate with extreme caution until danger of collision is over.

Comment:

Rule 8(a) requires avoiding action to be taken in ample time in all conditions of visibility. When the visibility is restricted it generally is necessary to take action to avoid a close-quarters situation at an earlier stage. However, action should not be taken without first making a full assessment of the situation. Rule 7(c) states that assumptions shall not be made on the basis of scanty information, especially scanty radar information. If a fog signal from another vessel is heard the OOW should keep in mind that the vessel is within two miles (audible range of a whistle) although the direction of the vessel is very difficult, if not impossible, to determine.

As a general guide it has been suggested that, using a twelve-mile range scale in the open sea, radar observations should be assessed as an approaching target crosses the outer one-third of the screen. Action should be taken by one of the vessels (preferably both before four miles). If not, substantial action should be taken before the target reaches the inner one-third of the screen (Fig. 4-3).

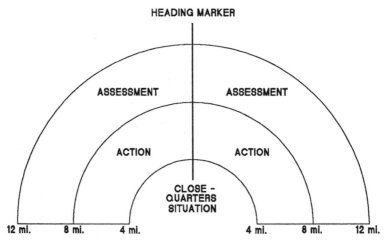

Fig. 4-3. Assessment, action, and close-quarters situations sectors of the twelve-mile range scale. (Courtesy of A. N. Cockroft and J. N. F. Lameijer from Guide to Collision Regulations.)

Visibility is difficult to determine at sea. Are precautions for restricted visibility commenced when visibility reduces to five miles or two miles? By observing the radar and visually seeing when vessels or other objects disappear from sight the OOW can determine when restricted visibility procedures should commence. If there is any doubt the OOW should call the master. The procedures that should be complied with in restricted visibility follow:

1. Reduction to a safe speed and engines on standby.
2. Master and engine room informed.
3. Radar operated and plotting commenced.
4. Prescribed fog signals sounded.
5. Hand steering engaged.
6. VHF receiver switched to channels 13 and 16 unless local conditions require another listening watch channel.
7. Lookouts (audiovisual) posted as far forward and as low down as possible.

8. Navigation lights switched on.
9. Echo sounder operated, if in soundings.
10. Specified watertight doors shut.
11. If position is in doubt, possibility of anchoring considered.
12. More than one officer may be called to assist at the discretion of the master.

The log entry that should be made is as follows:

0805   Vis. decreases to .5 mi. Notified master, placed eng. on SBE, commenced sounding fog signals, radars and running lights on, posted lookout fwd, switched to hand stg. All precautions taken.
0810   Master on the bridge
0900   Vis. increases to approx. 8 miles. Resumed normal steaming. Master left bridge.

VHF PROCEDURES

Boards of investigation in their reports of findings concerning collisions times say it would have been prudent for the two vessels to try to establish contact via their radio-telephones for the purpose of establishing a passing agreement. The term "pass" should be avoided as it can apply to meeting, crossing and overtaking situations.

How do you talk to other vessels or stations on VHF and how do you identify the vessel you are speaking to?

For VHF calls to other vessels, place yourself on vessel being called:

"Containership that has me broad on its port bow 5 miles, this is the tanker *Capella;* I am altering course to starboard to cross astern of you. Over." (Fig. 4-4.)

or

"Containership that has me broad on its starboard bow five miles, this is the tanker *Capella;* When will you change course to starboard in order to cross astern of me? Over." (Fig. 4-5.)

or

"Vessel that has me dead ahead 10 miles, this is the tanker *Capella.* My position is 12 miles south of the BA buoy. When will you change course to starboard so we can meet port to port? Over."

or

"Securité for all vessels in the Nantucket to Ambrose traffic lane, this is the tanker *Capella.* My position is fifteen miles west of the Lightship Nantucket and my rudder is locked hard over to starboard. Out."

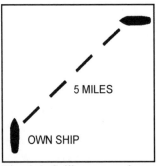

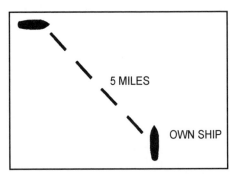

Fig. 4-4. Calling a vessel on your starboard bow.

Fig. 4-5. Calling a vessel on your port bow.

CALLING THE MASTER FOR CONTACTS

Watch officers should ensure they make the correct call to the master when reporting the status of contacts. OOWs must keep in mind, especially during the mid-watch, that they may be waking the master out of a dead sleep. The position of contacts should be reported in relative terms. True bearings and true courses should not be included in the report unless the master requests them. The order listed below will make such reports clear and concise.

1. Determine greatest threats. Use visual bearings with radar range.
2. Prepare to call master in accordance with night orders.
3. When calling master report contacts as follows:
    (a) contact position relative to ship
    (b) distance away in miles
    (c) bearing drift (left, right, or steady)
    (d) CPA: relative to ship, distance at CPA, and time to CPA
4. Maneuver vessel in accordance with master's instructions and the Rules of the Road or concurrence with your proposal.

Mention must be made of SEASPEAK. SEASPEAK, a universal language for seafarers, is guided by the spirit and letter of the IMO *Standards of Training and Watchkeeping* (1978), regulations II./2.16 and II./4.16. It is suitable for deck officers of all nations. It complements the IMCO *Standard Marine Navigational Vocabulary* (1977) and takes into account other relevant IMO regulations and resolutions.

SEASPEAK integrates four elements into a single system:
1. Procedures and conventions for using VHF radio, including the manner of initiating a call, agreeing on a working VHF channel, maintaining contact, and terminating a call, and also the special conventions for speaking letters of the alphabet, numbers, time, position, etc.
2. Certain standard usages including fixed-format messages (e.g., for MAYDAY, MAREP, and POSREP calls, etc.) and standard phrases, such as, "How do you read?" "Say again," "Stay on," "Over," "Out," etc., which are precise replacements of the many uncontrolled alternatives of everyday speech.
3. Rules for organizing the transmissions and constructing the messages so as to maximize understanding and minimize ambiguity, including indicating in advance the intent of each message (question, warning, information, etc.), controlling message patterns and information content, and using simple routines for checking the accuracy of message reception.
4. A maritime vocabulary.

The design criteria for SEASPEAK were that it must:

• be in the internationally agreed maritime language, English,
• meet the practical requirements of the bridge officer and shore authorities,
• reduce confusion and ambiguity in speech communications,
• follow existing regulations and incorporate existing maritime usage,
• make it possible to express in a simple and precise manner any and all of the communication needs of professional seafarers, and
• be simple to learn, both for native speakers and for non-native speakers. SEASPEAK meets these criteria by simplifying, regularizing, and organizing the procedures and language to be used.

A typical SEASPEAK conversation might be as follows:

"Black tanker, position: fairway buoy. Black tanker, position: fairway buoy. This is *Rattler,* Golf X ray X ray X ray; *Rattler,* Golf X ray X ray X ray. On VHF channel one-six. Over,"
"*Rattler,* Golf X ray X ray X ray, This is *Rose Maru,* Juliett Alfa Alfa
Alfa, black tanker, position: fairway buoy. Over,"
"*Rose Maru.* This is *Rattler.* Switch to VHF channel zero-six, Over."
"*Rattler.* This is *Rose Maru.* Agree VHF channel zero-six, Over."
"*Rose Maru.* This is *Rattler.* Question: what is your ETA? Nothing more. Over."

Fig. 4-6. Alidade *(above)* and Azimuth Circle *(below)* for taking visual bearings.

"Rattler. This is *Rose Maru.* Answer: my ETA is one-five-four zero
GMT. Nothing more. Over,"
"Rose Maru. This is *Rattler,* Understood. ETA: one-five-four-zero
GMT. Thank you. Out."

SUMMARY

In summary it is recommended that OOWs:
1. Take frequent visual bearings (Fig. 4-6).
2. Make use of VHF: put yourself on ship calling.
3. Make proper report to master:
   (a) Contact's relative bearing
   (b) Contact's range
   (c) Contact's bearing drift (steady, left, or right)
   (d) CPA, relative to ship: distance and minutes to CPA
   (e) Wait for further instructions or concurrence of your proposal
       from master; if none, comply with his standing or night
       orders and the COLREGs.
4. Use proper helm orders:
   (a) Switch to hand steering (when five miles away).
   (b) Give order for starboard or port, then amount of rudder
       according to the situation.
5. Keep the master informed.
6. If in doubt, ask the master to come to the bridge early enough to
   avoid a close encounter of the worst kind and not to be a witness.

CONCLUSION

A practical application of the Rules of the Road can be accomplished
through a systematic approach as follows:
1.Locate all vessels visually and by Radar.
   a. Rule 5—"Every vessel shall at all times maintain a proper
      look-out by sight and hearing as well as by all available means
      appropriate in the prevailing circumstances and conditions so
      as to make a full appraisal of the situation and of the risk of
      collision."

2.Determine if risk of collision exists (which vessels are threat
   vessels).

   a. Rule 7(a)—"every vessel shall use all available means appro-
      priate to the prevailing circumstances and conditions to deter-
      mine if risk of collision exists."
   b. Rule 7(d)(i)—"such risk shall be deemed to exist if the compass
      bearing of an approaching vessel does not appreciably change."

3.Determine if any vessels have privileges under the Rules.

    a. Rule 18—Responsibility Between Vessels
    b. Rules, Part C—Lights and Shapes
    c. Rule 35—Sound Signals in Restricted Visibility

4. Determine what Rules apply.

    a. International or Inland
    b. Rule 10—Traffic Separation Schemes
    c. Rule 11—Application
    d. Rule 13—Overtaking
    e. Rule 14—Head-on Situation
    f. Rule 15—Crossing Situation
    g. Rule 19—Conduct of Vessels in Restricted Visibility
    h. Rule 2(b)—Special Circumstances

5. Determine your responsibility.

    a. Rule 16—Action by Give-way Vessel
    b. Rule 17—Action by Stand-on Vessel
    c. Rule 2(b)—Special Circumstance Instance

6. Determine what action is required.

    a. Rule 8—Action to Avoid Collision

7. Take Action

    a. Rule 16—Action by Give-way Vessel
    b. Rule 17—Action by Stand-on Vessel

8. Monitor the effects of your action.

    a. Rule 8(d)—"The effectiveness of the action shall be carefully checked until the other vessel is finally past and clear."

CHAPTER FIVE

Shipboard Emergencies and Special Situations

A N emergency is defined as "a sudden need for immediate action."
Some of the emergencies described below require more immediate
action than others. Standing watch aboard merchant vessels has
often been compared to war—composed of 98 percent boredom and 2
percent action (or emergency). The watch officer (OOW) should always
keep in mind the possibility of an emergency and mentally rehearse what
immediate actions should be taken to save the vessel and its crew or to
minimize damage. The emergencies, listed below in alphabetical order,
are not all inclusive, and the recommended steps should not conflict with
procedures that might be listed in standing orders or special instructions
of the master.

EMERGENCIES

Abandon Ship

1. Inform master and engine room, and establish emergency
   communications.
2. Sound "abandon ship" signal upon master's orders (whistle and
   general alarm: seven short and one prolonged).
3. Maneuver ship to provide a lee for lifeboats and rafts and prepare
   for possible help evacuation; at night turn on deck lighting.
4. Diminish speed and secure overboard discharges.
5. If time allows get accurate position, distance, and direction to
   nearest land; get information to lifeboat commanders.
6. Gather chart, log book, *Nautical Almanac,* HO 229, plotting
   tools, sextant, pilot or other chart, and accurate timepiece and
   take to lifeboat.
7. Get emergency radio to lifeboat. Take portable GPS and VHF
   if available.
8. Transmit SOS.
9. When muster of crew is complete, abandon ship.
10. Find emergency position-indicating radio beacon (EPIRB) and
    lash to lifeboat. Lash all boats and rafts together.
11. Stay in area, activate EPIRB and stay together.

Bridge Control/Telegraph Failure

1. Establish emergency communications with engine room.
2. Inform duty engineer/engine room.
3. Switch to engine room control.
4. Inform master.

Collision

1. Sound five short blasts on ship's whistle and the general alarm, call master to the bridge.
2. Maneuver ship to minimize effects of collision. (Alter course to port for a give-way vessel on your port bow and who failed to give way.)
3. Close and check watertight doors and automatic fire doors.
4. Switch deck lighting on at night. Note time on course recorder.
5. Switch VHF to channel 16, make mayday call with position (lat and longitude) and also on channel 13, if appropriate.
6. Inform engine room and establish emergency communications.
7. Muster crew and passengers, if carried at emergency stations.
8. Make available vessels to GMDSS station, satellite terminal, and other automatic distress transmitters (update as necessary).
9. Sound bilges and tanks after collision.
10. Check for fire/damage.
11. Offer assistance to other ship. Obtain name, flag, port of registry, and voyage from/to. Broadcast DISTRESS ALERT and MESSAGE if the ship is in grave and imminent danger and immediate assistance is required, otherwise broadcast an URGENCY message to ships in the vicinity.
12. Check all adjacent spaces for fire; post cool-down watches.
13. Treat injured personnel.
14. Pump fireFighting water out. Watch stability.
15. Prepare line-throwing apparatus and pyrotechnics.
16. Ready lights/shapes.
17. Prepare emergency message for salvage/towing or abandon ship.

Collision With Navigational Aid

1. Stop vessel.
2. Check status of aid.
3. Take photos.
4. Check vessel's propeller.
5. Inform appropriate authority.

Fire

1. Sound emergency alarm (internal and external).
2. Notify all concerned of site of fire.
3. Close ventilation, automatic fire doors, and watertight doors.
4. Switch deck lighting on.
5. Inform master.
6. Inform engine room, ready pumps.
7. Make available vessel's position in radio room. Update as necessary.
8. Slow vessel and maneuver to put fire on lee side of vessel with relative wind abeam.
9. Secure power to fire area.
10. Secure ventilation to space (doors, fans, vents).
11. Use fixed system if installed. Cool adjacent bulkheads and over-heads with water.
12. Check all adjacent spaces for fire. Post cool-down watches.
13. Treat injured personnel.
14. Pump fire Fighting water out. Watch stability.
15. Prepare line-throwing apparatus and pyrotechnics.
16. Ready lights/shapes.
17. Prepare for salvage/towing or abandon ship.

Flooding

1. Sound emergency alarm (internal and external).
2. Muster damage control party.
3. Close and check watertight doors.
4. Inform master so decisions can be made in following procedures.
5. Inform engine room. Ready pumps.
6. Make available vessel's position. Update as necessary.
7. Commence pumping with installed system and/or portable pumps/educators.
8. Diminish speed and prepare a temporary patch, if possible.
9. Sound all tanks and spaces; take drafts.
10. Shore up adjacent bulkheads.
11. Send emergency message.

Gyro Failure/Compass Failure

1. Shift to manual steering.
2. Use magnetic compass course or any alternative means used as heading.
3. Inform master.
4. Inform person responsible for gyro maintenance.

5. Inform engine room.
6. Consider effect of failure on other navigational aids, use radar ranges and greater margins of safety.

Main Engine Failure

1. Use existing movement of vessel to depart from danger, use rudder and bow thrusters to best navigational advantage.
2. Inform master.
3. Turn on fathometer and prepare for anchoring if in shallow water.
4. Exhibit "not under command" shapes or lights. Sound signals.
5. Establish emergency communications with engine room.
6. Inform other vessels in vicinity.

Man Overboard

1. Release life ring with watertight or smoke signal.
2. Commence Williamson turn at night or in restricted visibility, otherwise round turn to the side the man went overboard is quickest. Also in cold water where hypothermia is a concern, a round turn is recommended. Standby engines.
3. Post lookouts to keep person or life ring in sight.
4. Inform master and engine room.
5. Sound three prolonged blasts and repeat as necessary.
6. Assemble rescue boat crew and ready boat. Use boat that will eventually be on lee side.
7. Have a crewman in wet suit standing by to assist in case of shipboard recovery. For shipboard recovery, lower cargo net and/or accommodation ladder.
8. Make vessel's position available by radio and update.
9. Ship maneuvered to launch/recover boats. Place vessel between wind and man.
10. If other vessels are in the area, make VHF call with PAN, PAN, PAN to clarify maneuvers or request assistance.

Steering Failure

1. Inform engine room and engage alternative/emergency steering/ prepare for anchoring if depths permit.
2. Inform master and turn on fathometer.
3. If steering not regained then:
    (a) Exhibit "not under command" shapes or lights.
    (b) Make appropriate sound signal.
    (c) If necessary, take way off ship.
    (d) Notify nearby ships.
4. Note time on course recorder.

Stranding

1. Stop engines.
2. Sound emergency alarm (internal and external).
3. Close and check watertight doors. Visually inspect compartments where possible.
4. Inform master and determine which way deep water lies.
5. Inform engine room, switch to high suction, ready pumps.
6. Switch VHF to channel 16.
7. Make sound signals and exhibit lights/shapes.
8. Check hull for damage.
9. Switch on deck lighting at night.
10. Ensure that bilges and tanks are sounded, drafts taken.
11. Have overside soundings taken and reduce draft of ship (calculate loss of displacement).
12. Determine nature of seabed and if possible attempt to back off if bottom conFiguration permits.
13. Make available vessel's position, update as necessary.
14. Prepare for deballasting, shifting of ballast, or jettisoning of cargo.
15. Watch for broaching.
16. Obtain tidal and weather data.
17. Ready line-throwing equipment.
18. Prepare to run out anchors to kedge; prepare for salvage operations.
19. Make ship's position available to GMDSS station, satellite terminal and other automatic distress transmitter and update as necessary.
20. Broadcast DISTRESS ALERT and MESSAGE if the ship is in grave and imminent danger and immediate assistance is required, otherwise broadcast an urgency message to ships in the vicinity.

SURVIVAL

Exposure to Sun (Heatstroke)

1. Keep covered with clothing and headgear.
2. Rig canopy and keep it wet.
3. Keep clothing wet for cooling by evaporation.
4. Minimize exertion.

Exposure to Cold (Hypothermia)

1. Layer clothing, preferably using wool with a waterproof outer layer.
2. Wear an exposure suit.
3. Keep head out of water and covered with a warm cap.

4. Minimize movement, but keep fingers and toes moving for good circulation.
5. Keep arms and legs against body to minimize heat loss.

See Figure 5-1.

WATER TEMPERATURE		AVERAGE DURATION OF SURVIVAL	
°F	°C	DRY SUIT	CLOTHING AND PFD
32	0	10 hr.	Less than 1 hr.
40	4	13 hr.	2 hr.
50	10	24 hr.	3 hr.
60	16	Indefinite	5 hr.
70	21	"	18 hr.
80	27	"	Indefinite

Fig. 5-1. Hypothermia survival chart.

SPECIAL SITUATIONS
HELICOPTER EVACUATION CHECKLIST

When Requesting Helicopter Assistance

1. Give accurate position, time, speed, course, weather conditions, wind direction and velocity, and radio frequencies (voice and continuous wave) available.
2. Give complete medical information on patient, including age, sex, pulse, blood pressure, breathing rate, temperature, past medical history, symptoms, and treatment already started. Obtain patient documents and passport.
3. If beyond helicopter range, advise of diversion intentions to arrange a rendezvous point.
4. Advise immediately of any changes in ship's schedule or the condition of the patient, especially if the patient dies.

Preparations Prior to Arrival of Helicopter

1. Provide continuous radio guard on 2182 kHz or specified voice frequency. The helicopter cannot operate CW.
2. Select and clear the hoist area, preferably aft, with a minimum radius of fifty feet. This must include securing loose gear, awnings, and antennae; cradling booms and securing their

running rigging; and a clean sweep-down of all weather decks to clear any dirt or debris that could be blown around by the rotor wash, blinding personnel or crippling the helicopter engines.

3. If the operation is at night, light the pickup area well, preferably with lights that are not blinding in intensity. Put lights on all obstructions in the hoist area. *Do not shine any lights onto the helicopter or in its direction.* All floodlights should be directed toward the deck.

4. Point the searchlight vertically to help the helicopter locate the ship, then secure as soon as the helicopter is in the vicinity.

5. Advise helicopter of location of hoist area well before its arrival and notify it of any obstructions or special considerations near hoist area.

6. There will be a high noise level under the helicopter, making voice communication almost impossible. Arrange a set of hand signals among the crew who will assist and brief all concerned of evolution. All personnel must have eye and ear protection, and all hats must be removed unless securely held by a chin strap.

7. Make sure the patient has all necessary medical records, seaman's documents, passport, money, glasses, medication, etc.

8. Have adequate fire-Fighting equipment available at hoist site, preferably large portable CO_2 units with hoses or Aqueaus Fire Fighting Form (AFFF) or other foam systems.

9. Change course so that the relative wind is about two points on the port bow, to keep stack gasses clear of fantail and facilitate helicopter approach. Adjust speed if necessary to provide adequate relative wind or to ease motion of ship.

10. Clear weather decks of all personnel not absolutely necessary for hoisting operation. Warn hoist crew to hit the deck at first sign of trouble from helicopter.

Hoist Operations

1. Have patient as close as possible to hoist area. *Time is important.*

2. If you do not have radio contact with the helicopter, when in all respects you are ready for the hoist, signal the helicopter in with a "come on" signal with both arms. At night, use flashlights to make this signal.

3. If a trail line is dropped by the helicopter hoist operator, use it to guide the basket or stretcher to the deck. Keep this line clear at all times. Do not allow it to get fouled or to be made fast to anything.

4. *Allow the basket, stretcher, or hoist wire to touch the deck and ground itself prior to handling. This wire can develop a static charge of up to 1,000 volts.*

5. If a litter is required, it will be necessary to place the patient in the litter provided by the helicopter, as it is designed for hoisting. Do this as quickly as possible.

6. If it is necessary to move the litter from directly under the helicopter, disconnect it from the hoist wire. *Do not secure the cable to the vessel or attempt to move the litter without unhooking. The helicopter will most likely lose control and crash.*

7. When the patient is strapped into the litter, properly seated in a basket, or in a hoisting sling, give the hoist operator a "thumbs up" signal to hoist.

8. Use the trail line to steady the litter or basket during the lift. When the end of the line is reached, just let go, do not attempt to toss it up.

HURRICANE EVASION

Note: Information in parenthesis applies to Southern Hemisphere, all other information applies to Northern Hemisphere.

1. *To locate eye.* Face into wind, eye is two points abaft starboard (port) beam.

2. *Dangerous semicircle.* Right (left) side of storm track, put wind broad on starboard (port) bow and run.

3. *Navigable semicircle.* Left (right) side of storm track, put wind broad on starboard (port) quarter and run.

4. *Ahead of track.* Put wind two points on starboard (port) quarter and run until in navigable semicircle. Veering wind: Shifting to right (left), in dangerous semicircle.

5. *Backing wind.* Shifting to left (right), in navigable semicircle.

A good rule of thumb is to keep the vessel clear of a sector that is 40° left and right of the hurricane's track projected ahead of the eye for 48 hours. For example, a hurricane tracking 270° (T) at 10 knots would have an arc extending 480 miles ahead of the eye from 230° (T) through 310° (T). This is a sector that a ship should avoid.

NAVIGATION IN TROPICAL STORM AREA

1. Inform master.
2. Inform engine room.
3. Adjust speed and course as necessary.
4. Ensure that all deck cargo, hold cargo, cargo gear, and loose gear on deck are doubly secured.
5. Warn crew to secure personal belongings.

6. Have safety lines rigged on deck.
7. Monitor weather reports and instruments.
8. Transmit weather reports.
9. Take on ballast.
10. Secure watertight doors, weather doors, ports, hatches.
11. Ship may handle best with sea astern or on the quarter, minimum headway. Keep in mind the cautions under "Hurricane Evasion."

ICE NAVIGATION

Preparations
1. Verify steel screw and spare.
2. Verify spare rudder.
3. Test watertight integrity and pump operations.
4. Stow cargo at least fifteen inches from sides to minimize sweat damage.
5. Trim by three feet at stern.
6. Remove all projections from hull near waterline.
7. Reinforce bow.
8. Stock up on damage control equipment and shoring.
9. Enclose and winterize lookout station.
10. Have extra mooring lines.
11. Have telephone poles as fenders.
12. Stock up on timber and wire for deadman mooring.
13. Have plenty of picks, shovels, ice axes, saws.
14. Rig ice anchor.
15. Run steam to discharges, topside for deicing.
16. Have extra provisions and arctic foul-weather gear.
17. Use antifreeze as necessary.
18. Have towing gear available.

Navigation
1. Shut all watertight doors.
2. Keep ice from accumulating topside. It affects stability.
3. Drain fire mains on deck.
4. Skirt to windward of the ice mass, if possible.
5. Keep a good lookout.
6. Enter ice mass perpendicular to edge at slow speed into a bight and not into a projecting tongue.
7. Maintain headway.
8. If you must collide with large chunks of ice, do so head on.

SEARCH AND RESCUE

1. Retransmit distress message.
2. Maintain continuous listening watch on all distress frequencies.
3. Consult *Merchant Ship Search And Rescue Manual* (MERSAR).
4. Communication between surface units and SAR aircraft should be on 2182 kHz and/or channel 16.
5. Plot position courses and speeds of other assisting units.

UNEXPECTED AND LARGE LIST

1. Sound emergency (General Alarm) signal.
2. Change course to head down sea.
3. Diminish speed.
4. Establish watch on channel 16.
5. Close and check watertight doors.
6. Obtain vessels position.
7. Turn on deck lights at night.
8. Check condition of cargo.
9. Master will decide whether to abandon vessel.

CONCLUSION

Shipboard emergencies and special situations can lead to tragedies at sea. The OOW must prepare for this eventuality and know what steps to take to assist the master. All one has to do is read the accounts of such tragedies at sea to realize how such assistance by the OOW may have averted the disaster (see chapter 9).

For the mariner on watch there is no substitute for proper prior planning, the three Cs of "communication, coordination, cooperation," and constant vigilance.

CHAPTER SIX

Shiphandling for the Watch Officer

SHIPHANDLING is both an art and science. It involves combinations of variables so numerous and complex that no amount of detailed predetermined instruction can bring a ship through a canal or dock it. Each time a ship moves, the precise influences acting on her are different from the way they were at any other time, and the ship responds to every one of those influences.

Consider the situation when a ship is a thousand yards (five cables) away from a berth under normal conditions and preparing for docking. If the correct evolution is known in advance, taking all factors into account and precise times stated for execution of the various steps, surprisingly few "bells" and rudder orders would be necessary to dock the ship. But what goes into the making of these few commands? How far in advance must each decision be made before the vessel can be expected to respond? How long does it take to acquire a *seaman's eye* and get the *feel* of the vessel?

In many respects a large ship is the most difficult of all vehicles in the world, or in space for that matter, with which to perform precise maneuvers. On land, vehicles have a vast range of positive traction under which to maneuver. In the air, due to the speeds of flight, an aircraft is almost always in an undisturbed medium. Its movement can be easily instrumented and its forces can be physically felt by the pilot. Turbulence is left far behind. In a vessel under way on water, however, all external forces such as the wind, current, waves, swell, shallow water, bank cushion, and bank suction will cause turbulence.

For a detailed discussion of shiphandling, *Shiphandling for the Mariner* by Daniel H. MacElrevey is recommended. This chapter will discuss only briefly shiphandling for the watch officer (OOW) as it pertains to helm orders, turning circles, rough weather, convoy and underway replenishment operations, anchoring, approaching a pilot station and berth, and vessel propulsion considerations.

HELM ORDERS

Helm orders must be clear, concise, and loud enough to be heard and understood by the helmsman. The helmsman must, in turn, repeat the order and then execute it. The watch officer must ensure the helm is placed at the desired rudder angle. Failure to do this has resulted in collisions and groundings. Finally, helm orders must be given correctly.

Commands to the Helmsman

1. Commands to the helmsman are always given in the following order: *direction, amount,* except for hard rudder.
2. To avoid confusion with orders to the engines the following words are used: *starboard/port* or *right/left* (right/left is preferred in the United States.)
3. All commands must be repeated word for word, exactly as given.

Examples:

Starboard/port (right/left) (degree) rudder. Cause the rudder angle indicator to read the specified number of degrees.

Hard starboard/port (hard right/left) rudder. Use right/left rudder to achieve the maximum amount of rudder. These will differ from ship to ship to achieve maximum rudder angle possible (usually 35°). Helmsman must use caution to avoid placing the rudder in the stops. On many vessels where hard rudder is 35°, full rudder is 30°.

Rudder amidships. Put the rudder on the centerline; no rudder angle.

Increase your rudder. Increase the rudder angle. Should be followed by the angle desired, for example, "Increase to right 30° rudder."

Ease your rudder. Reduction of rudder angle. Should be followed by the angle desired, for example, "Ease to left 15° rudder."

Shift your rudder. Change the rudder angle to the opposite direction at the same angle.

Mind your helm. Usually a caution to steer more carefully, but may be a warning to stand by for an order to follow.

Steady as you go. Steer the course indicated by the ship's heading when the order is given.

Meet her. Stop the swing of the ship without steadying on a specific course. Usually followed by the order, "Steady on course"

Steady on. States the course on which the ship's head is to be steadied. Normally given when the ship is swinging.

Steer. Usually given for only a minor (less than 5°) change of heading. The new heading has to be specified.

Starboard/port (right/left) steer course. Swing the ship's head in the direction stated and steady her on the course given. Usually given if course change is less than 10°.

Steering nothing to the starboard/port (right/left) of ____. Given
when the presence of some danger on one side makes it necessary to avoid a set in that direction. The helmsman must keep the
ship from swinging past the course in the direction warned against.
Keep her so. Continue to steer the course you are heading. Usually
given after the helmsman states the course he is steering.
Very well. Reply meaning, "The situation is understood."

Verifying the helm orders or the course being steered by the helmsman
cannot be overstressed. This is a most important task for the OOW, particularly when the ship is in restricted waters where the margins of safety are
very narrow.

TURNING CIRCLES AND RATE OF TURN

Fig. 6-1 shows a turning circle when the rudder is placed hard over to starboard. A vessel initially will heel inward (to starboard) and then outward
(to port in this turn). The heel will be more noticeable at higher speeds.

The turning circle and its components are defined as:

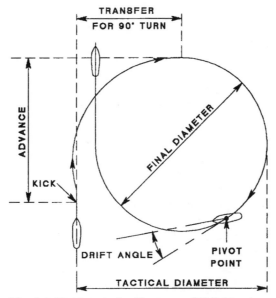

Fig. 6-1. Turning circle. (Courtesy of U.S. Naval
Amphibious School, Little Creek, Virginia.)

Turning circle. The path described by the ship's center of gravity
when turning. A full 360° with constant rudder angle and speed.

The turning circle will vary with amounts of rudder and with speeds used and in size and shape according to one's position on the ship's centerline. The angle for the bow is smaller than that for the stem. Mariners like the turning circle to be based on the position of the bridge whereas naval architects use the position of the ship's center of gravity (often close to the ship's midpoint on the centerline).

Pivot point. The point of rotation within the ship as she makes a turn or the position, on the centerline where the drift angle is zero. This point varies according to type of vessel but is generally about one-third the length the ship from the bow.

Advance. For any turn, the advance is the distance gained in the direction the same as that of the original course from the time the rudder is put over until the ship has turned through 90°.

Transfer. For any turn, the transfer is the distance gained in a direction perpendicular to that of the original course from the time the rudder is put over until the ship has turned through 90°.

Tactical diameter. For any amount of constant rudder angle, the tactical diameter is the distance made good in a direction perpendicular to that of the original course line from the time the rudder is put over until the ship is on a reverse heading. It is the transfer for a turn of 180°.

Final diameter. Diameter of a circle ultimately scribed by a ship that continues to circle with a constant rudder angle.

Drift angle. Angle at any point on a turning circle between intersection of the tangent at that point and a ship's keel line. An extreme case of large drift angles occurs in a Hovercraft during a turn. There is very little lateral resistance from the sea and the pivot point can be well forward of the bow.

Kick. (a) swirl of water toward the inside of a turn when the rudder is put over; (b) the momentary movement of the ship toward the side opposite the direction of the turn.

Acceleration and deceleration rates. The rates at which a ship picks up or loses headway after a change of speed.

During turns the rate of turn indicator (see Fig. 2-8) furnishes the OOW with an important relative visual cue as to how fast a vessel is turning. By watching the rate of turn indicator and the jackstaff and hearing the clicks of the gyrocompass (two clicks for each degree) the OOW may easily determine when to increase or decrease the rate. On modern gyros the clicks cannot be heard and the OOW must rely on the rate of turn indicator. The helm orders of "Steady as you go" or "Steady 345°" now can be monitored easily with the rate of turn indicator.

WEATHER

Note: Charles Thor, former Professor of Meteorology at the U.S. Merchant Marine Academy and the State University of New York Maritime College, Fort Schuyler, New York, wrote the following section for the OOW's guidance.

The importance of weather knowledge at sea cannot be overestimated. Weather has a significant effect on each and every voyage. It is extremely important for the deck officer to be weather-wise. The safety of crew and passengers, cargo, and frequently the ship itself, often is dependent upon making the proper weather decisions, both before departure and during the voyage itself.

Ships, they say, are operated in a hostile environment (Figs. 6-2 and 6-3). The boundary between the ocean and the atmosphere can be a dangerous place. Without being overly dramatic, this environment of high winds and waves, ice, and fog, on occasion is doing its best to sink a ship.

The specific weather responsibilities of the mate-on-watch follow:

1. At all times be knowledgeable regarding the current state of the weather.
    (a) Know the current wind direction and speed.
    (b) Know the current wave direction and height.
    (c) Know the current visibility.
    (d) Know the current barometric tendency.
2. At all times be knowledgeable regarding the forecast weather.
    (a) Know the twenty-four-hour forecast.
    (b) Be aware of the potential problems associated with the forecast weather.
3. Be competent regarding the marine surface weather observation. Be able to make these observations accurately, in a reasonable amount of time. Be able to log these observations and encode them if necessary.
4. Be able to acquire the latest weather warnings, forecasts, and advisories and present a proper weather summation or briefing to the master.
5. Be knowledgeable with respect to the climate and ocean currents, especially of the major ship routes.

Fig. 6-2. *Above.* A view from the bridge as a 150,000-ton tanker collides with an oncoming wave. *Below.* Head-on poundings by the sea can cause damage to the vessel that may necessitate reducing rpms. (Courtesy of the *San Francisco Examiner.*)

Fig. 6-3. Formation of ice on the vessel's superstructure will affect the vessel's stability.

Some details on these specific responsibilities follow:

1. *The current state of the weather.* Be able to determine the wind direction and speed from the state of the sea surface. This involves getting the wind from the waves, using the Beaufort wind scale (see Fig. 6-4). Also be able to determine the wind from readings of the anemometer which involves correcting the relative wind to the true wind, using either the "wind wheel," tables, or vector calculations.

    Be able to determine the wave direction and height. This involves being able to distinguish between sea and swell, and being able to identify secondary swells, etc.

    Be able to determine the visibility, especially during fog or precipitation situations.

    Be able to read the microbarograph.
2. *The weather forecast.* Be able to secure the weather map from the weather facsimile machine. Be knowledgeable regarding facsimile schedules, both reporting stations and transmission times. Understand the weather map, including highs and lows, isobars, and fronts. Comprehend the significance of the weather map, as it explains the current and forecast weather for the ship.

Force 0: wind speed less than
1 knot, sea like a mirror.

Force 1: wind speed 1–3 knots,
wave height .1m (.25 ft.) ripples
with appearance of scales, no
foam crests.

Force 2: wind speed 4–6
knots, wave height .2–.3m
(.5–1 ft.), small wavelets,
crests of glassy appearance,
not breaking.

Fig. 6-4. Sea state photograph for determining wind speed from Beaufort Wind
Force Scale. (Courtesy of NOAA, adapted from their May 1987 chart.)

Force 3: wind speed 7–10 knots, wave height .6–1m (2–3 ft.), large wavelets, crests begin to break, scattered whitecaps.

Force 4: wind speed 11–16 knots, wave height 1–1.5m (3.5–5 ft.), small waves becoming longer, numerous whitecaps.

Force 5: wind speed 17–21 knots, wave height 2–2.5m (6-8 ft.), moderate waves, taking longer form, many whitecaps, some spray.

Fig. 6-4. (continued).

Force 6: wind speed 22–27 knots, wave height 3–4m (9.5–13 ft.), larger waves forming whitecaps everywhere, more spray.

Force 7: wind speed 28–33 knots, wave height 4–5.5m (13.5–19 ft.), sea heaps up, white foam from breaking waves begins to be blown in streaks along direction of wind.

Force 8: wind speed 34–40 knots, wave height 5.5–7.5m (18–25 ft.), moderately high waves of greater length, edges of crests begin to break into spindrift, foam is blown in well-marked streaks.

Fig. 6-4. (continued).

Force 9: wind speed 41–47 knots, wave height 7–10m (23–32 ft.), high waves, sea begins to roll dense streaks of foam along wind direction; spray may reduce visibility.

Force 10: wind speed 48–55 knots (storm), wave height 9–12.5m (29–41 ft.), very high waves with overhanging crests, sea takes white appearance as foam is blown in very dense streaks, rolling is heavy and shocklike, visibility is reduced.

Force 11: wind speed 56–63 knots, wave height 11.5–16m (37–52 ft.), exceptionally high waves, sea covered with white foam patches; visibility still more reduced.

Fig. 6-4. (continued).

Force 12–17: will have wind speeds from 64–118 knots, hurricane with phenomena high waves over 45 ft., air filled with foam, sea completely white with driving spray and a greatly reduced visibility.

Be able to interpret the plain-language weather messages, including weather warnings, forecasts, and advisories.

Be able to "make the map" from the coded weather message.

3. *The marine surface weather observation.* There are no weather stations at sea. We are dependent primarily on ships in the merchant service for weather observations at sea. It is the mate-on-watch who has the responsibility for these observations.

Since the oceans cover 72 percent of the earth's surface, these marine observations are of tremendous importance to the weather forecaster. Accurate and timely observations make for accurate weather maps, which in turn make for accurate weather forecasts and warnings for marine areas.

Simultaneous shipboard observations are made four times daily at six-hour intervals. Observation times are: 0000, 0600, 1200, and 1800 GMT. The weather observation should require no more than twenty minutes of time, but it requires a very well-organized routine because more than a dozen or so items of the weather need to be observed. These weather items include several that are subjectively determined, such as, cloud type, amount, and height, and visibility

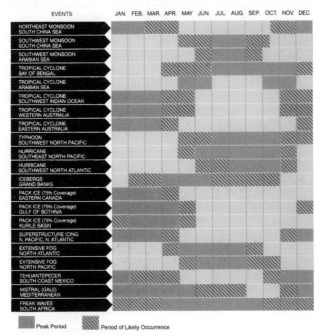

Fig. 6-5. Meteorological events by month. (Adapted from *Ocean Routes*, March 1985. Used by permission.)

and obstruction to vision. Finally the weather messagegram must be delivered on time, since it is obvious that "old" weather has no value to the weather service.

4. *The weather briefing.* Be able to explain the weather forecast and the weather map to the ship's master, and to your relief. Be prepared to make recommendations regarding alterations in the ship's course, and operations, vis-à-vis forecast weather changes.
5. *Climate and ocean currents.* Be familiar with "pilot charts" and meteorological events by month (Fig. 6-5).

WEATHER CONCERNS FOR
CERTAIN BRIDGE EVOLUTIONS

Preparing for and Standing the Watch

Be aware of the weather situation before going on watch.
Receive a proper weather briefing from the mate you relieve.

Bridge Equipment

Know how to change the paper on the weather facsimile machine and tune it.
Know when and how to change the microbarograph paper.
Know the location of all weather instrumentation: microbarograph, psychrometer, wet and dry bulb thermometer, bucket thermometer, wind wheel, etc., and of all weather charts, logs, pilot charts, manuals, etc.

Voyage Planning and Recordkeeping

Incorporate ship's weather routine.
Include weather logs.

Shipboard Emergencies

Make the special weather observation that is required after significant or sudden weather change.

Arrivals and Departures

Coordinate the visit of the port meteorological officer.
Secure the needed weather instrumentation and manuals, charts, etc.
Mail the weather log to the National Weather Service at the conclusion of the voyage.

Item No. 181 (Rev. 78)   SUBJECT: HEAVY WEATHER REPORT – S.S. _____   To: _____   VOY. # _____

Marine   Passage – From: _____

On Boarding at Sailing: Cargo ____ Tons: Fuel Oil ____ Tons in ____ OD/B ____ Tons Deep Tanks and Settlers.

Water Ballast ____ Tons in ____, Fresh Water ____ Tons in Dom. & Dist., Tanks.

Sailing Draft   : Forward ____ Ft. ____ In., Aft. ____ Ft. ____ In., Mean ____ Ft. ____ In.
Salt/Fresh Water

DATE	CSC	RPM	SLIP	WIND	SEA	BEHAVIOR OF SHIP	CHANGES CSC/RMP/BALLAST

MASTER _____

PAGE # _____

NOTE: ENTRIES ON HEAVY WEATHER ARE TO BE RECKONED FROM MIDNIGHT.

*COURSE ON AT 12:01 AM AND AVERAGE RPM FOR PREVIOUS WATCH (8:00 PM TO MIDNIGHT)

Fig. 6-6. Heavy weather report. (Courtesy of EXXON.)

HEAVY WEATHER

In heavy weather the seas may become so violent as to make it necessary to change priorities from maintaining the passage to saving the ship. A heavy weather report (Fig. 6-6) should be maintained by the vessel. To avoid damage and prevent foundering or capsizing, the vessel must heave-to. A vessel may head into the sea, run before the sea, or stop engines and drift. The three methods and factors to consider are:

Head into the Sea-Factors to Consider

Wave impact on bow; maintain minimum speed (usually about six to eight knots) to allow steerage way and to prevent excessive pitching or pounding.

Waves breaking on board.

Pitching may cause excessive hogging and sagging stresses. Steering cannot allow vessel to fall off and allow possibility of broaching.

With ship head on to wind and seas the decks will be wet continuously.

Run before the Sea—Factors to Consider

Steering is more difficult.

Speed on the vessel must be greater than wave speed to prevent vessel being pooped by overriding seas from astern.

Steering cannot allow vessel to fall off and allow possibility of broaching.

With wind and seas astern the decks will be drier and the vessel may roll more.

There must be plenty of room to leeward.

Stop Engines and Drift—Factors to Consider

There must be plenty of room to leeward. The rate of drift will vary from two to five knots.

The ship must have all watertight doors secured and be well buttoned up.

Drifting may be most advantageous near the center of a tropical cyclone where seas are confused.

The vessel's metacentric height must be adequate since pitching and rolling will be heavy.

Damage to vessel from the seas will be minimal.

The following general advice from the *Admiralty Seamanship Manual* for heavy weather is worth quoting here.

Do:
1. Make sure that you are kept informed continually about expected changes of weather.
2. Know the factors affecting the stability of your ship and take steps to improve stability, if necessary, *before* encountering heavy weather.
3. See that the ship is made thoroughly seaworthy before leaving harbor, or before the approach of a storm.
4. Consider the effect of the ship's motion on the activities being carried out by all the various members of the ship's company.
5. Appreciate the signs of an approaching tropical storm and take the necessary action to avoid it.
6. Alter course, if possible, in a beam sea to break the synchronization of the period of the waves with that of the ship's rolling.

Don't:
1. Drive a ship too fast into a head sea—particularly a fast, lightly built ship.
2. Fail to reduce speed soon enough in a head sea or swell through being unable to visualize the consequences or fear of being considered too cautious.
3. Run too fast before a following sea, particularly when the length of the ship and that of the sea are about the same.

CONVOYS

The U.S. Navy has long realized the importance of a strong merchant marine and is concerned about the decline of ships within the U.S. Merchant Marine. For any overseas conflict, more than 95 percent of all supplies must be carried on merchant vessels. Therefore, with U.S. Navy insistence, three Maritime Preposition Ship Squadrons have been established and regularly exercise in convoy operations. Merchant officers must be prepared to operate in convoys (Fig. 6-7) and practice the art of maintaining station within the convoy formation. Formations normally approximate the standard grid shown in Figs. 6-8 with spacing of 2,000 yards between vessels and allowed deviation from station being 5° in bearing and 400 yards in range. Convoys may also operate in circular formations (Fig. 6-9) with vessels being on station when within a designated sector (usually 35° width and 2,000 yards in length).

OOWs should realize when they must slow down; increase speed, alter course left or right; or combine these elements to regain station. Use of the radar and visual bearings to maintain station should be practiced along with the use of a stadimeter in case radar cannot be radiated for ranging purposes. Many times the U.S. Navy will impose conditions of non-emission of any radios or radars to keep detection of a convoy by the potential enemy as remote as possible. In that eventuality maneu-

Fig. 6-7. Convoy operations. (Courtesy of MEBA District Two.)

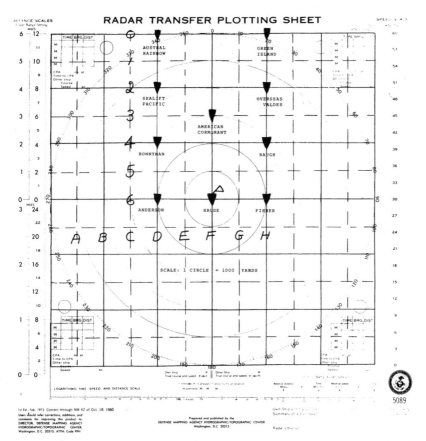

Fig. 6-8. Standard grid formation used in convoy exercises for vessels assigned to Maritime Pre-Position Squadron TWO in Diego Garcia (distance between ships is 2,000 yards).

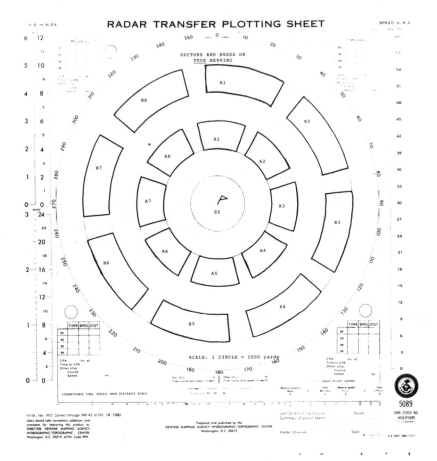

Fig. 6-9. Circular formation (form 70) used in convoy exercises for vessels assigned to Maritime Pre-Position Squadron TWO in Diego Garcia.

vering signals, usually made by VHF, may be executed by flag hoist or flashing light. Watch officers must remain knowledgeable in recognizing flag and flashing light letters and numerals. Publications that are used in convoy formations that the OOW should be familiar with are HO 102 (International Code of Signals), ATP-2, Vol. II and in Diego Garcia COMPSRONTWO SOP VOL. II.

UNDERWAY REPLENISHMENT

During convoy operations or exercises it may be necessary to go alongside a navy oiler or stores ship or a merchant tanker for underway replenishment. Your vessel also could go alongside another vessel for transfer of personnel by highline. If you are asked to go alongside another vessel, set the replenishment course into the wind and sea. If seas are too rough to head into, you can place them astern, although this will make steering more difficult. In any case the best helmsman should be at the wheel during underway replenishment. The approach should position the vessel on the beam at a distance of 200 yards (1 cable). Speed should then be matched by adjusting rpms. The vessel can then gradually close in to the proper distance off the replenishment ship. Experienced mariners can use the "coast-in method" illustrated in Fig. 6-10. Replenishment speeds vary between ten and sixteen knots, the most common speed being fourteen knots. Distance alongside varies from 80 to 140 feet. During the approach and while alongside after steering must be manned by a qualified helmsman and engineer in case of a steering failure and the need to shift control to after steering. The rate of turn indicator, course steered, rpm indicator, and Doppler should all be monitored by the OOW during underway replenishment operations.

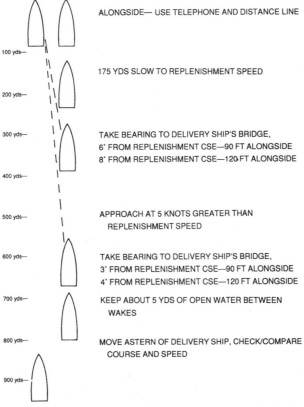

Fig. 6-10. Underway replenishment, coast-in method. (Courtesy of U.S. Naval Amphibious School, Little Creek, Virginia.)

Fueling astern wherein a tanker will stream a hose astern to be taken aboard by the receiving vessel has advantages in heavy weather and when refueling alongside is too risky.

When refueling or highlining alongside, the vessel can be kept in position rather easily. An increase or decrease of rpms can keep the vessel abreast correctly if distance off is good. If distance off must be reduced then the conning officer should alter course by 1° into the vessel and reduce rpms. If distance off must be increased then the conning officer should alter course by 1° away from the vessel and increase rpms. Once distance off has been regained, then rpms must be adjusted accordingly. Conning practice alongside should be made available by the master to the chief mate and all OOWs.

ANCHORING

Anchoring is an evolution that all masters should allow their deck officers to execute. When anchoring, take the following factors into consideration.

Preparation

1. Use largest scale chart available. If two charts are required, a shift of charts should not have to be made during a critical portion of the approach.
2. Read sailing directions concerning the approach and anchorage area. Check the wind to be anticipated during approach. Ensure anchorage area is suitable for the size of the ship.
3. Look over the chart carefully, noting especially soundings, conspicuous landmarks for visual bearings, landmarks that can be used for parallel indexing, and the type of bottom for holding characteristics.
4. Calculate any tides and currents that may affect the vessel during the approach.
5. Lay off tracks to the anchorage on the chart and distance circles or arcs on the track from 1,000 yards (1/2 mile), 800 yards, 600 yards, and then every 100 yards to the drop point. (Take into consideration the distance from the bridge to the anchor on the bow if you strive for perfection. Knowing this distance is imperative if the vessel has her superstructure aft.)
6. Mark charts with all required information including margins of safety, parallel index information, areas of danger, wheel-over positions with advance and transfer, and the drop bearing and range from a radar conspicuous object at the anchorage (see Fig. 3-20).

7. Extrapolate the above information into your conning or bridge notebook (see Fig. 3-21).
8. Inform the chief mate and the chief engineer of the expected time of maneuvering and anchoring.
9. Determine ship's draft and test fathometer at scale appropriate to soundings on the chart. Determine depth curves the vessel may use in its approach to the anchorage. Make up passage plan (see Fig. 3-19).
10. Determine which anchor the vessel will use, how many shots (shackles) needed to set the anchor, and how many shots (shackles) needed to veer to. Use the quality of the bottom to assist in these determinations. It is recommended that an anchor buoy be rigged on each anchor. Anchor buoys can be three-foot lengths of 2" x 4" wood painted red for the port anchor and green for the starboard anchor. Attachment to the bill of the anchor can be by twenty-one-thread 1(1 1/2") line and have a length of five fathoms greater than the depth. If an anchor is lost it may be easily located by this buoy and its line.

Approach

1. Ensure that all stations are manned and ready. After steering also should be manned by a qualified helmsman and an engineer.
2. Ensure that the chief mate or mate designated is forward and the anchors are clear and ready to let go. Ensure there is power and water on deck.
3. Take fixes every three to five minutes and alter course as necessary to adjust for leeway and maintain track. Fixes should be by visual bearings and radar ranges to radar conspicuous objects.
4. Keep the designated mate on the bow and keep the engine room informed of distances to go.
5. Monitor all instruments on approach such as Doppler and rate of turn indicator. Ensure speed over ground is adjusted so as not to overshoot or undershoot anchorage.
6. Monitor approach when nearing drop bearing. Monitor any parallel index lines to maintain track.
7. Check conning or bridge notebook (see Fig. 3-21) with chart to ensure everything is going according to plan.
8. Ensure anchor is walked out to above water's edge and is on the brake if the depth of the water is less than ten fathoms. Otherwise at the anchorage the anchor should be backed out under power to within a few fathoms of the bottom before being placed on the brake.

9. As steerageway is lost, use the bow thruster to maintain the ship's head.
10. Constantly monitor approaching drop bearing. Commence backing down to check headway.

At Anchorage

1. Ensure that the ship is at the drop bearing.
2. Ensure the ship is dead in the water or has slight sternway by observing doppler, overboard discharges, stern wash coming up the ship's side, and chips of wood thrown from the bridge wing.
3. Let go the anchor with instructions to set the anchor at two or three times the depth. Ensure that the anchor buoy has been cast overboard when anchor is let go.
4. Keep track of the strain and direction of the anchor as it is veered out to desired amount (four to seven times the depth of the water). Strain should be reported as none, slight, moderate, or heavy. Direction should be stated by the o'clock method with 12 o'clock being dead ahead.
5. Take round of bearings, ensure the ship is at anchorage, lay off radius of swing, ensure anchor buoy is watching, hoist anchor ball, rig drift lead, and ring off engines. Set anchor watch. Windlass should be disengaged after setting the brake and securing the stopper.

APPROACHING PILOT STATION

For a thorough discussion concerning the approach to the pilot station the OOW should read chapter 1 of Daniel H. MacElrevey's *Shiphandling for the Mariner.* Factors the OOW should keep in mind include:
1. Give clear concise VHF communication to pilot station with repetition of ETA, side for pilot ladder, height of pilot ladder above the water, and required speed of own vessel.
2. Complete pre-arrival checks and inform all concerned.
3. Ensure rigging of pilot ladder in accordance with IMO regulations. Do not forget to confirm its rigging and have another mate and seaman standing by for pilot embarkation.
4. Slow vessel down to required speed (usually about four knots) and alter course to provide a lee for the pilot boat.
5. Ensure completion of master/pilot information exchange form (see Fig. 7-1) for presentation to the pilot upon his arrival on the bridge. The OOW must be part of this exchange between

the pilot and the master since he is a vital member of the bridge team as the vessel proceeds into restricted waters.

APPROACHING A BERTH

During the approach to a berth in pilotage waters too many officers of the watch believe their sole responsibility is to keep the pilot supplied with coffee, relay helm and engine orders, and log the time when the vessel passes a buoy or a major navigational aid. The OOW is a vital member of the bridge team, whose duties encompass far more than the three tasks above. The OOW must be vigilant and alert to all aspects of vessel operations and must be familiar with the plan and the pilot's intentions. Factors the OOW must take into consideration during the vessel's approach to the berth include:

1. Be familiar with the pilot's plan.
2. Relay the pilot's or master's orders to the helm and monitor the helmsman's execution to ensure the correct amount of rudder is applied in the correct direction.
3. Ensure the pilot's or master's engine commands are correctly executed and answered by the engine room.
4. All orders from the pilot or master should be repeated loudly by the officer of the watch, executed and then announced loudly when executed.

    Pilot: "Right (starboard) 20°. rudder."

    Watch Officer: "Right (starboard) 20°. rudder."

    Watch Officer: (when rudder angle indicator indicates rudder at right (starboard) 20°.)
    "Rudder is right (starboard) 20°."
5. Obtain concurrence of the master when to go "fore and aft." The bow should be manned and the anchor ready for letting go. Inform bow and stem which side to the vessel will be going as soon as possible. Keep the engine room informed.
6. Monitor parallel index lines and obtain fixes every three to six minutes. Keep the master and the pilot advised of whether vessel is left, right, or on track.
7. Keep the master and the pilot advised of distances to go to wheel-over positions (course changes). Take into account advance and transfer and announce clearly when the vessel is at the wheel-over position.

8. Be alert to other vessels and small craft that may endanger your vessel. Keep the pilot and the master advised of all such traffic.
9. Monitor VHF communications that may affect your vessel.
10. Keep records of all bridge evolutions. Use your bridge notebook and bell book to record events. You can never record too much, but recordkeeping must not detract from your most important tasks of maintaining an alert and vigilant watch to ensure the safe navigation of your vessel.

PROPULSION CONSIDERATIONS

The OOW should be familiar with the characteristics of the vessel's engineering plant. While off watch, tour the engine room with your normal underway engineering watch officer; or, in port, have the chief engineer or first assistant give you a tour. In addition, try to observe procedures and practices in the engine room during maneuvering. Time at the throttle under the supervision of the chief or first assistant would make an OOW more aware of what is going on down below and how important it is to keep the engine room informed as to what is going on above decks. Engineers commonly feel that mates are in general unappreciative of their efforts during maneuvering. An appreciation by the OOW of what is going on down below is an essential ingredient for the safe navigation of the vessel.

The officer of the watch must know the characteristics of different types of engines, described below.

Engine Types

1. Steam reciprocating
   (a) Response is fast.
   (b) Astern horsepower is equivalent to ahead horsepower.
   (c) This type is seldom used in modem ships.
2. Diesel
   (a) This is the most common type of propulsion for all but the very largest ships today.
   (b) Quick starts and stops of propeller while maneuvering are possible.
   (c) Minimum maneuvering rpm is sometimes as much as 30 percent of maximum rpm.
   (d) This type of engine may be difficult to start in reverse when making good headway.
   (e) Older types of diesels are limited as to the number of starts that can be made in a given period of time.

3. Steam turbine
   (a) This engine takes time to build up or reduce rpm.
   (b) Backing power of steam turbines is limited. Most astern turbines give less than two-thirds the rpm of the ahead turbine.
   (c) When using a "touch ahead" to regain steering, the gradual buildup sometimes increases headway before the propeller race is strong enough to reestablish steering.
   (d) Turbines are capable of very low rpms ahead or astern. This affords greater capability when working engines against a mooring line or anchor.
4. Turbo-electric or diesel-electric
   (a) Full power is quickly available ahead or astern.
5. Azimuthal propulsion

The development of diesel-electric drive technology has enabled a design breakthrough, in which a diesel engine inside the ship's hull powers an electric-drive system outside the hull. In the resulting Azimuthal Propulsion System, a pod suspended under the stern of the ship holds the propeller and electric drive. On the RMS *Queen Mary 2* (QM2) propulsion consists of four 21.5 MW electric propulsor pods (two fixed and two azimuthing). The forward pair is fixed, but the aft pair can rotate through 360°, obviating the need for a rudder.

Propellers

Prior to getting under way from a pier or anchorage watch officers should ensure the propeller is clear (wheel clearance). Debris, flotsam, or jetsam may have drifted in the vicinity of the propeller and the area should be visually checked by the watch officer just prior to getting under way. This is often called wheel clearance. While docking or undocking, OOWs should stay alert to possible reports from the stern that a line has become fouled in the propeller. The OOW should also be aware of the characteristics of the vessel's propeller, which begin with the definition of pitch.

Pitch is the distance traveled by any point on a blade parallel to the shaft through one complete rotation of the shaft. Each propeller may rotate in open water or be shrouded in a tunnel and Kort nozzle. There are four general types of screw propellers—all having pitch.

1. *Fixed,* also known as constant or uniform. On a fixed pitch propeller each blade has the same pitch for all points on all blades.
2. *Variable* pitch propellers have blades that are variable in one or both of the following ways:

(a) With axially varying pitch, the pitch changes from the leading edge to the following edge.

(b) With radically varying pitch, the pitch changes from the hub to the tip.

3. *Adjustable* pitch propellers have blades the position of which can be altered relative to the hub by rotating the blade to a new position and then rebolting it on the hub.

4. *Controllable* pitch propellers have blades the position of which can be altered relative to the hub by rotating each blade in unison via hydraulic/mechanical linkages in a hollow propeller shaft to a geared mechanism in the hub where gear motion causes each blade to alter pitch equally. This is accomplished while the shaft is rotating in only one direction. This type of propeller allows for change in direction by altering pitch from ahead to reverse without having to reverse shaft rotation.

CONCLUSION

Many say shiphandling is a science and an art. It requires time and experience. Different ships, different long splices is said about ships. This is true about handling different vessels. Although general principles apply to all vessels, each one requires a seaman's eye and a feel of the vessel.

CHAPTER SEVEN

Arrivals and Departures

A RRIVAL at a port can be very hectic with many vessels converging at the pilot station in waters that are becoming more and more restricted. Many accidents occur in these waters. Investigations of these incidents clearly reinforce the absolute need for bridge organization. Bridge discipline, skill, sound procedures, and strong watch organization are absolutely essential. The following excerpt from the standing orders of Maersk Line, Limited, emphasizes the need for such organization:

BRIDGE ORGANIZATION

- By bridge discipline the company means the cooperation and sharing of responsibility which exists between deck officers, helmsman, and lookout. The company expects all deck officers to do their utmost to provide the best possible bridge discipline.
- It is essential that navigation under all conditions is carried out with great precision and discipline, as it is only in this way that it is possible to acquire the general knowledge and the competence which is a condition of being able to react confidently with sufficient speed and take correct action if something unforeseen happens. The master has overall responsibility in this, as well as in all other matters, and it is one of his responsibilities to organize and detail, officers, for the watch bill. The master decides to what extent and in what rotation the officers off watch shall assist on the bridge in the various conditions under which the ship may navigate.
- When the master requires the services of several deck officers on the bridge, each of them should know his station and be fully aware of his duties, whether to operate the engine telegraph, use radar, or plot positions, etc., and he should assume his duties without receiving specific orders.
- Under normal conditions of navigation, it is part of good bridge discipline for those on duty on the bridge to inform each other of everything concerning the navigation in a clear and precise manner.
- The officer of the watch continues to be responsible for the safe navigation of the ship despite the presence of the master on the

bridge, until the master informs him specifically that he has assumed responsibility. The fact that the master has taken over the navigation does not relieve the officer of the watch of the duty to assist and to follow closely the master's navigation and also to plot the ship's position on the chart as often as is necessary in view of local conditions. It is the duty of the officer of the watch to notify the master immediately if he thinks the master's navigation does not follow the planned track.

- On arrival and departure, it is preferable to have the officer who is on watch, or who is to come on watch, on the bridge. Change of watch must not take place in conditions where particularly great demands are made on navigation or in narrow waters and in connection with arrival/departure.
- In narrow waters the master should consider whether in addition there ought to be two officers on the bridge. In such cases, one officer shall be solely responsible for fixing the ship's position, while the other will assist the master in checking positions and also the courses and the navigation.
- When visibility of less than five (5) miles is encountered, the master should consider whether in addition there ought to be two officers on the bridge. In such circumstances, one of the officers shall be solely engaged in watching the ship's progress by means of the main radar and from the station he shall report in a loud and clear voice all information of importance to the navigation, such as position fixes, the positions of other ships, and their course and speed.
- The other officer plots the positions reported from the main radar on the chart and then checks them by means of SAT NAV, echo sounder, or other available means.
- When visibility of less than five (5) miles is encountered, and the ship is in narrow or congested water, there must always be two officers on the bridge in addition to the master.

COMMUNICATION

- In large ships where communication by normal speech is made difficult, owing to great distance from bridge wings to wheelhouse and noise from the engines, etc. the use of walkie-talkies is required so that the officer need not leave his station at the telegraph and the helmsman in order to receive orders from pilot or master.
- All orders received shall be repeated in a loud and clear voice.

MAKING READY FOR ARRIVAL

- In order to ensure that all aids to navigation are operational before the ship enters narrow waters or harbor areas, the officer of the watch shall carry out tests/checks in ample time.
- The company's checklist for tests and checks before arrival shall be completed and signed.

Landfall

The master will allow sufficient time when approaching land to ensure that the advance planning of the navigation is carried out using charts of suitably large scale which amply cover the relevant area.

Echo Sounder

The echo sounding depth recorder shall be used and checked frequently during the entire approach.

Anchoring

The selected anchorage should be plotted on the chart and the master should satisfy himself that there is sufficient room to swing even in unfavorable weather conditions.

In this connection account should be taken of the ship's length, the scope of the chain and the fact that in new ships the bridge is aft.

Windlass

The windlass should be made ready well before arrival. It is important that timely request for power is made by arrangement with the watch-keeping engineer and also that anchor lights are tested well in advance if the ship is to anchor at night. When the anchor is about to be let go, it is important to remember, particularly in large ships, that the officer on the forecastle head will often be the person in the best position to decide when the ship is stopped and making no way through the water.

Position Fixing

When at anchor, the ship's position shall be established, preferably by reliable terrestrial observations. This position shall be verified at suitable intervals with due regard to existing conditions and depth of water.

BOARDING OF PILOT AT SEA

- The master may employ the services of a pilot whenever and wherever he considers it necessary and where qualified professional pilots are available.
- The pilot should be contacted in ample time to determine whether a pilot hoist is acceptable or whether accommodation ladder and/or Pilot ladder shall be rigged.

APPROACHING PORT AND ARRIVAL

The instructions relating to navigation and approach of land shall also apply to arrival at port.

CHARTS AND SAILING DIRECTIONS

Charts and sailing directions should be carefully studied in advance so that conspicuous objects capable of being used for position fixing and orientation may be readily identified.

Local Traffic

Information about local traffic, ferries, etc., should, whenever possible, be studied beforehand.

Current and Wind Conditions

- These shall be studied before arrival so that appropriate steps can be taken as required. Particular attention should be paid to current conditions, since the point of impact of the current in the case of cross currents will invariably shift on large ships.
- Always remember to observe the direction of the set when passing aids to navigation and compare with available predictions.
- Tidal predictions are not always entirely exact, being subject to meteorological conditions.

Engines

Always remember to inform the watchkeeping engineer at least one hour before maneuvers for entering port are intended to commence.

Mooring

Make sure that power is on winches and mooring lines are on deck and available in ample time.

NAVIGATION WITH PILOT ON BOARD

When circumstances warrant employment of a pilot for a prolonged passage aboard, the master (preferably together with the senior navigation officers) should thoroughly discuss the passage plan with the pilot upon his boarding. Harbor conditions requiring special attention such as insufficient buoyage, effects of currents, draft of vessel, etc., must be clearly understood by all navigating officers; just as it is understood that the pilot's presence on the bridge does not relieve the master of his responsibility for the safe navigation of his ship.

Company policy requires that all navigation aids such as radar, depth sounder, satellite navigators, etc. are to be functioning during piloting periods, regardless of the time of day or visibility.

A constant running plot of the ship's position must also be maintained.

PREPARATIONS FOR ARRIVAL IN PORT

Preparations for arrival in port should include the following:

1. ETA sent to pilot station at appropriate time with all relevant information required.
2. Available port information, sailing directions, and other navigation information, including restrictions on draft, speed, entry time, etc., studied.
3. All appropriate flag/light signals displayed.
4. Minimum and maximum depths of water in port approaches, channels, and at berth calculated.
5. Draft/trim requirements determined.
6. Cargo/ballast rearranged if necessary.
7. Large-scale charts for port's pilotage water prepared.
8. Latest navigational messages for area received.
9. All hydrographic publications fully corrected up-to-date.
10. Tidal information for port and adjacent area extracted.
11. Latest weather report available.
12. Radio check for pilot/tugs/berthing instructions.
13. VHF channels for various services noted.
14. Availability of pilot ladder hoist on correct side.
15. Master/pilot information exchange form ready (Fig. 7-1).
16. All navigational equipment tested, stabilizers housed.
17. Engines tested for satisfactory operation ahead and astern.
18. Steering gear tested in primary and secondary systems.
19. Course recorder, engine room movement recorder, and synchronization of clock checked.

VESSEL PARTICULARS

BULBOUS BOW	BOW THRUSTERS INSTALLED	WALKING OUT ANCHORS
☐ YES ☐ NO	☐ YES ☐ NO	☐ NECESSARY ☐ UNNECESSARY
ANCHOR SHOTS	MAXIMUM RUDDER ANGLE	RUDDER AREA
☐ PORT ☐ STBD	DEGREES	PERCENT

OTHER UNUSUAL ITEMS

EQUIPMENT LIMITATIONS, FAILURES, etc.

ELECTRONIC AIDS (CHECK IF INSTALLED AND OPERATIONAL)

☐ RADAR 3 cm	☐ LORAN "C"	☐ R.D.F.
☐ RADAR 10 cm	☐ DOPPLER	☐ VHF MAIN
☐ A.R.P.A.	☐ RATE OF TURN	☐ VHF EMERGENCY
☐ SATELLITE	☐ DEPTH ALARM	☐

MOORING WINCHES FITTED WITH

LENGTH	SYNTHETIC	WIRES

SQUAT EFFECTS (LOADED, EVEN KEEL)

UNDERKEEL CLEARANCE (ft.)	6.0		4.0		2.0	
SHIP SPEED (KNOTS)	8	4	8	4	8	4
MAX. SINKAGE BOW DOWN (ft.)						

PILOT COPY

USE SAFETY MARGINS

MASTER/PILOT CHECK LIST (DISCUSS WHEN PILOT BOARDS)

PILOT'S NAME

COMMUNICATIONS ESTABLISHED (*INDICATE VHF CHANNEL*)	RIVER	HARBOR	PORT CONTROL

- ☐ INTENDED NAVIGATION PLAN FOR THE PASSAGE
- ☐ SPEED REQUIRED FOR THE PASSAGE
- ☐ EXPECTED TRAFFIC CONDITIONS/PASSING -OVERTAKING RESTRICTION
- ☐ TIDE, CURRENTS, WEATHER FORECAST/LIMITATIONS
- ☐ STATUS OF NAVIGATIONAL AIDS
- ☐ ANY SPECIAL REQUIREMENTS
- ☐ POSITION TO MEET/RELEASE TUGS
- ☐ POSITION TO EMBARK/DISEMBARK MOORING MASTER/SEA PILOT
- ☐ BERTH/ANCHORAGE LOCATION
- ☐ SEQUENCE OF PLACING/RECOVERING MOORING LINES
- ☐ OTHER (Describe)

NOTE *Use Reverse Side For Sketching Position Of Tugs And Mooring/Unmooring Sequence.*

MASTER/PILOT INFORMATION EXCHANGED

DATE	TIME
MASTER'S SIGNATURE	

VESSEL COPY

TUG POSITION

TUGS	NUMBER	HORSE POWER	USING ☐ OWN WIRE ☐ SHIP'S WIRE

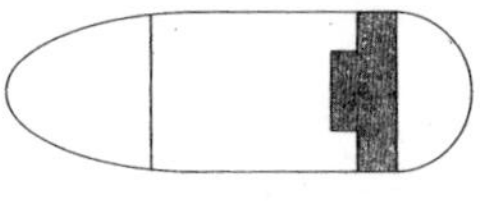

MOORING ARRANGEMENT

NUMBER OF LINES ______

SEQUENCE ______

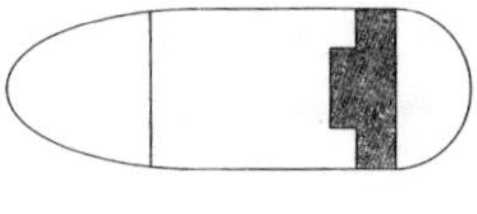

VESSEL COPY

MASTER/PILOT INFORMATION EXCHANGE CARD

VESSEL NAME	DATE
PORT	
BUILT AT	YEAR
TONNAGE NET	GROSS

VESSEL DIMENSIONS

LENGTH	OVERALL	BETWEEN PERPENDICULARS	
DISTANCE	BRIDGE TO BOW	BRIDGE TO MANIFOLD	BRIDGE TO POOP
HEIGHT	KEEL TO TOP OF MAST		
BREADTH			

DRAFTS

FORWARD	MID SHIP	AFT	INCREASE FOR 1° LIST

GYRO COMPASS ERROR		DISPLACEMENT (TONS)	
DEGREES EAST	DEGREES WEST	PRESENT	SUMMER

MANEUVERING SPEEDS (KNOTS)

ENGINE ORDER	RPM		SPEED			
			LOADED		LIGHT	
	AHEAD	ASTERN	AHEAD	ASTERN	AHEAD	ASTERN
FULL						
HALF						
SLOW						
DEAD SLOW						

FULL AHEAD RPM TO FULL ASTERN ______ SECONDS

PLANT	BRIDGE CONTROL	BOW THRUSTER
☐ STEAM ☐ DIESEL	☐ YES ☐ NO	
ASTERN POWER % AHEAD	MAXIMUM TIME ASTERN MINUTES	CRITICAL RPM

PILOT COPY

SPEED AND ECONOMY ARE SECONDARY TO SAFETY

Fig. 7-1. Master/pilot information exchange form.

20. Manual steering engaged in sufficient time for helmsman to become accustomed before maneuvering commences.
21. Berthing instructions received, including anchoring/berthing, which side to, ship or shore gangway, size and number of shore connections, booms (derricks) required, mooring boats/mooring lines, and accommodation ladder.
22. Ship's crew at stations for entering into harbor.
23. Mooring machinery tested, mooring lines, etc., prepared.
24. Adequate pressure on fire main.
25. Internal communication equipment, signal equipment and deck lighting tested.

The best method of ensuring all preparations have been made for arrival is to make up an arrival checklist for your vessel. The arrival checklist used for the simulator 40,000 ton tanker *Capella* is shown in Fig. 7-2.

SS Capella   ARRIVAL CHECKLIST

Date:	Port:	Draft F:	A:	M:

01. Passage to berth planned on form and large scale up-to-date charts	
02. Latest navigational warnings received	
03. Latest weather report received	
04. Pilot/Master exchange of information form completed	
05. VHF channels for various services noted. VHF tested and operative	
06. Bell Book, VHF log and Log Book prepared and available	
07. Bearing circles/alidades in place	
08. Bearing and radar repeaters aligned with master gyro.	
09. Radars, depthmeters, doppler log and course recorder operative	
10. Binoculars, megaphones and walkie-talkies ready for use	
11. Signal lights and flags ready. Whistle tested	

12. ETA sent to Pilot Station and pilot embarkation arranged	
13. Pilot ladder and equipment ready for lee side embarkation	

14. Telephone to engine room tested	
15. Appropriate notice of 'Arrival' given to engine room	
16. Bridge and engine room clocks synchronized	
17. Power and water on deck	
18. Bow and stern thrusters initialized	
19. Engine order telegraph tested	
20. 'Arrival' time signalled and arrival position on chart	
21. Engines tested astern	
22. Relevant watertight doors shut	

23. Telephone to steering compartment tested	
24. Steering gear tested using each pump independently	
25. Bridge and steering gear compartment gyro repeaters aligned	
26. Steering compartment manned by competent helmsman	

27. Chief Officer and Bosun called	
28. Telephone to forecastle tested	
29. Anchors cleared away and prepared for letting go	
30. Anchor ball/lights tested and ready for use	

31. Bridge to aft telephone tested	
32. Mooring lines and handlers ready fore and aft	

BERTH NO. & LOCATION	NO. & SIZE OF SHORE CONNECTIONS
WHICH SIDE TO	MOORING LINES DESIRED
SHIP OR SHORE GANGWAY	TUGS

Fig. 7-2. Arrival checklist.

MASTER/PILOT INFORMATION EXCHANGE

Master/pilot information exchange must include the following:

Pilot supplied by master with relevant shiphandling information
(draft, trim, turning circles, peculiar maneuvering characteristics
in restricted water depth/channel width, and other data). This
information may be displayed at the conning position.

Proposed track, plan contingencies, alternative plan, and available
anchor berths along route explained by pilot and agreed with by
master. Charts compared.

If required, appropriate master/pilot information exchange form may
be used.

Safe progress of the ship in relation to agreed track and plan monitored by master and OOW and the execution of orders checked.

Berthing/unberthing plan, including the availability and use of tugs
and other external facilities, agreed upon by pilot and master.

Tide, set, wind force and direction, and visibility expected along route
are discussed.

Pilot informed of position of lifesaving appliances provided for his use.

All of the above should be indicated on the master/pilot information
exchange form. Once the pilot boards, the OOW, after being a party to
the information exchange between the master and pilot, should keep the
following in mind:

1. The pilot should be regarded as a local expert. In most cases,
    this is true.
2. Pilots are vulnerable to human error. They make mistakes,
    sometimes during the most critical stages of maneuvering and in
    waters where the potential for casualty is highest.
3. For the master, navigation with the pilot in waters where the
    threat potential is high is one of the most severe tests of his
    responsibility. It requires skill, discipline, strong watch organi-
    zation, and sound procedures.
4. Preliminary observations of the pilot by the master with the
    assistance of the OOW must be made as follows:
    (a) Has the pilot handled ships like this before?
    (b) Is the pilot familiar with maneuvering characteristics? *(If the
    answer is no to [a] and [b] above, it should be a warning
    signal to the master.)*
    (c) What is the pilot's plan? Does the master concur? Are the
    watch mates aware?

(d) Does the pilot appear to be ill, tired, nervous, or emotionally upset?

(e) To monitor the plan the master should use local check points along the track to help determine whether the vessel is where she should be at any given time.

(f) The influence of set and drift may be greater than the pilot anticipated and some adjustment may be required.

All other elements in the approach to the anchorage, pilot station, and berth that should be of concern to the watch officer can be found in the preceding chapter. On approach to the anchorage or pier it is essential that the OOW carry out the orders of the conning officer (master or pilot or docking pilot) expeditiously. The OOW must be extremely alert and vigilant and monitor all indicators to ensure compliance. Once the ship is secure at the berth the bridge must be secured.

SECURING BRIDGE

The following steps should be taken to secure the bridge:

1. Turn off navigation lights. If anchored, ensure anchor lights are on fore and aft and anchor ball is raised. Turn on deck lights as required.

2. Ring up FWE. Secure bow thruster. Secure steering system.

3. Turn off radars, fathometer, and instrument indicator lights. Turn down VHF volume controls. Clear and lock satellite navigator.

4. Take down arrival flags and signals. Make up halyards. Ensure proper in-port flags are flying. Place working flags in wheelhouse pigeonholes. Make up and secure any arrival signals used and stow. Cover gyro wing repeaters and bow thruster controls.

5. Place azimuth circles/alidades in racks. Stow binoculars, flashlights, walkie-talkies (ensure turned off), navigation instruments, etc., in designated spaces. Place charts in appropriate desk drawer. Place logbook and record books in stowage's for same.

6. Sign and mark gyro course recorder chart with port and date when turned off.

7. Log arrival draft. Make up passage report and noon position when required, and deliver passage report to chief engineer; noon position to bridge, master, and chief engineer.

8. Lock all wheelhouse doors, chronometer case, log desk locker, binocular drawer, and walkie-talkie stowage.

IN-PORT WATCH

The ship is secure alongside or at anchor, and time in port is sufficient to enable breaking the sea watches and commencement of in-port watches. Even though the dangers to a vessel are fewer and the watch officer is now standing eight-hour watches, the OOW cannot be lulled into a false sense of security. The safety of the vessel is still the OOW's responsibility.

In-port watchstanding still requires a high degree of vigilance and common sense. During the day all sorts of people (longshoremen, stevedores, Coast Guard, company officials, classification surveyors, passengers, repair workers, etc.) may be boarding. Meanwhile cargo operations may be going on and the mate on watch must be aware of all in-port evolutions. During night watches the vessel may become so quiet that the urge to catch a few winks in the captain's chair or on the chart room settee may become too tempting to resist. Whatever evolutions are going on or not going on, the safety of the vessel must remain paramount in the OOW's mind. In preparation for an in-port watch the OOW must obtain enough rest in advance especially since it will be an eight-hour watch. Too many mates who may have, the 00-08 watch come back from being ashore just in time to relieve the watch. A tired watch officer may not be alert or vigilant enough to observe a potential hazard to the vessel. The OOW must keep in mind the responsibilities described below.

WATCH OFFICER'S DUTIES IN PORT

Officer-in-Charge

In the master's absence, the most senior ranking deck officer aboard is the officer-in-charge. The master or officer-in-charge must see to it daily that all officers on duty are up and tending to their duties when anchored, moored, or berthed alongside.

Watch Officer (OOW)

A licensed deck officer must be on watch at all times while the vessel is in port and in active status. The OOW is not to leave the ship at any time until properly relieved by a licensed deck officer.

Scope of Responsibility

The OOW is responsible to the master for the safety and security of the ship and all personnel aboard. The OOW is responsible for knowing and complying with all applicable laws and regulations at the port in which the vessel is anchored or berthed.

Preparations for Relieving the Watch

The following items should be kept in mind when preparing to relieve the watch:

The OOW must determine the state of the tide, time of change, and currents to be expected.

If the ship is anchored, the OOW must confirm its position, comparing it to the position fixed on anchoring. The officer should ascertain that the vessel is within the circle of radius of swing and go to the fo'c'sle to check visually the direction and strain on the chain and if the anchor buoy is still watching.

The OOW must check the mooring lines or anchor chains and status of the engines, and must be aware of any special port or terminal regulations personnel on duty, licensed officers aboard, posted sailing time, and all particulars regarding the loading and discharging of cargo, or ballasting activities the OOW will have to supervise.

The OOW must read and initial the orders concerning cargo handling and ballast prepared by the master or chief officer.

The OOW must obtain or have prompt access to the keys to all locked compartments on the vessel.

Checking Valve Settings

When cargo on a tanker or ballast is being handled, the relieving OOW must be satisfied that the cargo handling valves are set properly on deck and in the pump room. The officer must ensure that their status conforms with the layout required by the operation.

Checking Mooring Lines

The OOW must ensure that mooring lines are kept taut and the vessel is maintained in her proper position at the berth to avoid breasting away from the berth and strain on any hoses and gangways.

Fire Preparedness

To prepare for the possibility of fire, the OOW has the following responsibilities:

The OOW must see that the emergency fire wires are rigged and ready for use on a tanker.

The OOW must be sure that the fire detection system has been inspected and it is operating properly.

The OOW must ensure that fire hoses are connected to hydrants and foam equipment is in place, ready for use.

Rigging Cargo Hoses

The OOW on a tanker must see that cargo hoses are properly hung off. The OOW must ensure that mooring lines, topping lift falls, and runners are always made fast to bitts or cleats and *never* to winch gypsy heads.

The OOW on a tanker must see that bonding wires are connected properly when required.

Scupper Plugs on a Tanker

The OOW must see that scupper plugs are in place whenever cargo or ballast is being handled or when bunkers are being loaded or transferred.

Gangway Safety Net

When berthed alongside, gangway conditions permitting, a gangway safety net must be properly rigged and tended as necessary. The gangway must be illuminated properly and the angle not so steep as to make boarding or disembarking hazardous. On the pier the gangway rollers should be free to move as the vessel moves. A board under the rollers may be necessary. A safety line, life ring, and waterlight must be in the vicinity. The OOW, or his or her seaman, should be available at the gangway, especially when at anchor and a launch carrying crew members or officials is approaching.

Communications with Engine Room

The OOW must determine from the engineer-on-watch the time that the propeller will be turned during warming or cooling the main engine. The officer will then maintain a watch on the mooring lines or anchor chain and stand ready to signal the engine room should the propeller thrust cause undue strain on the mooring lines or anchor chain. The OOW must take whatever precautions are necessary to ensure the vessel remains secured.

The OOW must notify the engineer-on-watch whenever the atmospheric temperature threatens to fall to 35°F so that precautions can be taken to prevent freezing damage to pipes and deck machinery.

The OOW must be alert for excessive stack emissions when in moorings or in berth and must immediately contact the engineer-on-watch if excessive smoke is observed.

Anchorage

While the vessel is at anchor, either in a port anchorage or at a sea terminal, the master or chief officer should be on board.

The OOW must check anchor bearings frequently and use radar during low visibility to determine if the ship is dragging anchor. Bearings should be taken at least every twenty minutes and all fixes should be plotted to ensure the vessel is within the radius of swing (distance bridge to fo'c'sle and scope of chain).

When the ship is at anchor during low visibility, the OOW must see that the proper sound signals are made fore and aft.

Clean Water Inspection/Oil Pollution aboard a Tanker

The OOW must check the waters around the vessel frequently to ensure no cargo is leaking from the hull. If a leak is discovered, determine its source and stop the leak as soon as possible. Any cargo spills or leaks must be noted in the deck logbook and reported.

The OOW must be alert to prevent any situation during cargo or bunkering operations that might lead to an accidental oil spill. He or she must be prepared to stop all cargo or bunkering operations to minimize the spill if it occurs. If oil leaks onto the seas due to a spill, the OOW must contact the proper authorities as soon as possible.

The OOW must ensure no refuse is thrown overboard while the vessel is in a harbor, inland waters, or sea terminals.

Bunkering

The OOW is expected to be fully informed on what bunkering operations are to be carried out and must be prepared to conduct or assist in any aspect of bunkering.

When bunkers are to be taken, the master, in conjunction with the chief engineer and first officer, must assess the ship's total workload, converting operations such as cargo handling, ballasting, repairs, bunkering, and manpower. Based on these factors, the master, with the agreement of the chief engineer, should assign supervision of the bunker loading operation all or in part to an engineering or deck officer.

When any bunkering operations are assigned to the deck department, the following procedures are to be followed:

1. Prior to loading ship's bunkers, the lineup must be checked simultaneously by a deck and engine officer.

2. The deck officer must notify the engineering officer immediately upon commencement of loading which tanks are loading and the bunker fuel oil temperature.
3. When loading bunkers into ship's tanks which are in service, fuel oil temperature cannot exceed 150°F or fall below a temperature at which viscosity increases above the easy pumping limit. Bunker loading must be stopped or loading diverted into an out-of-service tank until the shore adjusts the temperature to within this range.
4. The connecting and disconnecting of bunker hoses must be supervised by a deck officer.

Arrivals and Departures

Appropriate entries on the bunkering operation must be recorded in the deck logbook.

In-Port Security

The OOW must ensure that only authorized persons are permitted to board the vessel. A careful watch must be kept in port to prevent contraband from being loaded and to prevent stowaways, terrorists or other undesirable persons from boarding. The warning sign to unauthorized persons to keep off the ship must always be displayed at the head of the gangway.

A seaman must be stationed on a gangway and cargo hose watch at all times while the vessel is alongside a dock to prevent boarding by unauthorized persons and to attend hoses. He or she must not leave the vicinity of the gangway unless properly relieved. If a guard service is used at a port, this in no way relieves the OOW of these security duties.

Unauthorized persons must not be allowed aboard the ship. Salesmen or vendors will not be permitted aboard unless given permission. Friends or relatives of vessel personnel must not be permitted aboard ship except as provided by company policy.

Authorized persons are those having legitimate business with the vessel, such as repairmen, dock workers, agent's employees, company employees, pilots, and government authorities. Authorized persons must present a valid pass or other identification.

Authorized persons must not be allowed to enter areas other than those where their business is conducted.

Compartments not in use will be locked during time in port. This includes fan rooms, steering engine rooms, wheelhouse, chart room, and storerooms. In quarters and other locations where portholes are needed for ventilation, they will be left open only as far as the dog rings to prevent unlawful entrance.

Navigating equipment such as sextants, binoculars, alidades/azimuth circles, portable tools, and other pilferable items must be collected and placed under lock while in port.

In ports where piracy may be a possibility the OOW must be extremely vigilant. Keep pirates and terrorists off your vessel by making it obvious that the ship is alert and it is impossible to board undetected. Always take these precautions:

Have at least three fire hoses rigged and ready for discharge over the stem.

Post a visible lookout with a radio on the stem to warn for approaching boats.

Use as much lighting as possible during darkness to allow early detection of approaching boats.

Post extra lookouts on deck when the vessel is at anchor or in port. Make sure they are highly visible to potential pirates.

Serious injury to the crew is very rare during pirate attacks, even in areas where pirate attacks are common. But if pirates do board your vessel do not aggravate the situation, surrender the ship's money and allow the pirates to escape.

As soon as safety permits, an urgent report must be sent to local authorities and the company with full details.

Cargo Operations

During cargo operations, no matter what the cargo is, the OOW must be aware that the company exists for the safe loading, carriage, and discharge of the vessel's cargo. The company's economic survival depends upon the OOW's vigilance during cargo operations. Loading and discharging occur in port and protection of the cargo must be paramount. Exceptions must be written where appropriate, and the chief officer's cargo orders must be complied with strictly. In the last stages of loading or discharging the thoughts of the watch officer must turn to preparations for departure.

DEPARTURE

The use of the voyage plan, conning notebooks and predeparture checklist (see Fig. 7-3) is intended as a practical navigational procedural system with emphasis on preplanning the vessel's intended routes throughout the

PRE-DEPARTURE GEAR CHECK-LIST

Start Check-List one (1) hour before getting underway.

Check Off:

_____ Synchronize all Bridge and Engine Room clocks.

_____ Test Engine Room telegraph(s) in all positions.

_____ Test whistles, both steam and air, including manual control.

_____ Test General Alarm.

_____ Test steering systems, both steering motors and NFU unit.

_____ Check gyro compass(es) and all repeaters. Ensure that the master gyro is operating, the locks are off, and the speed/latitude settings are correct. Synchronize all repeaters to the master gyro. Compare dock heading with the gyro and magnetic compass heading. Report any large errors. Check illumination of all repeaters.

_____ Check course recorder. Make sure it is wound, is running, has sufficient paper, and is set on proper quadrant, course, and GMT time. Mark chart with date, time, port, and initials.

_____ Check fathometer. Place in operation and make sure indicator and recorder are operating properly. Test alarm system.

_____ Set bridge bell logger on GMT. Mark chart with date, time, port, and initials. (C-8's and C-9's)

_____ Check VHF radios. Turn on and test each set. Turn one set to Channel 13, one to 16 (U.S. waters only). Check listening watch on 2182 KHZ Unit.

_____ Check radars. Operate both radars. Synchronize headings and turn for optimum operations. Check ranges and bearings with charted objects.

_____ Place clean azimuth circles on clean bearing repeaters.

_____ Illuminate all wheelhouse and navigation bridge wing indicators.

_____ Check UHF walkie-talkies. Make sure each unit is working and batteries are charged.

_____ Test sound-powered telephones to Engine Room, bow, and stern.

_____ Clean binoculars and place in proper location.

_____ Display proper signals according to law, local requirements, and custom. This includes flags, special lights, and day shapes.

_____ Test navigation lights to make sure both elements of all lights are operable. Turn off all outside deck lights before S.B.E.

_____ Energize bow thruster (if applicable) and have operational before S.B.E.

_____ Lay out charts, publications, and tools in the order they will be used. Have tide tables, current tables, light list, and radio aids opened to appropriate page and marked. Have corrections readily available.

_____ Check SAT/NAV position with chart.

_____ Test LORAN and lock on to available stations.

_____ Rig and test Aldis signal light. Place loudhailer and/or megaphone(s) on inbound nav. Bridge wing.

_____ Make sure the helmsman is competent and at helm before S.B.E.

_____ Comply with 33 CFR 164.25 (U.S. waters only) as follows:
   (a) Test primary and secondary steering gear.
   (b) Test all internal vessel control communications and vessel control alarms.
   (c) Test standby or emergency generator properly functioning.
       Name/Rate Engineer reporting _____
   (d) Test storage batteries for emergency lighting and power systems.
       Name/Rate person reporting _____
   (e) Test main propulsion machinery, ahead and astern.
       Name/Rate Engineer reporting _____

_____ Notify Chief Mate and Chief Engineer in writing of inoperative equipment; also alert Master.

                            Date/Time _____

Master _____   Port   _____

                            LDO Signature _____

Fig. 7-3. Pre-departure gear checklist.

voyage. It incorporates a checking procedure to guard against one person's errors and ensures that positive action is taken to check the vessel's position at frequent stipulated intervals by more than one method, especially prior to a change of course.

The voyage plan should be completed for each voyage. However, at the discretion of the master, the necessity for completing a voyage plan for every voyage leg can be influenced by the following:

1. Continuity of personnel in the bridge team.
2. Familiarity with voyage routing when trading between the same ports.
3. Assignment of personnel to the bridge team who are unfamiliar with the intent of the plan and checklist.

As appropriate for the intended voyage, all vessels must carry adequate and up-to-date charts, *Sailing Directions, Coast Pilots, Light Lists, Notices to Mariners, Tide Tables, Current Tables,* and all other nautical publications necessary.

After taking into consideration all of the previous guidelines it is time to make up the voyage plan. The master and navigator (usually the second mate) must discuss the plan after the second mate makes it up, and all OOWs should be part of this process. The voyage plan must incorporate preparation for sea, transit in pilotage waters, disembarkation of pilot, coastal navigation, and deep-sea navigation.

Preparation for Sea

1. Switch on and synchronize gyro and repeaters.
2. Check headings of magnetic compass and repeaters.
3. Switch on fathometer.
4. Activate speed/distance recorder.
5. Turn on electronic navigational aids.
6. Switch on and tune radar for operation.
7. Synchronize ship's clocks.
8. Activate course and engine movement recorder. Sign and note date and time.
9. Test primary and emergency navigation lights.
10. Ensure propeller and rudder clear of obstruction. (Wheel clearance.)
11. Check "not under command" and anchor lights and shapes.
12. Test steering in primary and secondary systems.
13. Test autopilot and change over arrangements.

14. Test telegraphs and ensure main engines ready.
15. Test bridge communications equipment-internal, external, and portable.
16. Test signaling lamps.
17. Test whistle.
18. Test window wipers/clear view screens.
19. Ensure deck power available.
20. Make arrangements for pilot embarkation/disembarkation including overside lighting, heaving line, life buoy and condition of ladder/hoist.
21. Have telescope/binoculars available.
22. Ensure charts and navigational publications corrected up-to-date and courses laid off.
23. Prepare passage plan and conning notebook.
24. Where carried, have bridge bell book available.
25. Ensure crew at stations for leaving harbor.
26. Have anchors cleared away and ready for use.

Transit in Pilotage Waters

1. Ensure bridge equipment operating and monitored by OOWs.
2. Ensure all required stations manned and ready.
3. Supervise and monitor helmsman.
4. Clearly establish who has conn (pilot or master).
5. Obtain vessel's position and constantly monitor track.
6. Comply with Rules of the Road and harbor regulations.

Disembarkation of Pilot

1. Inform master of probable time of disembarkation.
2. Send ETA/ETD to pilot station.
3. Agree upon side from which pilot will disembark.
4. Ensure ancillary equipment for pilot disembarkation is ready and checked.
5. Ensure deck officer is available to conduct pilot from bridge to disembarkation point and supervise the disembarkation until pilot boat is away.
6. Inform engine room of expected disembarkation time.

Navigation, Coastal Waters/Traffic Separation Schemes

1. Have available corrected charts and hydrographic publications.
2. Lay courses well clear of obstructions.
3. The following factors must be taken into consideration:
   (a) advice/recommendation in the *Sailing Directions;*

(b) depth of water and draft;

(c) tides and currents;

(d) weather, particularly in areas renowned for poor visibility;

(e) degree of accuracy of navigational aids and navigational fixes;

(f) daylight/nighttime passing of danger points; and

(g) concentration of fishing vessels.

4. Fix position at regular intervals, particularly when navigating in or near a traffic separation scheme.

5. Use with caution the position of buoys or other floating aids.

6. Check error of gyro/magnetic compasses whenever possible.

BRIDGE SAILING OR SHIFTING CHECK-OFF

ONE and ONE-HALF (1½) HOURS BEFORE SAILING

    Check propeller and give clearance to Engine Room.

ONE (1) HOUR BEFORE SAILING

_____ 1. Check on necessary personnel calls for sailing.

_____ 2. Set Bridge clocks. Give time check to Engine Room. Test engine order telegraph, telephones, console alarms.

_____ 3. Test whistles (three electric, one manual station) and general alarm.

_____ 4. Test electric steering systems. Leave on last side tested. Turn wheel over at least every 15 minutes once unit is energized.

_____ 5. Test navigation lights. (Leave off until underway)

_____ 6. Check master gyro compass settings and settings on all Bridge repeaters. Set the gyro course recorder on GMT and mark port and date on chart. Check magnetic compass with gyro heading. Place azimuth circles on Bridge repeaters.

_____ 7. Energize and check for proper operation: radars, fathometer, lorans, and RDF. Unlock satellite navigator and set. Ensure all instrument indicator lights are operative.

_____ 8. Lay out binoculars, flashlights, walkie-talkies (check battery power), charts and navigating instruments.

_____ 9. Check VHF Channel 13 and Channel 16. Set any third channel required to be guarded; set all volume controls.

_____ 10. Hoist necessary flags and any other required signals, and lay out others that may be required. (Use working flags from wheelhouse port lower pigeon holes)

_____ 11. If sailing, obtain crew muster check from Purser, and that ship papers and port clearance are aboard.

_____ 12. If sailing, search assigned Bridge area spaces for stowaways.

_____ 13. Energize bow thruster 20 minutes prior to sailing.

    Note: *Keep all notes in Bell Book [Movement Book], starting with navigation gear test. Once gear is tested, do not leave the Bridge unattended. Docking stations will normally be 15 minutes prior to sailing time.*

_____ 14. Turn out all deck lights. If sailing during dark hours, ensure no lights are exposed from forward side and sides of midship house. Turn on navigation lights at last line.

_____ 15. As soon as possible after vessel is clear of berth, get a stowaway search report from each department head.

_____ 16. Make up Departure Report and deliver to Chief Engineer.

Fig. 7-4. Bridge sailing or shifting check off.

```
                        M.V. PRESIDENT F.D. ROOSEVELT
                        PRE-ARRIVAL/DEPARTURE GEAR TEST
```

The following guidelines are to be followed for pre-departure gear tests and for pre-arrival tests for entering U.S. Coastal Waters. The completed form is to be signed and filed away for the voyage.

The only log entry required is: "ALL TESTS HAVE BEEN PERFORMED IN ACCORDANCE WITH 33 CFR 164.25". In the case of a pre-arrival test the Latitude and the Longitude of the test area shall also be entered.

1. _____ CLOCKS - Ensure that the Bridge and E/R clocks are synchronized.

2. _____ COMPASSES - Verify that master compasses and all repeaters are aligned.

3. _____ PHONES - Ensure that phone and public address systems are operational between Bridge, Engine Room, and mooring stations.

4. _____ STEERING - In conjunction with the duty or first engineer test both steering systems in hand and non-follow up modes. Ensure that rudder angle indicators are functioning.

5. _____ THROTTLE - Test wheelhouse throttle only when on Engine Room manual control, with duty engineer in Control Room.

6. _____ RADIOS - Have the forward VHF tuned to the local traffic control channel. The after VHF should be on 13 and monitoring 16. Check UHFs with E/R and another deck officer.

7. _____ COURSE RECORDER - Verify the proper operation of the recorder. See that it is set to the proper heading and GMT. Your initials with the date/time group should be on the chart face.

8. _____ DEPTH SOUNDER and RECORDERS - Energize and initial recorders.

9. _____ RADARS - When crane drivers have departed their cabs, place both radars in the TX mode and align heading flashers. Set up the ARPA's to reflect the correct data, i.e.: speed log in-put, North up.

10. _____ NAV. LIGHTS - Energize and visually verify operation. Also, any special lights required.

11. _____ SPEED LOG - Verify accuracy and run through the test modes. Set in the "GEA" position unless otherwise directed.

12. _____ NAV. GEAR - Sat/Nav should be programmed with the current route. LORAN should be set to the best stations, if any.

13. _____ CHARTS and PUBLICATIONS - Appropriate charts and pubs should be laid out and ready for the upcoming voyage. Only the current and up-coming course lines should be on the charts to be used.

14. _____ FLAGS - In the daytime, have the appropriate flags hoisted or ready to be hoisted. Special signals and normally flown flags are enumerated in the *Bridge Navigation Manual*.

15. _____ BELL LOGGER - Date and initial bell logger after verifying correct time.

FIFTEEN (15) MINUTES PRIOR TO SAILING TIME

16. _____ MISC. - Clean azimuth circles should be available. Whistle and General Alarm should be tested and the whistle left in the AFTER position.

FIVE (5) MINUTES PRIOR TO SAILING TIME

17. _____ MAIN ENGINE - When cranes and wheel are clear, place subtelegraph in S/B position informing E/R readiness to roll on air. After the engine has been rolled on air ask for wheelhouse control.

18. _____ BOW THRUSTER - Have E/R energize bow thruster, after checking to see that control levers are in midship position. INFORM MASTER OF READINESS OF ENGINE AND BOW THRUSTER.

19. _____ LIGHTS - Douse all unnecessary lights.

Fig. 7-5. MV *President F. D. Roosevelt* Pre-Arrival/Departure Gear Test. (Courtesy of American President Lines.)

ANY DEFICIENCIES SHOULD BE BROUGHT TO THE ATTENTION OF THE DEPARTMENT HEAD CONCERNED AND LATER FOLLOWED UP TO SEE THAT THE CORRECTIONS HAVE BEEN MADE. ANY DEFICIENCIES THAT WOULD PREVENT OUR DEPARTURE SHOULD BE BROUGHT TO THE ATTENTION OF THE MASTER, WHEN IT IS ASCERTAINED THAT REPAIRS CANNOT BE EFFECTED PRIOR TO OUR SCHEDULED DEPARTURE TIME.

The above items were tested and found to be operating satisfactorily, except where specifically noted.

DATE _____ TIME _____ PORT _____

LAT _____ NORTH (U.S. PORTS) LOD SIGNATURE_____

LONG _____ WEST (ONLY) M/V PRESIDENT F.D. ROOSEVELT, VOYAGE_____

(*Courtesy of American President Lines*)

SS Capella   **DEPARTURE CHECKLIST**

Date:	Port:	Draft F:	A:	M:
01.	Passage plan on form and large scale chart of area			
02.	Chartwork instruments and accessories ready for use			
03.	Bell Book, VHF log and Log Book prepared and available			
04.	Bearing circles/alidades in place			
05.	Binoculars, megaphones, and signal light ready for use			
06.	Bridge front window clearview screens/wipers tested			
07.	Navigation lights and light failure alarms tested			
08.	Special purpose and n.u.c. lights tested. Flag hoists ready			
09.	Whistle and general alarms tested			
10.	Master gyro stabilized and compared with magnetic compass			
11.	Gyro repeaters, radar, course recorder, SatNav, Omega inputs aligned			
12.	Radars operative and checked on all ranges			
13.	SatNav, Omega, Loran, RDF and Doppler operative			
14.	Depthmeters operative and shallow water alarm set and checked			
15.	VHF channels for services noted. VHF and walkie-talkies tested			
16.	Internal telephones tested			
17.	Appropriate notice of departure given to engine-room			
18.	Bridge clock time checked. Synchronized with engine-room clock			
19.	Power and water on deck			
20.	Engine order telegraph tested			
21.	Rudder and propeller sighted clear of obstructions			
22.	Shaft turned if necessary			
23.	Bow and stern thrusters energized			
24.	Relevant watertight doors shut			
24.	Telephone to steering compartment tested			
25.	Steering gear tested in all modes			
26.	Bridge and steering compartment heading repeaters aligned			
27.	Arrangements made for manning after steering on departure from berth			
28.	Pilot/Master exchange of information form completed			
29.	Relevant personnel called			
30.	Mooring machinery and line handlers ready fore and aft			
31.	Hoses disconnected and clear			
32.	Pilot ladder and equipment ready for use			
33.	All visitors ashore			
34.	Departure draft and density obtained			
35.	Muster and stowaway search completed			
36.	After steering manned by competent helmsman			

Beadon

Fig. 7-6. Departure checklist—factors for a watch officer to consider.

7. Be aware of the likelihood of encountering unlit small craft at night.
8. Consult appropriate publications for effect of tidal streams and current.
9. Be aware of the effect of squat on underkeel clearance in shallow water.
10. Monitor broadcasts by any local navigation services.
11. Take into account the 1972 International Regulations for Preventing Collisions at Sea, Rule 10, when navigating in, or near the vicinity of, IMO-approved traffic separation scheme.

Navigation, Deep-Sea

1. Corrected charts and hydrographic publications must be made available.
2. Ocean passage charts should be prepared at least forty-eight hours before sailing time and discussed with the master.
3. Ship's position shall be fixed regularly and at least twice daily. (Note: Celestial observations in high latitudes are subject to false horizon error.)
4. Check gyro/magnetic compass error once a watch. (Note: Gyro/ magnetic compass in high latitudes is subject to greater error.)
5. Participate in area reporting system such as Automated Merchant Vessel Emergency Rescue (AMVER).

Figs. 7-4 and 7-5 show different variations of departure check-off lists that can be used by the OOW in preparing the vessel for sea. The factors the OOW must consider during departure are shown in Figure 7-6.

CONCLUSION

The importance of checklists cannot be overemphasized. When the term checklists or check off is used, it does not imply a simple checkmark. A checklist requires initials or signatures so the responsible person can be identified. The change of watch check off discussed in Chapter 1 (tables 1-2 and 1-3) is critical for the safety of the vessel. If the author had initialed and signed a change of watch checklist in his first watch (see Preface) the traumatic series of events described may have been averted.

CHAPTER EIGHT

Bridge Simulation Training

THE advent of radar simulators provided the mariner with the opportunity for training in restricted visibility for collision avoidance and navigation purposes. The first radar simulators in the 1960s used analog computers and analog coastline generators. Digital computers now drive modem radar simulators, which are composed of a modern bridge design and a capability to be expanded into a full mission bridge simulator.

In 1967 the first physical shiphandling simulator (using 1:25 scale model ships on an eight-acre lake) was built at the Marine Research and Training Center of Port Revel near Grenoble, France. In 1967 the Japan Radio Communications Company Ltd. (JRC) documented a visual display provided by television monitors framed in the front windows of a wheelhouse that could roll, pitch, and heave. The video signal was taken with a television camera that moved in a 1:1000 scale model of a harbor and followed the computed ship motion.

The first application of a computer was the Swedish Maritime Research Center (SSPA) simulator in 1968. This simulator used computer-generated graphics which were presented eventually on seven television screens. In 1968 the TNO-IWECO, Institute of Mechanical Engineering, simulator in Delft, Holland, used a point light source wherein the shadow of a three-dimensional scale model was projected onto the screen.

The emergence of larger ships and vessels with unusual maneuvering characteristics has supported the development of bridge simulators. The development also has been given impetus by concerns for research, shiphandling, port approach, passage planning, and training in bridge procedures. Because it is so close to shipboard reality, a bridge simulator is an effective method for training seafarers. However, there is controversy in the maritime community concerning its use as a *substitute* for shipboard service and experience.

Common to all simulators is the mathematical model of ship characteristics, a realistic bridge, and the visual scene out of the bridge windows. Many simulators use computer-generated imagery. Computer-generated imagery day/night and pure nocturnal simulators constitute the majority of the systems that have been produced to date. Nocturnal simulators are more cost efficient and less expensive than the day/night versions. The Racal-Decca simulator, installed in 1977 at the Warsash College of Maritime Studies, had a 110° field of view and projected 16 lights on a flat screen using computer-controlled projectors. Messerschmitt-Bolkow-Blohm (MBB) built the first large screen nocturnal simulator at the Bremen Nautical Academy in 1978.

Simulators are often judged by their field of view (110°, 120°, 180°, 220°, 240°, 360°), their projection system, and whether they are part task or full mission. Full mission simulators, which are more complex and costly, provide among their many options:

Individual and team training as required.
Integration of the skills and knowledge developed by the supplementary facilities.
Realistic setting for true representation of ship response under a variety of conditions.
Full flexibility of scenarios.
Capability for equipment degradation and/or casualties.

Projection systems or image generator sources include computer generated imagery (CGI) for daylight scenarios, computer-controlled video spotlight projection for nocturnal scenarios, point light source/shadowgraph, modelboard/video, and hybrid/unique.

SIMULATOR TRAINING

From 1970 to 1976 shipping companies observed that nearly all navigation casualties involved well-found ships operated by well-trained crews, that most casualties occurred in confined waters with a pilot on board, and at the time of the casualty, the vessels were not operating under adverse weather conditions or being committed to unfamiliar maneuvers. The International Chamber of Shipping (ICS) in their report #15 of January 1976 stated that the two principal factors causing navigation casualty are failure to keep a good lookout and weaknesses in bridge organization.

In 1977 the College of Maritime Studies in Warsash, UK, in conjunction with Shell Tankers Ltd., developed the first ship simulator bridge organization and teamwork courses. Initially the courses were for masters, port captains, and pilots. Later courses were extended to other deck officers. The UK Department of Transport was the first authority to grant two weeks' remission of sea time to students who completed the course.

Bridge Watchstanding Training Using the CAORF Simulator
In a report by the National Transportation Safety Board, dated September 9, 1981, and titled "Special Study—Major Marine Collisions and Effects

of Preventive Recommendations," the leading causes of 33 marine collisions from 1970 through 1980 were: improper navigation (73 percent), equipment failure (18 percent), and other causes (9 percent). The board noted that proper navigation includes the practice of determining, at any particular moment, the ship's position, speed, course, the time of encounter when approaching contacts, and the future courses to be steered to reach the desired encounter. This involves the use of radar, visual cues, whistle signals, aids to navigation, radiotelephone communications, and maneuvering data.

As a result of this study, the National Transportation Safety Board made the following recommendations:

To the U.S. Coast Guard:

> Expedite the study of the feasibility of requiring the installation of automatic recording devices aboard applicable ships to preserve vital navigational information.
>
> In cooperation with the U.S. Maritime Administration, identify and incorporate into licensing and certification programs the general emergency shiphandling procedures expected to be followed by vessel operators when ships experience vital control system failures.

To the U.S. Maritime Administration:

> In cooperation with the U.S. Coast Guard, develop a model simulator training program to reduce ship collisions caused by vital control system failure, which could be incorporated into licensing and certification programs.

The U.S. Maritime Administration sponsored, and the author developed, a training program at the United States Merchant Marine Academy designed to enhance the watchstanding knowledge, skills, and bridge procedures of its senior deck and dual (deck/engine) third officer candidates. The Bridge Watchstanding Training Program, using the Computer Assisted Operational Research Facility (CAORF) bridge simulator, combines classroom instruction and simulator exercises with instructional feedback. Part task training on the simulator was initiated in 1980, and included the topics of shiphandling, Rules of the Road, and port arrival planning. Initially, the program had only one instructor.

Since the International Marine Simulation Forum Conference of 1984 (MARSIM 84), and since two cadet bridge teams attended a two-week cadet bridge watchstanding course at the College of Maritime Studies in Warsash, UK, training at the U.S. Merchant Marine Academy has been changed. Now it consists mainly of whole task training with a voyage concept. The role of the instructor has also been changed: three or four instructors are used to operate the simulator and role-play as master and pilot. A portion of the training (Rules of the Road), which was in the original program, was retained due to the importance of this subject. The voyage training now consists of departure from New York, arrival in New York, two weeks of training in Rules of the Road, anchoring in Limon Bay, Panama, departure from anchorage in Limon Bay, transit Singapore Straits, California coast watch, arrival at Port Internationale, departure Port Internationale, Arrival San Francisco, and departure Valdez. The bridge simulator has proven to be an even more valuable tool, although it is felt that the at-sea experience is, and always will be, a necessary major part of the training program.

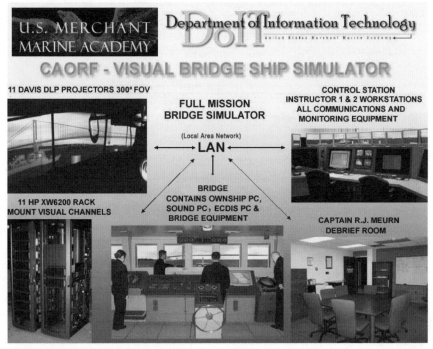

Fig. 8-1. Major CAORF subsystems.

Fig. 8-2. *Above.* CAORF bridge (port view). *Below.* CAORF bridge (starboard view).

Fig. 8-3. CAORF chart desk with chart, passage plan navigation record log, conning notebook, change of watch check off, and VHF log. Above the chart desk, from left to right, Navtex, fathometer, LORAN, and GPS.

U.S. Merchant Marine Academy Whole Task Training

At the U. S. Merchant Marine Academy, Bridge Watchstanding (Simulator-Based Training) is a three-credit course designed to enhance the potential third mate's decision-making skills as they apply to traffic and voyage planning situations. Practical application of Rules of the Road and development of correct bridge procedure is emphasized. Open sea and harbor conditions are simulated for day as well as night. Each watch team has two hours on the simulator and a class hour per week. Each watch team is composed of four cadets, who rotate their duties each scenario as OOW, navigator, radar observer, and helmsmen.

The course is designed to make available to students a valuable resource (Figs. 8-1, 8-2, and 8-3) that can sharpen the midshipman's bridge watchstanding skill to the highest level prior to graduation. This also will help the academy to meet the increased IMO requirements for sea time.

All course training is interrelated and there is time to reinforce objectives with multiple arrivals at different ports. The role-playing by different qualified instructors as pilot, master, and control station operator provides for more thorough debriefs with different observations of midshipmen performance.

Whole task training with role-playing by multiple instructors (all of whom have an unlimited master's license) appears to maximize effective use of the simulator. In addition, all members of the cadet watch team are contributing and benefiting more from this type of training.

From a training point of view, maximum use of training on the simulator is being obtained. Continued research should validate these observations. The course framework is in table 8-1.

TABLE 8-1
U.S.M.M.A. Bridge Watchstanding Course

Voyage New York to Port Internationale

Week	Time on Simulator for Each Watch Team	Event
(1)	½ hour ¾ hour	Bridge and vessel familiarization Vessel at Stapleton; prepare for sea; pilot boards; master on bridge; weigh anchor; pilot disembarks at pilot station; full away; master departs bridge (day)
(2)	1 hour	Prepare for arrival and arrive New York (night)
(3)	1 hour	At-sea Rules of the Road scenarios; unrestricted visibility (day and night)
(4)	1 hour	At-sea Rules of the Road scenarios; various steering failures and reduced visibility (day and night)
(5)	1 hour	Prepare for arrival and arrive Cristóbal anchorage (sunrise); begin grading watch teams
(6)	1 hour	Prepare for departure Cristóbal (sunset)
(7)	1 hour	Transit Singapore Straits and transfer of watch (night)
(8)	1 hour	California coast watch in vessel traffic lane and transfer of watch (day)
(9)	1 hour	Arrival preparation and transit Santa Cruz Channel for Port Internationale (day)
(10)	1 hour	Departure preparation and depart Port Internationale (night)
(11)	1 hour	Arrival preparation and arrive San Francisco (day in fog)
(12)	1 hour	Emergency departure from Valdez, Alaska due to tsunami (day)

Table 8-1. USMMA Bridge Watchstanding course.

SIMULATION AND THE DEBRIEF

At CAORF there is a great deal of emphasis on realism during the simulation and a thorough and detailed debriefing. During simulation, role-playing by the master and pilot must be true to life as possible. The scenarios should be realistic in that instructors must not use outlandish

Fig. 8-4. The debrief.

names for other vessels, purposely give the students a hard time, or make collisions unavoidable no matter what the student does. If the instructor allows any immature tendencies to infiltrate the scenario, realism is lost and the simulator will become a video game where the student is in a no-win situation. Scenarios must be conducted professionally by mariners who have a master's license and preferably have sailed as master.

Debriefing sessions should last at least an hour with the student doing most of the talking, explaining step by step how and why he or she performed each evolution. The instructor (Fig. 8-4) should allow the student to discover why a particular evolution did not work or did work as planned. At no time should the debriefing be demeaning to the student. The instructor should not say, "you should not have done this or that" or "that was a wrong decision;" rather suggestions should be made based on the instructor's experience. Voyage plans also should be examined and critiqued along with the charts, logbook, bell books, check-off sheets, track printouts, and conning or bridge notebooks. Finally, all aspects of the student's performance should be evaluated as in Fig. 8-5. The overall objective is to increase the student's confidence. It would be easy but self-defeating to destroy the student's sense of worth and newfound ability. The instructor must be tactful and keep in mind at all times that the objective is to sharpen the student's bridge watchstanding skills to the highest level.

BRIDGE RESOURCE MANAGEMENT
Cadet Watch Team Grading Form

DATE: 9/11/07	TEAM: (A-2)	ARRIVAL CRISTOBAL

WATCH OFFICER: __FARRAGUT__
NAVIGATOR: __BOWDITCH__
RADAR OBS: __SCANER__
HELM: __RIZZO__

(ANCHOR IN LIMON BAY, CRISTOBAL)
TIME LET GO ⚓ __0651__
OWNSHIP BEARING __180°__ AND
RANGE __1 CABLE__ FROM PLANNED ANCHORAGE

EXECUTION
Total 40 Points – 2 Points Per Item

1. Comp. with Master's standing orders......	9
2. More than one method of fixing used......	2
3. Proper internal comms./terminology......	1
4. Proper VHF procedures....................	
5. Master/Engine room kept informed.......	1.5
6. Arrival checks properly completed........	2
7. Proper helm orders given..................	1
8. Frequency & method of pos'n fixing......	2
9. Margins of safety maintained..............	2
10. Optimum use of all navigation aids......	1.5
11. Correct collision avoidance taken........	2
12. Safe speed maintained at all times........	2
13. Efficient visual lookout maintained.......	1.5
14. Anchoring properly prepared & executed	2
15. Optimum use of bridge personnel........	2
16. Bell Book properly maintained...........	2
17. Log Book properly maintained...........	2
18. VHF Log properly maintained...........	1.5
19. Navigation Log properly maintained.....	1
20. Port regulations complied with	1

EXECUTION SCORE | 34

MONITORING
Total 20 Points – 2 points per Item

1. Track (charted fixes and PI)...............	2
2. Visual Bearings...........................	2
3. Traffic....................................	2
4. VHF......................................	2
5. Helm.....................................	1.5
6. Fathometer / Bridge Instruments.......	1.5
7. Visibility / Weather......................	2
8. ETA's & W/O	2
9. Passing of Information....................	2
10. Watch Officer............................	2

MONITORING SCORE | 19

APPRAISAL & PLANNING
Total 30 Points – 2 Points Per Item

1. All relevant pubs. Studied	1.5
2. Satisfactory plan on form	
3. Tracks, DRs, W/Os & courses on chart	2
4. Dangers & margins of safety marked........	2
5. Tidal times, hts. & UKC calculated.........	1
6. Parallel Index planed & marked on chart...	2
7. Currents marked and effects considered.....	2
8. ETA's and distances planned...............	1.5
9. VHF ch. noted and RP's marked...........	1
10. Frequency & method of fixing planned....	1
11. Port regulations considered	1
12. Weather expectations and forecasts.........	2
13. Ships Maneuvering capabilities considered	2
14. Contingency plans documented.............	1
15. Safe anchorages marked.....................	2

APPRAISAL & PLANNING SCORE | 24

ORGANIZATION & TEAMWORK
Total 10 points – 5 points per item
1. Watch Officer Situational Awareness...... | 4
2. Teamwork..................................... | 4

ORGANIZATION & TEAMWORK SCORE | 8

SUMMARY

APPRAISAL & PLANNING (30)..............	24
EXECUTION (40)...............................	34
MONITORING (20)...........................	19
ORGANIZATION & TEAMWORK (10).....	8
TOTAL POINTS (Out of 100)	85

AUTOMATIC DEDUCTIONS

½ point each minute late to anchorage..................	1
10 Points for grounding..........................	0
10 points for collision or allision	0
5 points for near miss or extremely unsafe navigation.....	0
ADJUSTED (FINAL) SCORE	84

COMMENTS: CRISTOBAL SIG STA (CH 12) NOT NOTED ON PLAN. UKC AT EACH WAY POINT NOT CALCULATED CORRECTLY IN METERS. MAX SPD OF 10 KTS AT BKWTR ENTRANCE NOT NOTED ON PLAN & CHART NOR COMPLIED WITH. CONTINGENCY ANCHORAGES NOT INDICATED ON PLAN OR CHART. VHF CALLS & HELM COMMANDS NOT CORRECT. FATHOMETER NOT MONITORED NOR NOTED FOR EACH FIX. ORG & TEAMWORK EXCELLENT. ....Instructor: _____

Fig. 8-5. Cadet watch team grading sheet.

CONTROL STATION REQUIREMENTS

Simulators have become more sophisticated with expanding capabilities. They are used for training and research on a routine basis throughout the world. Many of the education institutes and private operators offer their simulators for one or both of the above uses. This increased competition coupled with the availability of advanced computer hardware and software has led to the highly sophisticated marine simulators in use today. Operators must have state-of-the-art equipment to market their services successfully. Manufactures and purchasers of these simulators usually set as their first priority the realism from a fidelity and mathematical model point of view followed by the bridge layout and equipment. Many times the control station requirements are dealt with as an afterthought. In some instances the institution purchasing the simulator waits to hire an instructor until after the purchase contract is signed. The instructor therefore has very little input into the design, and as a result little thought is given to the instructor's needs to properly monitor the trainee during an exercise. What is needed for a thorough debriefing, which will ensure maximum use of the simulator in accomplishing training objectives, is missing. The following must be considered when designing an observation, control, and debriefing facility:

1. General Layout
2. Gallery
3. Monitoring
   - visual scene
   - bridge team activity
   - navigation
   - situation display
   - status display
4. Communications
   - internal
   - external
5. Playback capability
   - print out
   - video
6. Debriefing room

GENERAL LAYOUT

The simulator instructor must be free of all duties and distractions associated with operating the simulator to monitor the trainees precisely. For this reason it is desirable to have a control station operator working with the instructor. Thus, the instructor can devote his or her full attention to

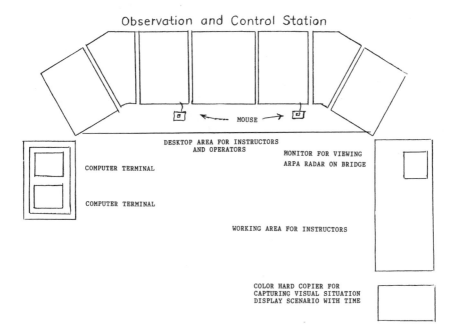

Fig. 8-6. Bird's-eye view of observation/control station.

observing the bridge team and making decisions on what vessel move-ments or casualties could take place. The control station must have suffi-cient room for these two individuals. The controls should be located so one person could act as instructor and operator if the situation required. A horseshoe arrangement satisfies both of these requirements with comfort and efficiency. (see Fig. 8-6.)

Some of the equipment, such as VHF, sound-powered telephone printout control should be duplicated to facilitate its use by either the instructor or operator. The operator should be able to assist the instructor by handling some of the internal communications aboard the vessel while the instructor uses the VHF for communications from another vessel.

Immediately in front of the operator and instructor station there should be a flat working surface. Reference material can be laid out for ready access. This working surface also gives the instructor desk space for taking notes during the exercise.

A large working area or chart table must be in the immediate vicinity of the control station. The instructor can then lay out the appropriate chart of the exercise area for reference and plotting bearings and distances. Plotting instruments must also be readily available.

GALLERY

Behind the instructors station there should be a gallery consisting of one or two rows of seats. These seats should be located so students or observers can see the visual scene clearly, the bird's-eye view, the radar repeaters, and the activity of the individuals on the bridge. The instructor needs only to turn in his or her seat to be able to talk to and explain the exercise to the students or point out what the bridge team is doing. Simulators without a gallery are limiting the use of the simulator exercise to only the students on the bridge who are actively participating in the exercise.

MONITORING

It is essential that the instructor be able to monitor easily the same visual scene as the students, all the activities on the bridge, the navigation that is being accomplished, and all the controls and instruments on the bridge.

The visual scene must be located in front of the control station so the instructor can monitor the scene without leaving his or her station. The horseshoe arrangement makes this possible especially on those simulators that have a wide field of view.

Bridge team activity can be monitored visually by the use of a one-way window or television camera arrangement. The use of a one-way window arrangement has the disadvantage of only giving one view of the bridge which may be blocked by students on the bridge. Also, monitoring is difficult during night-time scenarios. By using one or more low-light television cameras on the bridge the instructor can carefully select the area of the bridge that he or she wishes to observe. CAORF has four cameras giving simultaneous views of the forward and after sections of the bridge, the gyro repeater on the starboard bridge wing and a camera that can zoom in on the chart table or the port bridge wing repeater. All of these scenes are displayed on monitors directly in front of the instructor. In addition any one of these views can also be displayed on a large monitor which can easily be seen from the gallery. (see Fig. 8-7.)

Audio monitoring can be accomplished by placing microphones on the bridge (bugging) or by the use of cordless lapel microphones used in conjunction with an appropriate amplification system. Bugging may permit dead spots and conversations that take place away from the microphones cannot be monitored by the instructor. Lapel microphones eliminate that problem. The instructor also must have control of the volume of the monitoring system.

It is desirable that the navigation of the bridge team be monitored closely as it is being done. On many simulators the instructor becomes aware of the methods used by the navigator only at the debrief when the chart is laid out. Having a microphone and a low-light television camera

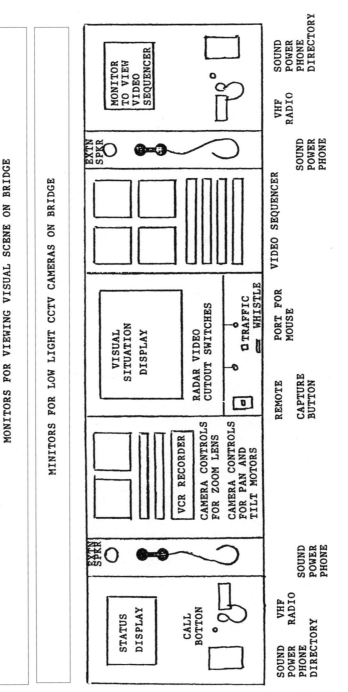

Fig. 8-7. Monitoring and communications capabilities.

located directly above the bridge chart table with the capability of panning and zooming allows the instructor to monitor the navigation as it is being done. The location of the monitor and camera controls should be located directly in front of the instructor at the control station.

A visual situation display or bird's-eye view of the exercise is necessary. It should show own ship, all other ships in the vicinity, coast lines, aids to navigation, dangers and any other reference points, such as traffic schemes that the instructor feels is necessary. The ability to change the scale of this view also is desirable. The instructor can then switch between full view of the exercise operating area and the immediate area around the vessel for close-quarters situations. The monitor for this view must be located so that it can be observed clearly by the instructor, operator, and gallery. This situation display must have a mouse-driven cursor, so the instructor can measure bearings and ranges from own ship to other ships or objects. A mouse should be located for the instructor and another for the operator.

Monitoring the status of the ship's instruments, systems, and the environment is extremely important. The most important instruments for the instructor to monitor are the ARPA and radar. This should be done by having a repeater of the units on the bridge at the operator-instructor station. It should be placed so both the instructor and gallery have a clear view of the screen. The instructor can then observe what mode the unit is being used in, what targets are being tracked, the scale being used, whether the unit is being used properly, or if the data being supplied to the student by the unit is being interpreted correctly.

A ship's system and environment status display is necessary. This monitor should display the simulator time, range, and bearing of the cursor on the visual situation display from own ship, wind, current, depth of water, heading, course being made good over ground, speed over ground, engine rpm, rudder position, bow thruster percent, and any system failures. This information should be well organized and easily read by the instructor.

COMMUNICATIONS

Communications between the instructor-operator station and the bridge must include all the normal communications systems internal and external to the ship. This would include sound power telephones, UHF, and VHF radios. These systems should be duplicated so that both the instructor and operator have easy access to them. It is important that these communications systems be able to indicate to the instructor the location aboard the ship the student is calling and the radio frequency on which the student is transmitting.

PLAYBACK CAPABILITY

Playback capabilities are an important component of the instruction scheme if a thorough debrief is to take place. The primary tools used by the instructor during the debrief is a printout of the situation display or bird's-eye view and the printout of the status display. Being able to print out the situation display at different stages of the exercise on different scales is an advantage. If the instructor is able to select one of several scales for this printout one of the selections should be the same scale as the chart the students are using. This printout can be used as an overlay on the chart during the debrief. The status display should be printed out at regular intervals during the exercise.

Videotaping the television displays can be useful. It can be used to play back to students during the debrief or to document good and bad procedures to be used during future briefings or lectures.

DEBRIEFING

Debriefing is a vital component in simulator training and should take place immediately after the conclusion of the exercise. For this reason the debriefing room (see Fig. 8-8) should be immediately adjacent to the

Fig. 8-8. Captain Robert J. Meurn Debrief Room.

bridge simulator and operator-control station. It must be furnished with a large table sufficient to all the participants, layout charts, bird's-eye views, passage plans, and student's notes. Other items that should be present are a whiteboard, projector with screen, VCR, small-ship models for demonstrating maneuvers, and plotting equipment.

TRAINING ON THE SIMULATOR

For bridge teams on the simulator the bridge team charter should be integral in their training and during debriefs. It incorporates the following concepts:

- All members of the group are equal.
- The project must be defined clearly and everyone must understand its purpose.
- Each member in turn is entitled to express one idea at a time.
- A hasty conclusion may conceal a better solution.
- No other member should criticize an idea put forward by a member.
- Respect for ideas expressed by listening to them.
- Use of common methods and tools allows the team to advance in the same direction.
- No energy should be wasted by focusing on the symptom.
- The success of the team is proportional to the participation of its members.

The student's attitude during simulator training is of paramount importance. If you had to quantify attitude in a formula to reveal its importance in bridge watchstanding it would be:

$$C = (K + S) \times A$$
Competency = (Knowledge + Skills) x Attitude

If Attitude is 0, then Competency is 0, even if you have all the knowledge and skills that are required.

BRIDGE OF THE FUTURE

In speculating about the bridge of the future one could ask any number of relevant questions: Will the bridge of the future be a control center designed for efficiency only? Will bridges be designed for one ship operating on one particular run? Will these bridges be designed to take into consideration the current U.S. concept of manning under various watch conditions? (See table 8-2 for these manning requirements.)

Obviously, it would be difficult to foretell what the bridge of the future will be. What is clear is that shipowners and equipment manufacturers are making a concerted effort to adopt a design that would require only one man on a cockpit-type bridge. This design, unfortunately, disregards the need for a lookout, which is required under present statutes. It also is doubtful whether a watch officer could satisfactorily fulfill his responsi-

TABLE 8-2
Levels of Normal Manning

	Open Sea		Pilotage Waters		Docking	
	Maximum	Minimum	Maximum	Minimum	Maximum	Minimum
Clear Visibility	Mate-on-watch Helmsman	Mate-on-watch Helmsman standing-by*	Pilot Captain Mate-on-watch Chief mate Helmsman	Pilot Mate-on-watch Helmsman	Docking master Pilot Captain Mate-on-watch Mate Helmsman	Docking master Captain Mate-on-watch Helmsman
Poor Visibility	Captain Mate-on-watch Chief mate Mate Helmsman	Mate-on-watch Helmsman standing-by*	Pilot Captain Mate-on-watch Chief mate Mate Helmsman	Pilot Captain Mate-on-watch Helmsman	Docking master Pilot Captain Mate-on-watch Mate Helmsman	Docking master Captain Mate-on-watch Mate Helmsman

*Helmsman standing-by is defined as a qualified helmsman not physically located at the steering controls, but within verbal communications with the mate-on-watch.

Courtesy *Marine Engineering Log* (May/June 1985)

Table 8-2. Levels of normal manning.

bilities especially at night under restricted visibility or in congested waters without the benefit of another person as lookout.

Although a case can be made by the proponents of this type of bridge that the sophisticated equipment aboard makes the need for a separate lookout less obligatory, opponents of the scheme contend that the more automation on the bridge, the more time the watch officer spends monitoring the equipment, and the less time he has available for lookout duties.

While only time will resolve this dispute, even those involved should be aware that safety must be the most important goal. Shipowners cannot overlook this fact in their attempt to decrease costs by automating the bridge and reducing crew size. Even now, it is evident that technological advances and reduced manning only increase the responsibility of the watch officer. Apparent too is the need to train these watch officers to the highest possible standard. The most effective and cost-efficient way to accomplish this training is using a simulator that is as close as possible to the design of the bridge on which each officer will be serving. An added benefit of undertaking this simulator training will be the contribution it makes to research to determine the optimal bridge design and the ideal manning requirements in various operating conditions.

CHAPTER NINE

Case Studies

I N more than 90 percent of the groundings and 75 percent of collisions and fires/explosions human error is present.[1] Accidents attributable to human error derive from two major sources: failure to navigate safely and failure to use available equipment correctly.

In spite of advances in technology marine accidents continue to happen. Mariners must be made aware of how accidents happen and must be proficient in safe shipboard practices so that they will intuitively and instinctively act correctly in the event of an emergency. Accident investigations should indicate a chain of errors and identify the area of training deficiency. Examining the accidents described in this chapter with this in mind should prove helpful to any prospective watchstander. Even though two of the cases are more than twenty-five-years old the lessons to be learned are still relevant to break a future error chain.

CASE ONE:
ANDREA DORIA/STOCKHOLM COLLISION

ANDREA DORIA VERSION

This account of the *Andrea Doria/Stockholm* collision disaster starts some twelve hours before the fatal tragedy when, at 11:30 on the morning of July 25, 1956, Captain Gunnar Nordenson, commanding officer of the Motorship *Stockholm*, moved his ship away from her Swedish-American berth in New York and headed for the open sea and Europe.

At the same time, from a pier half mile down stream, Baron Raoul De Beaudean was executing the identical maneuver with his luxury liner *Ile de France*. Little did Captain De Beaudean realize the vital part his ship would play in the tragedy that would play out some twelve hours later on the Atlantic Ocean.

---

[1] D. T. Bryant, A. F. M. Bievre, and M. B. A. Dyer-Smith, *Investigating Human Factors in Marine Casualties*. Paper presented at the Navigation and the Human Factor Seminar, United Kingdom, December 10, 1987.

The *Stockholm* fell in behind the *Ile de France* as the ships worked their way to Ambrose Light at the main entrance to New York Harbor. Here they dropped their pilots shortly after 1:00 p.m. and set course toward Nantucket Lightship some 200 miles to the east.

The *Ile de France* at a speed of 22.5 knots was four knots faster than the *Stockholm.* By 3:00 p.m. she had pulled far ahead of the *Stockholm* and was rapidly disappearing from view.

At about the same time, the senior officer of the watch on the Italian luxury liner *Andrea Doria,* inbound to New York from Genoa, Italy, notified his commanding officer, Captain Piero Calamai, that fog was closing in rapidly around the ship. The captain went to the bridge and immediately ordered the ship's engines placed under standby conditions, thus reducing her speed from 23 to 21.85 knots. The automatic timer had already been set to sound the fog whistle every two minutes.

The *Andrea Doria's* Sperry Gyrocompass Course Recorder Graph indicated that the ship had passed Nantucket Lightship at 10:10 p.m. when the course was changed to a compass heading of 269°, the normal compass heading for the 200-mile run to Ambrose Lightship. Because of the dense fog the officers did not see the lightship visually as they passed one mile to the south. However, they did have the lightship positioned on the radar screen and heard the distinctive coded foghorn signals.

Because traffic to and from Europe used Nantucket Lightship as their first or last contact with New York, the route between these two lightships was known in maritime circles as "Times Square." Therefore, after passing Nantucket Lightship, Captain Calamai and Second Officer Franchini, the senior officer of the deck, began to carefully monitor the radar screen. Third Officer Giannini, the junior watch officer, remained on the starboard bridge wing.

At 10:45 p.m., twenty-six minutes before the collision, a single target appeared on the *Andrea Doria's* radar screen. Later this target proved to be the *Stockholm.* The target was at a distance of seventeen miles bearing four degrees over the *Andrea Doria's* right, or starboard bow. As the target approached the angle of bearing continued to increase. Although the radar target was not being plotted, the continual increase of the bearing angle indicated the ships were on almost parallel courses headed in opposite directions. The fact that all traffic in the area would normally be east and west further convinced Captain Calamai that the ships were on nearly reciprocal courses. At this time he decided it would be a starboard-to-starboard (right side to right side) meeting situation with a CPA of about three-fourths of a mile.

At 11:05 p.m., or six minutes before the collision, the radar showed the *Stockholm* to be at a distance of four miles bearing 14° over the *Andrea Doria's* right starboard bow. At this moment the course recorder graph showed the *Andrea Doria* executed a slight change in course of 4° to her port, or left. This Captain Calamai later said he did so to place more water between the ships as they met each other right side to right side (starboard to starboard). Three minutes before the collision when the radar target indicated that the *Stockholm* was just two miles away and had neither been sighted visually nor heard, Captain Calamai left his second officer at the radar and joined the third officer on the right (starboard) wing of the open bridge. The third officer searching for the radar target with binoculars said to the captain, "Why don't we hear him? Why doesn't she whistle?"

Just then they both saw the glow of lights. The glow was at a distance of about one mile bearing between twenty and twenty-five degrees over the *Andrea Doria's* starboard bow. (This took place no more than one hundred seconds before the collision). Still under the impression that the ships were on reciprocal courses, Captain Calamai felt there was ample room for the safe starboard-to-starboard meeting that he had planned and he maintained course and speed.

Less than a minute later, or just seconds before the collision, when the *Stockholm's* lights became distinguishable, Captain Calamai found to his dismay that the *Stockholm* was turning sharply to her right—toward and into the *Andrea Doria.*

Captain Calamai recognized instantly that conditions were in extremis. Without hesitation he ordered a hard-left turn and maintained the speed on his engines to cross the *Stockholm's* bow more quickly at a perpendicular angle in a final desperate effort to avoid a collision.

At practically full speed, the *Stockholm* plunged headlong halfway through the *Andrea Doria,* just as she was beginning to respond to her helm in the evasive hard-left turn that had just been ordered. The *Stockholm* entered the *Andrea Doria* at a point directly under the starboard bridge wing while Captain Calamai and his third officer looked on in horror (see Fig. 9-1 and Fig. 9-2). The *Andrea Doria* had been mortally wounded.

The *Andrea Doria* lies in 240 feet of water. During dives in 2006, David Bright determined that its keel had been breached by the *Stockholm's* ice-reinforced bow, making its sinking inevitable.

STOCKHOLM VERSION

The *Stockholm's* contention of how the accident happened was the antithesis of the *Andrea Doria's* account. Third officer, Carstens-Johannsen, who was in charge of the *Stockholm's* bridge at the time of the collision gave the following account of what happened while under oath at the official inquiry.

At about 11:00 p.m., he obtained a radio direction bearing fix (RDF) entering the time as such in the ship's log book. As a result of this RDF fix, he found the *Stockholm* had drifted to the left, or north of her projected course. Therefore, he ordered a slight change in course to the right to correct, or compensate for this drift to left. The *Stockholm's* course

Fig. 9-1. MV *Stockholm* ramming into the SS *Andrea Doria* on July 25, 1956. (Courtesy of J. C. Carrothers and U. S. Naval Institute.)

recorder graph indicates a three-degree change in course to the right, from a compass heading of 92° to 95°, was executed at 11:05 p.m. The third officer said that just as he ordered this compensating change in course following his 11:00 p.m. RDF fix, he picked up the *Andrea Doria* at a distance of twelve miles by radar. He also said the radar target was bearing slightly over the *Stockholm's* port, or left bow.

Carstens-Johannsen stated the night was clear with good visibility and the engines were running under "all clear full speed ahead" orders.

The third officer further stated that after the radar showed the distance between the ships had been reduced from twelve to ten miles he began a series of radar plots at regular intervals. Every radar plot confirmed the fact that it would be a port-to-port (left-side-to-left) meeting situation. Then, three minutes before the collision, the *Andrea Doria* eventually exposed herself from out of a fogbank right at the point where his radar plotting told him she would appear. He then said that the *Andrea Doria* was showing a weak red port, or left-side light with masthead and range lights open. At this instant the radar told him the *Andrea Doria* was at a distance of 1.8 or 1.9 miles bearing between 15° and 25° over the *Stockholm's* port bow. Although there was ample room for a left-side-to-left-side meeting, he ordered a 22½° (2 point) right turn away from the *Andrea Doria* as a further precautionary measure.

While the *Stockholm* was executing this 22½° right turn, which the course recorder graph shows consumed two minutes, the telephone rang. After the *Stockholm* had steadied on her new heading, which the course

Fig. 9-2a. MV *Stockholm*. (Courtesy of Mariner's Museum, Newport News, VA.)

Fig. 9-2b. SS *Andrea Doria*. (Courtesy of Mariner's Museum, Newport News, VA.)

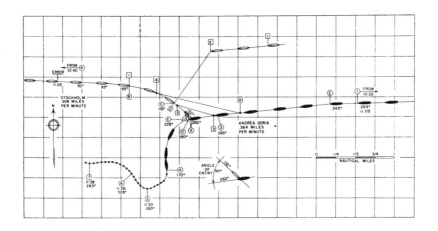

STOCKHOLM's Testimony

ANDREA DORIA's Testimony

1 to 1   Third Officer sights the ANDREA DORIA at a distance of 1.8 miles, being 20 degrees over the STOCKHOLM's port bow, and orders 22½-degree right turn.

2 to 2   The STOCKHOLM completes right turn and Third Officer checks the DORIA's lights. He then turns to answer telephone.

3 to 3   Seconds later, Third Officer finishes telephone conversation and again checks the DORIA's lights. He now finds the DORIA is in a collision situation and is attempting to race across the STOCKHOLM's bow. He orders hard right turn and full speed astern on both engines.

X   The collision occurs with the ANDREA DORIA after the STOCKHOLM has turned 13 degrees.

A to A   Captain Calamai and his Third Officer sight glow of the STOCKHOLM's lights. Believing the ships to be on parallel courses, the DORIA's captain maintains speed and course

3 to 3   Seeing that the STOCKHOLM is turning sharply to her right—towards and into the ANDREA DORIA—Captain Calamai orders hard left and maintains speed on engines

X   The collision with the STOCKHOLM occurs just as the ANDREA DORIA begins to answer the helm.

Fig. 9-2. Approaches of the MV *Stockholm* and the SS *Andrea Doria*. (Courtesy of J.C. Carrothers and U.S. Naval Institute.)

recorder graph shows occurred one minute before the collision, the third officer again checked the *Andrea Doria's* lights and satisfied himself that she would now pass well astern of the *Stockholm*. He then turned away to answer the telephone.

Seconds later, at the end of the telephone conversation with the lookout in the crow's nest who reported "lights to port," he again checked the lights of the *Andrea Doria*. To his horror, he found the ships had totally changed relative positions. The *Andrea Doria* was now showing her green, or right starboard, side light as she was attempting to race across the *Stockholm's* bow. Realizing instantly that conditions were in extremis, he ordered a hard-right turn and rang up an all-out emergency, full-speed astern on the engine order telegraphs. It was apparent that the *Stockholm* had slowed down little, if any, before plunging headlong into the *Andrea Doria's* starboard side. The *Stockholm* was not on standby engines and the motorman on watch was not immediately available to respond to the full speed astern order.

The third officer contended that he did not see the *Andrea Doria* cut across the *Stockholm's* bow because he had taken his eyes off her to answer the telephone. However, the lookout in the crow's nest alleged that after his telephone conversation with the third officer he watched the *Andrea Doria* close out her red port side light and show her green starboard side light as she turned to her left in an attempt to race across the *Stockholm's* bow (see Fig. 9-3). For this to occur would have necessitated the *Andrea*

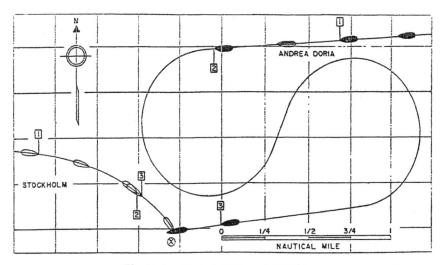

The Andrea Doria's 2,500 mph "S" Turn

1 to 1 — Three minutes before collision, Doria appears out of fog at distance of 1.85 miles bearing 20 degrees over Stockholm's port bow. Turn of 22.5 degrees ordered by 3rd Officer.

2 to 2 — One minute before collision, Stockholm completes right turn. Third Officer checks Doria's lights, turns to answer telephone.

3 to 3 — Seconds later 3rd Officer finds Doria in a collision course, attempting to race across his bow. Hard right turn and full speed astern ordered. Collision seconds later.

Information based on "Collision Course" report.

Fig. 9-3. The *Andrea Doria's* 2,500 mph "S" turn.

Doria to execute an "S" turn and increase her speed to 2,500 mph.
To refute the 2,500 mph "S" turn and to corroborate Carstens-Johannsen visual sighting of the *Andrea Doria's* red port side light over the *Stockholm's* port bow, the *Stockholm* owners contended that the approach of both vessels was as depicted in Figure 9-4.

Both ships started their turns three minutes before the collision, which occurred at the end of the turns when the ships were on the headings indicated. The *Andrea Doria* executed a long-three minute turn of

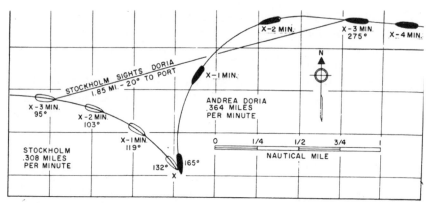

Fig. 9-4 The long three-minute turn

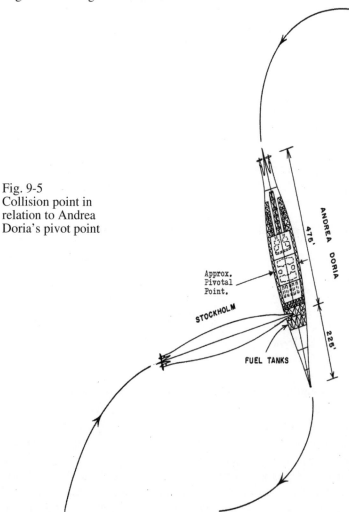

Fig. 9-5
Collision point in
relation to Andrea
Doria's pivot point

110° to port going from a compass heading of 275° to a heading of 165°. The accident happened at the end of this long port turn.

Figure 9-4 is an illustration of this contention. The *Andrea Doria*'s reduced speed of 21.85 knots is indicated in the one-minute (X-4 Min) period prior to X-3 Min. She would have been required to double her speed to reach this collision position. Furthermore, in no way can the condition of the *Stockholm*'s bow after the collision be reconciled to the roll-type collision illustrated here.

Finally, the Swedish American Line claims that the *Stockholm* by plunging into the starboard side of the *Andrea Doria* "broke the left turn and pivoted the ship to the right." However, Figure 9-5 clearly shows that the *Stockholm* plunged into the *Andrea Doria* at a point far forward of the pivotal point. Therefore, she would have been thrust further on her left turn and certainly not pivoted to the right.

CRUX OF THE *STOCKHOLM'S* DEFENSE

A monumental factor in the *Stockholm's* overall defense hinged on the answer to the vital question of what time did the third officer alter the ship's course to compensate for drift he found as the result of his 11:00 p.m. RDF fix? Under oath, Third Officer Carstens-Johannsen testified that he picked up the *Andrea Doria* by radar at a distance of twelve miles, just as he ordered a slight change in course following his 11:00 p.m. RDF fix. The *Stockholm's* course recorder graph shows a three-degree change in course from 92° to 95° was ordered at 11:05 p.m., plus or minus seconds.

In cross examination the attorneys were quick to point out to the third officer that his testimony was "impossible and untrue." In effect they proved to him that at 11:05 p.m., when he ordered the slight change in course to compensate for drift he found as the result of his 11:00 p.m. RDF fix, the *Andrea Doria* was only four, and not twelve, miles away from the *Stockholm*.

Faced with this irrefutable fact the third officer simply explained that the 11:00 p.m. entry he made in the *Stockholm's* log book at the time of the accident should have been "about 11:00 p.m." Furthermore, he continued that he did not change course at 11:05 p.m. This indication on his course recorder graph was only a "yaw'" in the ship's steering. He also claimed that the Sperry expert, who had identified the change in course at 11:05 p.m., was wrong. The attorneys apparently accepted this explanation because, as far as could be determined, the issue was not mentioned again.

The third officer's denial of the 11:05 p.m. change in course placed him in an untenable position. Now it was necessary to revert to the last previous slight change in course at 10:40 p.m. (obviously made as the result of drift found in his 10:30 p.m. RDF fix) as the time he picked up the *Andrea Doria* by radar at a distance of twelve miles. After informing his readers of this in his book, *Collision Course,* Mr. Moscow continued that by calculations the "about 11:00 p.m." RDF fix was actually taken at 10:48 p.m. It was as a result of drift found at 10:48, writes Mr. Moscow, that the third officer altered course at 10:40 p.m. Neither of these contentions are acceptable. At 10:40 p.m. the ships were 20.66 miles and not twelve miles apart. How could the third officer alter course at 10:40 p.m. to compensate for drift he did not know existed until eight minutes later at 10:48 p.m.? These alleged facts were presented by the third officer's testimony, which allegedly "correlated closely" with the *Stockholm's* course recorder graph. They cover the last hour before the collision and are presented in chronological order so that the sequence of events may be better understood.

1. At 10:10 p.m. the third officer altered course from a compass heading of 87 to 89 degrees to compensate for drift found twenty minutes later as the result of his 10:30 p.m. RDF fix.
2. The third officer picked up the *Andre Doria* by radar at a distance twelve miles just as he ordered a slight change in course from a compass heading of 89 to 91 degrees at 10:40 p.m. to correct for drift found eight minutes later as the result of his 10:48 p.m. RDF fix which he thought was "about 11:00 p.m." (At 10:40 the ships were 20.66 miles apart.)
3. The third officer waited for three minutes, until the distance between the ships had been reduced to ten miles, before starting to plot the oncoming *Andrea Doria* by radar. Note: To correlate the *Andrea Doria's* actions with the foregoing, while recognizing that the *Stockholm* was running at a speed of 18.5 knots, it would have been necessary for the *Andrea Doria* to have increased her speed to 194.72 knots to reduce the distance between the ships from 20.66 to 10 miles in three minutes. The *Andrea Doria* would then have resumed her normal speed of 21.85 knots when the third officer allegedly started his plotting procedure.
4. The third officer then plotted the oncoming *Andrea Doria* at the regular and prescribed intervals until, three minutes before the collision, the *Andrea Doria* finally exposed herself from out of the fog right at the spot where his radar plotting told him she would appear.

ANALYSIS OF THE CAUSE OF THE COLLISION

On July 25, 1956, at 11:11 p.m., the eastbound *Stockholm* plunged halfway through the westbound *Andrea Doria* at a position 180 miles east of Ambrose Lightship. Fifty-one people perished on impact, the

Andrea Doria sank some 10 hours later, and the *Stockholm* limped back to New York less 75 feet of bow. Thirty years of controversy followed concerning whether it was a right-to-right, head-on, or left-to-left approach and if it was foggy or not. Books, such as *Collision Course* and *Saved* by nonmariner authors did little to reveal the truth. The *Andrea Doria* sunk and the *Stockholm,* with a new bow, went on to sail under East German flag and today ironically sails under Italian flag.

John C. Carrothers, a retired chief engineer from Deep River, Connecticut, first discovered the cause of the collision, which was reported in the July 1958 and August 1971 issue of the *U.S. Naval Institute Proceedings*. It now seems clear that John Carrothers is correct in saying that the cause of the accident was human error by the *Stockholm's* third officer.

Fig. 9-6 and Table 9-1 illustrate how the third officer probably misused his radar. The third officer may have assumed that his radar was on the fifteen-mile range scale when in reality the range scale was five miles. In those days, ranges were determined by counting range rings, which assumed a different range for each scale. The scale was not illuminated and there was no variable range indicator. At 11:05 p.m. when the third officer first detected the *Andrea Doria* on radar, it was at four miles (on the fourth range ring) and not twelve miles away. Through misinterpretation of the radar by thinking he was on the fifteen-mile scale he believed the *Andrea Doria* (displayed on the fourth range ring) was twelve miles away. In addition, the third officer testified he thought the contact was a navy ship coming at great speed indicating a wrong range scale. Six miles (twelve-mile range ring to six-mile range ring) in three minutes indicates great speed where as two miles (four-mile range ring to two-mile range ring) in three minutes reveals the correct closing rate of forty knots. In this case, the most likely cause was the failure to use available equipment correctly. Proper instruction in and practical use of radar as required. Consequently, attending a radar observer's course and endorsement of such completion is compulsory for those seeking a merchant marine officer's license.

The major factors in the cause of this collision have been addressed through the following:
- Inbound and outbound ships are required to use prescribed sea-lanes. This is regardless of whether they are within a major port approach area or in constricted waterways, such as the English Channel and the Singapore Straits.
- On most passenger and cruise ships, two officers must be on watch, instead of just one.
- Merchant Marine officers must be certified in the use of radar and obtain radar endorsement updates every five years.

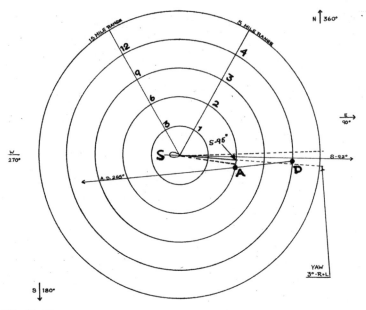

Fig 9.6 The Fatal Error.

Facsimile of Stockholm's radar screen. Five mile range each circle carries a value of one mile. On the 15 mile range each circle is valued at three miles. Broken lines illustrate how the graph showed the Stockholm was yawing 3° to port and starboard of her compass heading of 92°.

"S" to "D": Six minutes before collision. Stockholm allegedly picked up Andrea Doria at a distance of 12 miles bearing slightly over the Stockholm's port, or left, bow. Actually the Andrea Doria was only four miles away bearing slightly over the Stockholm's starboard, or right, bow. The only explanation for this is the error in radar range while the constant yawing caused the target to move back and forth from the port to starboard sides of the heading flasher of 92°. Note: With respect to distance it can be seen that the target appears in the identical spot on the screen in both the five and 15 mile ranges.

"S" to "A": Three minutes before the collision. Stockholm is now on a heading of 95°. Third officer assumes the Andrea Doria is six miles away while in reality she was only two miles distant. At this point, he ordered the 22-½° right turn which ended in disaster less than three minutes later.

RDF ↑ FIX	STOCKHOLM VERSION		CSE 087°	BY COURSE RECORDER WHAT REALLY DID HAPPEN	
	TIME	COURSE CHANGE	TIME		COURSE CHANGE
#1	2200-2206	NONE	TAKING FIX (2200-2206)	2207	C/C 089°
#2	2230-2237	C/C 089°	TAKING FIX (2230-2237)	2237	C/C 091°
#3	2248-2251	C/C 091°	TAKING FIX (2300-2306)	2306	C/C 094°

TUNING IN RADIO FREQUENCIES TO OBTAIN THEIR BEARING AND THEN PLOT ON A CHART. WHERE THEY CROSS IS A RDF FIX

THE THIRD RDF FIX TO COININCIDE WITH OBSERVING PIP OF ANDREA DORIA JUST AFTER FIX AND 12 MILES AWAY

ANDREA DORIA 4 MILES AWAY AT THIS TIME

DESCRIBED BY ALVIN MOSCOW AS A 90 SEC. YAW BEFORE CARSTENS ORDERED RIGHT 20° RUDDER AT 2309. REALLY WAS A 3° CHANGE OF COURSE TO KEEP ON COURSE AFTER THIRD RDF FIX 2300-2306

Table 9-1. Correlation of testimony of MV *Stockholm* to its course recorder graph.

- Every vessel must be equipped with VHF radio sets for bridge-to-bridge (ship-to-ship) radio-telephone communications. This facilitates the exchange of maneuvering intentions between ships.
- Range scales on radar are illuminated so that the watch officers using them can easily distinguish which scale is in use. This is to prevent misreading of distance between ships.
- Global positioning systems have replaced the time consuming radio-direction finder (RDF) and LORAN as navigational aids.
- With the Automatic Identification System (AIS), vessels are identified by their name, course, and speed. This is also true on ECDIS. Thus, there is no reason not to know which vessel you are calling and where she is located.

CASE TWO: *LASH ATLANTICO/HELLENIC CARRIER* COLLISION

The collision of two freighters in dense fog on the Atlantic Ocean on May 6, 1981, occurred after the master of one vessel ordered an evasive turn that placed his ship on a collision course, according to the National Transportation Safety Board (NTSB).

The 820-foot Prudential Lines barge carrier *Lash Atlantico* and the 470-foot Greek freighter *Hellenic Carrier* collided about fifteen miles off Kitty Hawk, North Carolina, causing some $8 million in damages, a board announcement stated.

There were no injuries, but a fuel oil spill of nearly 150,000 gallons necessitated a cleanup along North Carolina beaches that cost more than $500,000.

The board said the probable cause of the accident was the failure of the master and second mate of the *Lash Atlantico* to plot and accurately determine the relative movement of the Hellenic Lines vessel before ordering a course change to the right.

The following is the sequence of events that occurred on the *Hellenic Carrier* and the *Lash Atlantico* respectively, in the minutes prior to the collision:

Hellenic Carrier

0640 The northbound *Hellenic's* watch officer established radar contact with the *Atlantico* 10° off his starboard bow at a range of twelve miles.

0645 He calculated the closest point of approach (CPA) to the *Atlantico* to be approximately two miles off his starboard beam. To open

Fig. 9-7. The 5,881-ton *Hellenic Carrier* is sailing toward Norfolk, still in fog, with a large hole in her side after a collision with the 26,406-ton *Lash Atlantico* while about twenty-five miles southeast of Cape Henry. (U. S. Coast Guard photo, courtesy of Mariners Weather Log, May-June 1981.)

<table>
<tr><td></td><td>this distance, he brought the Hellenic left to a new course of 330°(T). Actually the CPA was 1.1 miles off his starboard beam.</td></tr>
</table>

0658	The *Hellenic's* lookout on the starboard bridge wing heard two whistles off the *Hellenic's* starboard beam.
0659	The *Hellenic's* watch officer sighted the *Atlantico* on his starboard beam for the first time. He ordered a left full rudder in a futile attempt to avoid the collision.
0700	Collision occurred (see Fig. 9-7). The *Hellenic* was proceeding at fourteen knots. The *Hellenic* neither sounded her fog signals nor attempted to contact the *Atlantico* on her bridge-to-bridge radio.

Lash Atlantico

0650	The southbound *Atlantico's* watch officer established radar contact with the *Hellenic*. He held the *Hellenic* 8° to 10° off what he believed was his port bow at a range of five miles. The District Court found, because of the faulty radar, that the *Hellenic* was actually 5° to 7° off the *Atlantico's* starboard bow.
0653	The *Atlantico* alters course to starboard 4° to a new course of 165° (T) to increase the passing distance for what was believed would be a port-to-port passage.
0654	Between 0654 and 0659, the *Atlantico* came farther right with numerous 4° and 5° course changes. During this time, the

Atlantico began sounding fog signals in accordance with the 72 COLREGS.

0659   The *Atlantico* sighted the *Hellenic* for the first time. About thirty seconds later, the captain ordered the engines stopped and a hard-right rudder.

0700   Collision occurred. The *Atlantico* was proceeding at slightly under eighteen knots. The *Atlantico* never attempted to contact the *Hellenic* on her bridge-to-bridge radio.

"Proper plotting would have shown that the course change—intended as an evasive action—was the incorrect maneuver and placed his vessel in the path of the northbound freighter," the announcement stated.

The safety board said that the excessive speed of both ships while approaching in fog that had limited visibility to about 1,000 feet had contributed to the accident.

Another contributing factor, the board found, was the failure of the chief officer on the *Hellenic Carrier* to closely observe the *Lash Atlantico* on radar for a five-minute period before the collision and to plot and determine the relative movement of that ship.

The board's investigation led it to conclude that if the *Lash Atlantico* had maintained its original course the ships would have passed starboard to starboard about one nautical mile apart without incident. The report noted that neither ship's personnel had plotted the position and times of radar contacts at frequent intervals so as to determine relative movement and the closest point of approach of the opposing vessel.

"It was not prudent for either ship to proceed at full speed under the reduced visibility which existed that morning," the report stated. It noted that the ships were closing at thirty-two knots, or more than 0.5 nautical miles per minute. The *Lash Atlantico's* stopping distance was about 5,000 feet, while the Greek vessel would take about 2.5 nautical miles and some twelve minutes to stop.

The board also said that under the limited visibility conditions, the watch officer of the *Hellenic Carrier* should have been sounding fog signals. In addition, the board noted that, although not required by law or international agreement, it would have been prudent for the two vessels to try to establish contact via their radio-telephones for the purpose of establishing a passing agreement.

Again the cause of the accident was failure to use available equipment correctly in that neither the radar nor VHF were used properly. As a result an alteration of course to starboard was made by the *Lash Atlantico* based upon scanty information. Again a similar approach and collision as in our previous case.

CASE THREE: GROUNDING OF THE *ROYAL MAJESTY*

About 2225 on June 10, 1995, the Panamanian passenger ship *Royal Majesty,* enroute Boston from Bermuda and carrying 1,509 passengers and crew members, grounded on Rose and Crown Shoal about ten miles east of Nantucket Island, Massachusetts.

The National Transportation Safety Board determined that the probable cause of the grounding of the *Royal Majesty* was the watch officers' overreliance on the automated features of the integrated bridge system. Majesty Cruise Lines failed to ensure that its officers were adequately trained in the automated features of the integrated bridge system and in the implications of this automation for bridge resource management. The procedures for its operation, and the second officer's failure to take corrective action after several cues indicated the vessel was off course, were contributing factors.

Additional contributing factors were the inadequacy of international training standards for watchstanders aboard vessels equipped with electronic navigation systems and integrated bridge systems and the inadequacy of international standards for the design, installation, and testing of integrated bridge systems aboard vessels.

The National Transportation Safety Board Conclusions

1. The weather, the mechanical condition of the *Royal Majesty,* except for the global positioning system receiver, the officers' certifications, drugs, and fatigue were not factors in the accident.
2. Although Coast Guard personnel observed no indications that the officers had been under the influence of alcohol, alcohol could not be conclusively ruled out as a factor in the accident because of the delay in collecting the blood and urine specimens.
3. About fifty-two minutes after the *Royal Majesty* left St. George's, Bermuda, the global positioning system receiver antenna-cable connection had separated enough that the global positioning system switched to dead-reckoning mode, and the autopilot, not programmed to detect the mode change and invalid status bits, no longer corrected for the effects of wind, current, or sea.
4. Openly routing the global positioning system antenna cable in an area where someone occasionally walked increased the risk of damage to the cable and related connectors.
5. Had the fathometer alarm been set to three meters, as was the stated practice, or had the second officer chosen to display the fathometer data on the control console, the second officer would have been alerted that the *Royal Majesty* was in far shallower water than expected and was off course. He would have been

alerted perhaps as long as forty minutes before the grounding, and the situation could have been corrected.

6. The watch officers' monitoring of the status of the vessel's global positioning system was deficient throughout the voyage from St. George's.

7. Deliberate cross checking between the global positioning system and the LORAN-C to verify the *Royal Majesty's* position was not being performed and should have been on the voyage from St. George's.

8. Even though it is likely that the watch officers were not aware of the limitation inherent in using the position-fix alarm to monitor the accuracy of GPS position data, it was inappropriate for them to rely solely on the alarm to warn them of any problems with the GPS data.

9. The sighting of lights not normally observed in the traffic lanes, the second officer's inability to confirm the presence of the BB buoy, and the sighting of blue-and-white water should have taken precedence over the automation display on the central console and compelled the second officer to promptly use all available means to verify his position.

10. The chief officer and the second officer did not observe good watchkeeping practices or act with heightened awareness of the precautions that are needed when a vessel approaches the Boston traffic lanes and landfall.

11. The master's methods for monitoring the progress of the voyage did not account for the technical capabilities and limitations of the automated equipment.

12. The watch officers on the *Royal Majesty* may have believed that because the global positioning system had demonstrated sufficient reliability over three-and-a-half years, the traditional practice of using at least two independent sources of position information was not necessary.

13. All the watchstanding officers were overly reliant on the automated position display of the navigation and command system and were, for all intents and purposes, sailing the map display instead of using navigation aids or lookout information.

14. Because the industry standard protocol did not provide a documented or standardized means of communicating or recognizing that a dead-reckoning positioning mode was in use by a hybrid, dead-reckoning-capable position receiver, Raytheon, and STN Atlas adopted different design philosophies about the communication of position-receiver mode changes for the Raytheon global positioning system and the navigation and command system.

15. STN Atlas should have, to help ensure safety and compatibility with different National Marine Electronics Association (NMEA) position receivers, programmed the *Royal Majesty's* navigation and command system to recognize the valid/invalid status bits in the NMEA data.

16. Had the navigation and command system autopilot been conFigured to compare position data from multiple independent position receivers and had a corresponding alarm been installed that activated when discrepancies were detected, the grounding of the *Royal Majesty* may have been avoided.

17. Because watch officers must verify proper equipment operation frequently, alternative sources of critical equipment status should have been displayed directly on the console or on repeaters located where they could be seen from the central console.

18. The brief oral alarm of the Raytheon global positioning system receiver, the remoteness of the receiver's location, and the failure of the installer to connect the global positioning system external alarm resulted in the inadequacy of the oral warning sent to the crew when the global positioning system defaulted to the dead-reckoning mode.

19. Failure modes and effects analyses of the *Royal Majesty's* integrated bridge system would probably have disclosed the shortcomings of the system's components.

20. The on-the-job training program employed by Majesty Cruise Line to train the *Royal Majesty's* watch officers in the operation of the integrated bridge system did not adequately prepare these officers to identify and respond to system malfunctions.

21. The *Royal Majesty's* integrated bridge system did not adequately incorporate human factors engineering.

22. There is a need to have performance standards for integrated bridge systems, and to require that the systems be inspected and certified.

It is obvious that there was failure to use navigational equipment properly and the watchstanding tasks listed in chapter one were not performed. See Changing the Watch, pg. 6 and Navigation Tasks, pg. 8.

CASE FOUR: *ADMIRAL NAKHIMOV/P. VASEV* COLLISION

This case is extracted from the paper, "The Role of Technology in the Development of Maritime Safety," presented by A. Yakushenkov, Manager, Department of Navigation and Ship Automation, Central Ship Research Institute, Leningrad, USSR, to the Fifth International Conference on Maritime Education and Training (IMLA) in Sydney, Nova Scotia, on September 21, 1988.

On August 31, 1986, the passenger liner, *Admiral Nakhimov* departed the port of Novorossiysk in the Black Sea bound for the Soviet resort port of Sochi, 115 miles to the southeast. The 17,000-ton liner was built in Germany and launched in 1929. Onboard were a crew of 346, 4 members of crew families, and 884 tourists. The weather was fair and the port approaches were under control of a local vessel traffic station equipped with shore-based radar. At 2220 the vessel traffic station (VTS) transmitted to the *Nakhimov* that radio-telephone contact was established between the station and the approaching 41,000-ton bulk carrier *P. Vasev*. The *P. Vasev* was en route to Novorossiysk from the Bosphorus with a cargo of wheat. The VTS operator advised the *Vasev* to keep out of the way of *Nakhimov*.

At 2230 the *Nakhimov* passed the port entrance and joined the recommended route of 154.2°(T). According to local rules, this route was to be kept by vessels for several miles before altering the course toward Sochi. After the course alteration, the master of the *Nakhimov* consulted with the watch officer and then left the bridge. The master was in his cabin reading a book when the watch officer established VHF contact with the *Vasev*. The OOW informed the *Vasev* of the *Nakhimov's* course and received a confirmation that the *Vasev* would keep clear. At 2305 the *Nakhimov* left the zone controlled by VTS. At this moment the ships again exchanged VHF communications and the *Vasev* confirmed the previous agreement. About 2307 the OOW of the *Nakhimov* determined the approach to be dangerous and altered course by 5° twice to the port and advised the *Vasev* to stop engines. At 2309 the *Nakhimov* altered the course another 10° to the port. At 2311 the *Nakhimov's* OOW gave a "hard-a-port" order to the helmsman. The helmsman just started to execute the order when the collision occurred.

The *Vasev* had contact with VTS when the distance between the vessels was 7.2 miles. From that moment the master of the *Vasev* was completely absorbed in the ARPA screen. No measures were apparently taken to avoid the dangerous approach. The master ignored his OOW's advice to reduce the ship speed to allow the *Nakhimov* to pass clear ahead. At 2305 the *Vasev's* master finally changed speed to half ahead, then at 2307 to slow ahead and 30 seconds later to stop engines. In reality the speed of the *Vasev* did not change. The distance between the vessels was now 2200 yards (11 cables). At 2310 the master ordered half astern and then full astern. At 2311 a hard-a-starboard order was given to the helmsman. No ship's response, however, was detected. At 2312 the collision occurred. The angle of impact was 110°, with the speed of the *Vasev* being 5 knots. The rudder was at hard-a-starboard.

The *Vasev* impacted the starboard midships part of *Nakhimov*. The *Nakhimov's* diesel generator room and engine room were practically ripped open, the size of the hole being about 90 square meters. After disconnection of vessels, the *Nakhimov* started to list to starboard. In seven to eight minutes, having a list more than 60°, the *Nakhimov* sank in 47 meters of water and settled to the bottom on her starboard side. Four hundred passengers perished, many of them trapped in flooded cabins. After the catastrophe both masters were arrested and put on trial. Both were found guilty by the court, and each was sentenced to imprisonment for 15 years with a penalty of 40,000 rubles.

What seems quite surprising in this catastrophe was the behavior of the *Vasev's* master. His lack of action until it was too late can be explained by wrong interpretation of situations generated by the ARPA display. It is possible that he observed only true vectors of his own ship and assumed erroneously that *Nakhimov* would pass him clearly ahead. Meanwhile he did not take into account, or just did not know, certain ARPA limitations. Prior to the fatal accident, the master had several successful ship-to-ship passes with the aid of his ARPA. He was sure that the ARPA was a panacea against ship collisions and relied blindly on the ARPA-produced data.

Here is a classic case of ARPA-assisted collision similar to the radar-assisted collision in 1956 made by the third mate of the MV *Stockholm.* Once again, this tragedy resulted from human error due to the failure to use available equipment correctly.

CASE FIVE: THE COLLISION OF THE *ZIEMIA LODZKA* AND *VERTIGO*

The following summary is quoted from the Casualty Report issued on 24 April 2006 by the Division for Investigation of Maritime Accidents, Danish Maritime Authority:

On the 7 December 2005, shortly after midnight, the fully loaded 17,458 GT Monrovia-flagged bulk carrier *Ziemia Lodzka* was proceeding south in Route T in the Great Belt, and the fully loaded Jamaica-flagged 15,502 GT bulk carrier *Vertigo* was proceeding north in Route H. (see Fig. 9-8, a and b.)

The weather was calm and the visibility was 3–4 miles. Both vessels were proceeding at normal sea speed, *Ziemia Lodzka* at about 12 knots and *Vertigo* at about 13 knots. Both vessels reported to VTS Great Belt when respectively passing the northern and the southern VTS reporting lines. The vessels observed each other on the radar and saw each other visually at a distance of more than three miles. (see Fig. 9-9).

When the vessels approached the narrow area off Agersoe Flak *Ziemia Lodzka* was positioned at the centre line of Route T and *Vertigo* was slightly offset to the west of the centre line of Route H. The vessels were on crossing courses with *Vertigo* bearing approximately 20° on the starboard bow of *Ziemia Lodzka*.

Ziemia Lodzka's master was in command on the bridge, and it was his intention to continue southwest in Route H. When passing buoy #33 he therefore executed a change of course to starboard, when the distance to *Vertigo* was 0.5–0.8 miles. (see Figure 9-10 a and b)

Vertigo's master was also in command on the bridge. He became in doubt of the intention of *Ziemia Lodzka*, and when *Ziemia Lodzka* commenced a starboard turn after crossing *Vertigo's* bow, he then executed a full turn to port. (see Fig. 9-11.)

This was approximately 15 seconds after the start of the turn of *Ziemia Lodzka*. At 0036 hours the vessels collided in position 55° 12.29 N -011°05.46 E. The port bow of *Ziemia Lodzka* struck the starboard side of *Vertigo*. (see Fig. 9-12a and b.)

Vertigo suffered heavy structural damage in the starboard side and foundered at position 55°13' N -011°05' E in 11 meters depth of water. The superstructure of the vessel was above water level.

The crew abandoned the vessel in the lifeboat and was taken on board *Stena Carrier*. There were no injuries.

Ziemia Lodzka suffered structural damages on port side of the bow and was anchored approximately three miles north of the collision position. The vessel continued its voyage in the evening of the same day for a discharge and repair yard in Poland.

Danish Marine Accident Report issued on 24 April 2006 stated that the *Ziemia Lodzka* failed to:

1. proceed at a safe speed
2. post a lookout
3. make timely VHF contact to the M/V *Vertigo*
4. fulfill her obligation as a give-way vessel

Training deficiencies and a chain of errors can be identified in this case as well as with all the case studies in this chapter.

Training deficiencies lead to human error and invitation of error chains. The person to break the error chain is the master, provided he/she is called in time to do something and not to be a witness. Sometimes, as can be seen by these case studies, the master is part of the error chain and it is up to the OOW or another member of the bridge team to break the error chain. In the case of the *Ziemia Lodzka/Vertigo* collision the following training deficiencies are evident:

1. Lack of knowledge of the Rules of the Road
2. When to post a lookout, what are the duties and responsibilities of a lookout. (See Section I, Appendix A, pg. 196)
3. How to identify the vessel you are calling on VHF and how to utilize the VHF in order to comply with the COLREGS.
4. What are the obligations of a stand-on and give-way vesselFacts are stubborn things. They do not cease to exist because they are ignored. In this case, it is a fact this was a crossing situation. The *Ziemia Lodzka* was the give-way vessel. The *Vertigo* had to alter course when in compliance with Rule 17(a)(ii) it became apparent the vessel required to keep out of the way *(Ziemia*

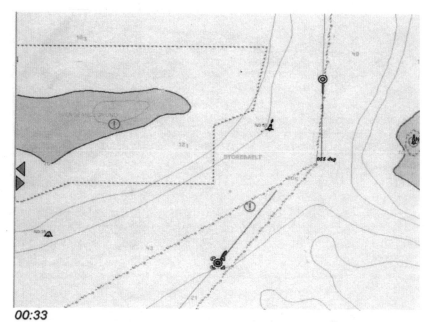

00:33

Fig. 9-8a. Ziemia Lodzka southbound approaching the northeast-bound
Vertigo three minutes prior to collusion. Vessels were 1.5 miles apart.
(Courtesy of Danish Maritime Authority [DMA] report of 24 April 2006.)

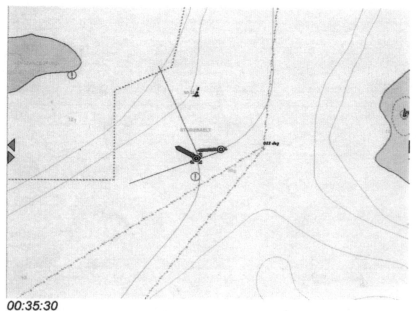

00:35:30

Fig. 9-8b. Thirty seconds prior to the collision. The Ziemia Lodzka's
rudder is full to starboard and the Vertigo's rudder is port 30°. (Courtesy
of DMA report of 24 April 2006.)

Fig. 9-9. Visual view of the Ziemia Lodzka from Vertigo at 00:32:00, four minutes prior to the collision. Note masthead light to right of the range light and green side light showing starboard side of Ziemia Lodzka. (Courtesy of CAORF Simulator, USMMA, Kings Point, New York.)

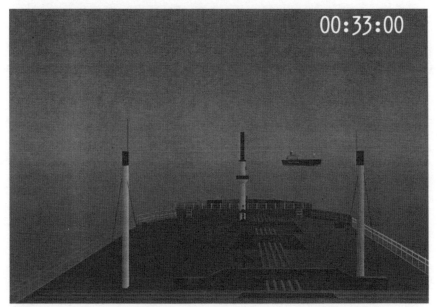

Fig. 9-10a. Visual view of Ziemia Lodzka at 00:33 (three minutes prior to the collision, driftin'! port to starboard across the Vertigo's bow.) (Courtesy of CAORF, USMMA, Kings Point, New York.)

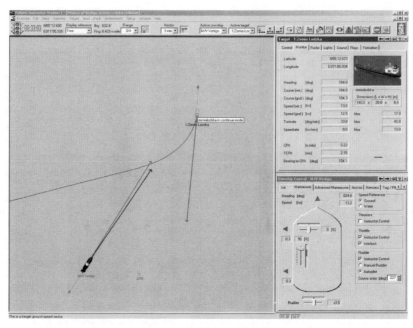

Fig. 9-10b. Bird's-eye view of both vessels at 00:33:03. CPA is now 0.22 miles in 2.15 minutes if both vessels maintain their course and speed. (Courtesy of CAORF, USMMA, Kings Point, New York.)

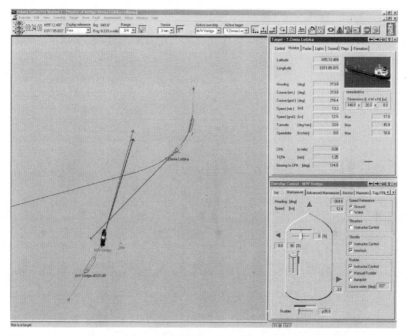

Fig. 9-11. Bird's-eye view of both vessels at 00:34, two minutes prior to the collision. According to DMA Report, page 15, the Ziemia Lodzka begins to alter course to starboard at 00:33:55, and the Vertigo begins to alter course to port in compliance with Rule 17(a)(ii). (Courtesy of CAORF, USMMA, Kings Point, New York.)

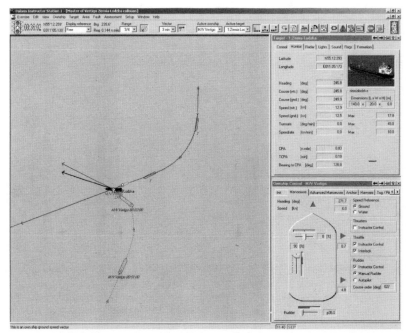

Fig. 9-12a. Bird's-eye view of collision at 00:36 at latitude 55°-12.38'
north and longitude ll°-05.3' east. (Courtesy of CAORF, USMMA, Kings
Point, New York.)

Fig. 9-12b. *Vertigo* foundered at eleven meters depth of water. (Courtesy of
Danish Maritime Authority [DMA] report of 24 April 2006.)

Fig. 9-13. Proposed air cushion merchant ship. The 420-foot vessel would have a beam of 140 feet and could cruise at eighty knots. (Courtesy of Bell Aerosystems and Thomas C. Gillmer from Modern Ship Design, Annapolis, MD: Naval Institute Press.)

Lodzka) did not take appropriate action in compliance with the rules.

The Master of the *Ziemia Lodzka* violated Rule 16—Action by Give-way Vessel—in that he did not take early and substantial action to keep well clear of the *Vertigo.*

In addition, in this case, GPS was utilized by both vessels with all sorts of lighted aids to navigation visible along with radar conspicuous objects available where by parallel indexing could have been utilized to maintain the vessels track. AIS was available to both vessels and neither vessel utilized their VHF to arrange how they would cross with one another. Time was wasted in obtaining GPS fixes and making assumptions. VTS available in the area was not utilized. The collision was avoidable and inexcusable.

An approved simulator course in a ship bridge simulator would provide the training necessary for the bridge team to detect and correct these deficiencies before the initiation of an error chain. At the very least, correct watchstanding procedures would be instituted during such training in order to break a future error chain.

CONCLUSION

Case studies help point out human errors and provide lessons for which every watch officer should profit. Human reaction to such cases generally is one of "that would never happen to me" or "I would never have committed that error." Until you are placed into an identical situation you cannot say for certain whether you would commit the same error.

For those whose prime interest in accident cases is safety and education, there is no satisfaction in pointing the finger of guilt. Yet, facts are facts, and they have an eloquence of their own. Accidents don't just happen; they are caused. By examining the causes, valuable lessons can always be learned, by and for the men who are and will be in charge of the watch on the bridges of ships.

Safe navigation to avoid accidents can be attainable with bridge organization through proper prior planning and compliance with the three Cs of communication, coordination, and cooperation. It is essential that watch officers support their masters in this regard. It is imperative that all watch officers and the master be familiar with all bridge equipment and bridge procedures, so as to navigate safely as a team.

Failure to use equipment correctly can be avoided with hands-on training. Correct actions that are intuitive and instinctive in the event of an emergency can be accomplished, even on ships of the future (see Fig. 9-13). The human-error problem can be solved with proper training both ashore and aboard ship. The most cost-effective method is through simulator courses and its use should be greatly increased in the interest of safety at sea.

Excerpts from the Standards on Training, Certification and Watchkeeping for Seafarers, 1978

Basic Principles to Be Observed in Keeping a Safe Navigational Watch

A. Parties shall direct the attention of ship owners, ship operators, masters, and watchkeeping personnel to the following principles, which shall be observed to ensure that a safe navigational watch is maintained at all time.

B. The master of every ship is bound to ensure that watchkeeping arrangements are adequate for maintaining a safe navigation watch. Under the master's general direction, the officers of the watch are responsible for navigating the ship safely during their periods of duty, when they will be particularly concerned with avoiding collision and stranding.

C. The basic principles, including, but not limited to, the following, shall be taken into account on all ships.

D. Watch Arrangements

   1. The composition of the watch shall at all times be adequate and appropriate to the prevailing circumstances and conditions and shall take into account the need for maintaining a proper lookout.

   2. When deciding the composition of the watch on the bridge, which may include appropriate deck ratings, the following factors, interalia, shall be taken into account:

      (a) the need to see that the bridge is at no time left unattended;

      (b) weather conditions, visibility, and whether there is daylight or darkness;

      (c) proximity of navigational hazards which may make it necessary for the officer-in-charge of the watch to carry out additional duties;

      (d) use and operational condition of navigational aids such as radar or electronic position-indicating devices and any other equipment affecting the safe navigation of the ship;

      (e) whether the ship is fitted with automatic steering;

      (f) any unusual demands on the navigational watch that may arise as a result of special operational circumstances.E. Fitness for Duty

The watch system shall be such that the efficiency of watch-keeping officers and watchkeeping ratings is not impaired by fatigue. Duties shall be so organized that the first watch at the commencement of a voyage and the subsequent relieving watches are sufficiently rested and otherwise fit for duty.

F. Navigation
1. The intended voyage shall be planned in advance, taking into consideration all pertinent information, and any course laid down shall be checked before the voyage commences.
2. During the watch the course steered, position and speed shall be checked at sufficiently frequent intervals, using any available navigational aids necessary to ensure that the ship follows the planned course.
3. The watchkeeping officer shall have full knowledge of the location and operation of all safety and navigational equipment on board the ship and shall be aware and take account of the operating limitations of such equipment.
4. The officer-in-charge of a navigational watch shall not be assigned or undertake any duties which would interfere with the safe navigation of the ship.

G. Navigational Equipment
1. The officer of the watch shall make the most effective use of all navigation equipment at his disposal.
2. When using radar the officer of the watch shall bear in mind the necessity to comply at all times with the provisions on the use of radar contained in the applicable regulations for prevention of collisions at sea.
3. In case of need the officer of the watch shall not hesitate to use the helm, engines, and sound-signaling apparatus.

H. Navigational Duties and Responsibilities
1. The officer-in-charge of a watch shall:
    (a) keep his watch on the bridge, which he shall in no circumstances leave until properly relieved;
    (b) continue to be responsible for the safe navigation of the ship despite the presence of the master on the bridge until the master informs him specifically that he has assumed that responsibility and this is mutually understood;
    (c) notify the master when in any doubt as to what action to take in the interest of safety;
    (d) not hand over the watch to the relieving officer if he has reason to believe that the latter is obviously not capable "of carrying out his duties effectively," in which case he shall notify the master accordingly.

2. On taking over the watch the relieving officer shall satisfy himself as to the ship's estimated or true position and confirm its intended track, course, and speed, and shall note any dangers to navigation expected to be encountered during his watch.

3. A proper record shall be kept of movements and activities during the watch relating to the navigation of the ship.

I. Lookout

In addition to maintaining a proper lookout for the purpose of fully appraising the situation and the risk of collision, stranding, and other dangers to navigation, the duties of the lookout shall include the detection of ships or aircraft in distress, shipwrecked persons, wrecks, and debris. In maintaining a lookout the following shall be observed:

1. The lookout must be able to give full attention to the keeping of a proper lookout and no other duties shall be undertaken or assigned which could interfere with that task;

2. The duties of the lookout and helmsman are separate, and the helmsman shall not be considered a lookout while steering, except in small ships where an unobstructed all-around view is provided at the steering position and there is no impairment of night vision or other impediment to the keeping of a proper lookout. The officer-in-charge of the watch may be the sole lookout in daylight, provided that on each such occasion:

   (a) the situation has been carefully assessed and it has been established without doubt that such arrangement is safe;

   (b) full account has been taken of all relevant factors including, but not limited to: state of weather, visibility, traffic density, proximity of danger to navigation, the attention necessary when navigating in or near traffic separation schemes,

   (c) assistance is immediately available to be summoned to the bridge when any change in the situation so requires.

J. Navigation with the Pilot Embarked

Despite the duties and obligations of a pilot, his presence on board does not relieve the master and officer-in-charge of the watch from their duties and obligations for the safety of the ship. The master and pilot shall exchange information regarding navigational procedures, local conditions and the ship's characteristics. The master and officer of the watch shall cooperate closely with the pilot and maintain an accurate check of the ship's position and movement.

K. Protection of the Marine Environment

The master and officer-in-charge of the watch shall be aware of the serious effects of operational or accidental pollution of the marine environment and shall take all possible precautions to prevent such pollution, particularly within the framework of relevant international and port regulations.

Recommendations on Operational Guidance for Officers in Charge of a Navigational Watch

A.   Introduction

This Recommendation contains operational guidance of general application for officers-in-charge of a navigational watch which masters are expected to supplement as appropriate. It is essential that officers of the watch appreciate that the efficient performance of their duties is necessary in the interests of safety of life and property at sea and the prevention of pollution of the marine environment.

B.   General

The officer of the watch is the master's representative and his primary responsibility at all times is the safe navigation of the ship. He should, at all times, comply with the applicable regulations for preventing collisions at sea (see "Clear, Weather" and "Restricted Visibility").

1.   It is of special importance that at all times the officer of the watch ensure that an efficient lookout is maintained. In a ship with a separate chartroom the officer of the watch may visit the chartroom when essential for a short period for the necessary performance of his navigational duties, but he should previously satisfy himself that it is safe to do so and ensure that an efficient lookout is maintained.

2.   The officer of the watch should bear in mind that the engines are at his disposal and he should not hesitate to use them in case of need. However, timely notice of intended variations of engine speed should be given where possible. He should also know the handling characteristics of his ship, including its stopping distance, and should appreciate that other ships may have different handling characteristics.

3.   The officer of the watch should also bear in mind that the sound-signaling apparatus is at his disposal and he should not hesitate to use it in accordance with the applicable regulations for preventing collision at sea.

C.   Taking over the Navigational Watch

1.   The relieving officer of the watch should ensure that members of his watch are fully capable of performing their duties,

particularly ensuring that their eyes have adjusted to night vision.

2. The relieving officer should not take over the watch until his vision is fully adjusted to the light conditions and he has personally satisfied himself regarding:

   (a) standing orders and other special instructions of the master relating to the navigation of the ship;

   (b) position, course, speed, and draft of the ship;

   (c) prevailing and predicted tides, current, weather, visibility, and the effect of these factors upon course and speed;

   (d) navigational situation, including, but not limited to, the following:

      1) operational condition of all navigational and safety equipment being used or likely to be used during the watch;

      2) errors of gyro and magnetic compass;

      3) presence and movement of ships in sight or known to be in the vicinity;

      4) conditions and hazards likely to be encountered during his watch;

      5) possible effects of heel, trim, water density, and squat on underkeel clearance.

3. If at the time the officer of the watch is to be relieved, a maneuver or other action to avoid a hazard is taking place, the relief of the officer should be deferred until such action has been completed.

D. Periodic Checks of Navigational Equipment

1. Operational tests of shipboard navigational equipment should be carried out at sea as frequently as practicable and as circumstances permit and in particular when hazardous conditions' affecting navigation are expected where appropriate these tests should be recorded.

2. The officer of the watch should make regular checks to ensure that:

   (a) the helmsman or the automatic pilot is steering the correct course;

   (b) the standard compass error is determined at least once a watch and, when possible, after any alteration of course; the standard and gyro compasses are frequently compared and repeaters are synchronized with their master compass;

   (c) the automatic pilot is tested manually at least once a watch;

   (d) the navigation and signal lights, and other navigational equipment are functioning properly.

E. Automatic Pilot

The officer of the watch should bear in mind the necessity to comply at all times with the requirements of Regulation 19, Chapter V, of the International Convention for the Safety of Life at Sea, 1974. He should take into account the need to station the helmsman and put the steering into manual control in good time to allow any potentially hazardous situation to be dealt with safely. With a ship under automatic steering it is highly dangerous to allow a situation to develop to the point where the officer of the watch is without assistance and has to break the continuity of the lookout to take emergency action. The change over from automatic to manual steering and vice versa should be made by, or under the supervision of, a responsible officer.

F. Electronic Navigation Aids
1. The officer of the watch should be thoroughly familiar with the use of electronic navigational aids carried, including their capabilities and limitations.
2. The echo sounder is a valuable navigational aid and should be used whenever appropriate.

G. Radar
1. The officer of the watch should use the radar when appropriate and whenever restricted visibility is encountered or expected and at all times in congested waters, having due regard to its limitations.
2. Whenever radar is in use, the officer of the watch should select an appropriate range scale, observe the display carefully, and plot effectively.
3. The officer of the watch should ensure that range scales employed are changed at sufficiently frequent intervals so that echoes are detected as early as possible.
4. It should be borne in mind that small or poor echoes may escape detection.
5. The officer of the watch should ensure that plotting or systematic analysis is commenced in ample time.
6. In clear weather, whenever possible, the officer of the watch should carry out radar practice.

H. Navigational Coastal Waters
1. The largest-scale chart on board suitable for the area and corrected with the latest available information should be used. Fixes should be taken at frequent intervals; whenever circumstances allow, fixing should be carried out by more than one method.
2. The officer of the watch should positively identify all relevant navigation marks.
3. Exhibit navigation lights.
4. Operate and use the radar.

It is important that the officer of the watch should know the handling characteristics of his ship, including its stopping distance, and should appreciate that other ships may have different handling characteristics.

K.   Calling the Master

The officer of the watch should notify the master immediately in the following circumstances:

1. If restricted visibility is encountered or expected;
2. If the traffic conditions or the movements of other ships are causing concern;
3. If difficulty is experienced in maintaining course;
4. On failure to sight land, or a navigation mark is sighted or to obtain soundings by the expected time;
5. If, unexpectedly, land, or a navigation mark is sighted or change in soundings occurs;
6. On the breakdown of the engines, steering gear or any essential navigation equipment;
7. In heavy weather if any doubt about the possibility of weather damage;
8. If the ship meets any hazard to navigation, such as ice or derelicts;
9. In any other emergency or situation in which he is any doubt. Despite the requirement to notify the master immediately in the foregoing circumstances, the officer of the watch should in addition not hesitate to take immediate action for the safety of the ship, where circumstances require.

L.   Navigation with Pilot Embarked

If the officer of the watch is in any doubt as to the pilot's action or intentions, he should seek clarification from the pilot; if doubt still exists, he should notify the master immediately and take whatever action is necessary before the master arrives.

M.   The Watchkeeping Personnel

The officer of the watch should give watchkeeping personnel all appropriate instructions and information which will ensure the keeping of a safe watch, including an appropriate lookout.

N.   Ship at Anchor

If the master considers it necessary, a continuous navigational watch should be maintained at anchor. In all circumstances, while at anchor, however the officer of the watch should:

1. Determine and plot the ship's position on the appropriate chart as soon as practicable; when circumstances permit, check at sufficiently frequent intervals whether the ship is remaining securely at anchor by taking bearings of fixed navigation marks or readily identifiable shore objects;

2. Ensure that an efficient lookout is maintained;
3. Ensure that inspection rounds of the ship are made periodically;
4. Observe meteorlogical and tidal conditions and state of the sea;
5. Notify the master and undertake all necessary measures if the ship drags anchor;
6. Ensure that the state of readiness of the main engines and other machinery is in accordance with the master's instructions;
7. If visibility deteriorates, notify the master and comply with the applicable regulations for preventing collisions at sea;
8. Ensure that the ship exhibits the appropriate lights and shapes and that appropriate sound signals are made at all times, as required;
9. Take measures to protect the environment from pollution by the ship and comply with applicable pollution regulations.

Recommendation on Principles and Operational Guidance for Deck Officers in Charge of a Watch in Port

A. Introduction
  1. This Recommendation applies to a ship safely moored or safely at anchor under normal conditions.
  2. The following principles and operational guidance should be taken into account by ship owners, ship operators, masters, and watchkeeping officers.
B. Watch and Its Arrangements
  1. Arrangements for keeping a watch when the ship is in port should:
     (a) ensure the safety of life, ship cargo, and port;
     (b) conform to international, national, and local rules;
     (c) maintain order and the normal routine of the ship.
  2. The ship's master should decide the composition and duration of the watch on the basis of the conditions of mooring, type of the ship, and character of duties.
  3. A qualified deck officer should be in charge of the watch except in ships under 50 gross register tons not carrying dangerous cargo, in which case the master may appoint who ever has appropriate qualifications to keep the watch in port.
  4. The necessary equipment should be so arranged as to provide for efficient watchkeeping.
C. Taking over the Watch
  1. The officer of the watch should not hand over the watch to the relieving officer if he has any reason to believe that the latter is obviously not capable of carrying out his duties effectively, in which case he should notify the master accordingly.

2. The relieving officer should be informed of the following by the officer being relieved:

 (a) the depth of water at the berth, ship's draft, the level and time of high and low waters; fastening of the moorings, arrangement of anchors, the scope of the anchor chain and other features of mooring important for the safety of the ship; state of main engines availability for emergency use;

 (b) all work to be performed on board ship; the nature, amount, and disposition of cargo loaded or remaining or any residue on board after unloading of the ship;

 (c) the level of water bilges and ballast tanks;

 (d) the signals or lights being exhibited;

 (e) the number of crew members required to be on board and the presence of any other persons on board;

 (f) the state of fireFighting appliances;

 (g) any special port regulations;

 (h) the master's standing and special orders;

 (i) the lines of communication that are available between the ship and the dock staff or port authorities in the event of an emergency arising or assistance being required;

 (j) other circumstances of importance to the safety of the ship and protection of the environment from pollution.

3. The relieving officer should satisfy himself that:

 (a) fastenings of moorings or anchor chain are adequate;

 (b) the appropriate signs or lights are properly hoisted and exhibited;

 (c) safety measures have been taken and fire protection regulations are being complied with;

 (d) he/she is aware of the nature of any hazardous or dangerous cargo being loaded or discharged and the appropriate action in the event of any spillage or fire;

 (e) no external condition or circumstances imperil the ship and that his/her own ship does not imperil others.

4. If, at the moment the watch is to be handed over, an important operation is being performed, it should be concluded by the officer being relieved, except when ordered otherwise by the master.

D. Keeping a Watch

The watchkeeping officer should:

1. Make rounds to inspect the ship at appropriate intervals;

2. Pay particular attention to:

 (a) the condition and fastening of the gangway, anchor chain, or moorings, especially at the turn of the tide or in berths where the water level rises and falls considerably, and, if necessary, take measures to ensure that they are in normal working condition;

(b) the draft, under keel clearance, and the state of the ship to avoid dangerous listing and trim during cargo handling or ballasting;

(c) the state of the weather and the sea;

(d) observance of regulations concerning safety precautions and fire protection;

(e) water levels in bilges and tanks;

(f) all persons on board and their location, especially those in remote or enclosed spaces;

(g) the exhibition of any signals or lights.

3. In bad weather or on receiving a storm warning, take the necessary measures to protect the ship, personnel, and cargo;

4. Take every precaution to prevent pollution of the environment by his own ship;

5. In an emergency threatening the safety of the ship, raise the alarm, inform the master, take all possible measures to prevent any damage to the ship, and, if necessary, request assistance from the shore authorities or neighboring ships;

6. Be aware of the state of stability so that in the event of fire, the shore fireFighting authority may be advised of the approximate quantity of water that can be pumped on board without endangering the ship;

7. Offer assistance to ships or persons in distress;

8. Take necessary precautions to prevent accidents or damage when propellers are to be turned;

9. Enter in the appropriate logbook all important events affecting the ship.

M/V *Capella* Bridge Standing Orders

The bridge standing orders created for the hypothetical training ship M/V *Capella* are typical of the verbiage contained in orders for actual ships, hence the use of male and female pronouns referring to bridge officers is intended to include officers of both sexes.

1.   Introduction

1.1   These standing orders shall not be constructed by anyone to indicate a departure from the Regulations for the Prevention of Collision at Sea, navigational laws of the United States of America, Regulations for the International Convention for Safety of life at sea, or the usual practices of good seamanship. Those are to be strictly adhered to at all times during normal vessel operation.

2.   Duties and Responsibilities

Passage Plan

2.1   The second officer is responsible for planning the navigational passage of the vessel in accordance with my instructions. The intended voyage shall be planned in advance and in accordance with my instructions and the recommendations contained in the attached paper Guide to the Planning and Conduct of Passages.

Bridge Watch System

2.2   When underway, bridge watches shall be maintained as follows:

```
0000 to 0400 (1200 to 1600)_____Second Officer
0400 to 0800 (1600 to 2000)_____Chief Officer
0800 to 1200 (2000 to 2400)_____Third Officer
```

2.3   The system may be temporarily modified, particularly on the occasion of the first watch when leaving port, to ensure that watchkeeping officers are not impaired by fatigue. The same system of watches as summarized above will be maintained whenever the vessel is at anchor. However, the requirements for anchor watches may be varied depending on the circumstances prevailing at the time.

General Watchkeeping Requirements

2.4 The bridge watch officer is in charge of the vessel during his/her watch period and is responsible to me for the safety of the vessel, crew and cargo. It is the watch officer's duty to see that all navigation laws, rules of the road, standing orders, etc., are complied with. The watch officer should be completely familiar with the vessel, her characteristics, operation, safety and fire Fighting equipment, badge and navigation equipment, including portable equipment and signals.

2.5 The watch officer is responsible for the conduct, actions, and performance of the personnel on his/her watch; instructing them in proper watchstanding duties; and ensuring that the instructions are carried out,

2.6 The watch officer must never leave the bridge at any time unless relieved by me or by another licensed officer.

2.7 The course and speed of the ship must not be changed without my authority, except as planned or to avoid immediate danger, in which case the watch officer must bear in mind that the engines are at his/her disposal and he/she should not hesitate to use them in case of need. In any event, any course and/or speed changes must be reported to me immediately.

2.8 The watch officer must be familiar with, and periodically review, the vessel data information and maneuvering characteristics which are posted and available with these standing orders.

2.9 All watch officers *must have a complete working knowledge of the regulations "For The Prevention of Collisions At Sea," and observe those rules at all times.* When taking any action as prescribed by the rules, be sure that the action is timely and sufficient, and has the desired result.

2.10 Notwithstanding anything contained in these orders, all watches are to be kept in accordance with the recommendations of the IMO document *"Keeping A Safe Navigational Watch."* A copy of the document is attached and it must be read by all watch-keeping officers.

3. Responsibility with a Pilot on Board

3. 1   Attention is drawn to the following extract from IMO Resolution A 285 (VIII):

Despite the duties and obligations of a pilot, his presence on board does not relieve the watch officer from his duties and obligations for the safety of the ship. He should co-operate closely with the pilot and maintain an accurate check on the vessel's position and movements. If he is in any doubt as to the pilot's actions or intentions, he should seek clarification from the pilot and if doubt still exists he should notify the master immediately and take whatever action is necessary before the master arrives.

3. 2   After the pilot's arrival on board, in addition to being advised of the maneuvering characteristics and basic details of the vessel for its condition of loading, the pilot should be consulted on the passage plan to be followed. The aim is to ensure the expertise of the pilot is fully supported by the bridge team. Once the pilot's intentions are known, the watch officer must continue to ensure the position of the vessel is plotted on the chart, all aids to navigation properly identified, tidal heights, and corrections are known; ship's personnel are alert and correctly execute orders.

4.   Calling the Master

4.1   *Never fail to call me at any time if in any doubt whatsoever.* Use any means at your disposal to contact me. If you cannot locate me in an emergency, sound one short ring on the general alarm bells.

4.2   Despite the requirement to notify me immediately in the following circumstances, the watch officer *should not hesitate to take immediate action for the safety of the ship where circumstances require.* In the absence of any specific orders to the contrary, I am to be called in the following circumstances when underway and at anchor:

Underway
(a) If restricted visibility is encountered or expected.
(b) If the traffic conditions or the movements of other ships are causing concern.
(c) If difficulty is experienced in maintaining course.
(d) On failure to sight land or a navigation mark or obtain soundings by the expected time.
(e) If, unexpectedly, land or a navigation mark is sighted or change in sounding occurs.

(f) On the breakdown of engines, steering gear, or any essential navigation equipment.
(g) In heavy weather if in any doubt about the possibility of weather damage.
(h) If the ship meets any hazard to navigation.
(i) In any other emergency or situation in which you are in any doubt.

At Anchor

(a) If the movements of other ships are causing concern.
(b) If the vessel is dragging her anchor(s).
(c) If the state of the weather and sea is expected to deteriorate.
(d) If restricted visibility is encountered or expected.
(e) On the approach of any unidentified craft attempting to come alongside.
(f) In any other emergency or situation in which you are in any doubt.

5. Presence of the Master on the Bridge

5.1 My presence on the bridge does not relieve the watch officer of the conn unless he /she is specifically advised that I have taken over.

6. Assuming the Watch

6.1 It is essential that watches are relieved punctually. The relieving watch officer must be on the bridge at least ten minutes prior to the time he/she is to take over the watch.

Assuming the Watch at Sea

6.2 Prior to assuming the watch at sea, the relieving watch officer must ensure that his/her vision is adjusted fully to the light conditions and he/she is personally satisfied regarding:
(a) Standing orders, night orders, and other special instructions relating to the navigation of the ship.
(b) The position of the ship and the depth of water.
(c) The true, magnetic and gyro courses being steered, the errors of the gyro and magnetic compasses, the direction and rate of prevailing and predicted tides, currents and winds, and the amount of leeway and set being applied.
(d) The engine control mode, horsepower or rpm in use, and the speed made good through the water and over the ground.
(e) The DR track for the watch, with any proposed course changes. Landmarks or navigation aids to be sighted.

(f) Presence and movement of vessels, lights or objects in sight, and status of bearings on them.

(g) Navigation equipment in use. Their operational status and an evaluation of information obtained from them.

(h) Conditions and hazards likely to be encountered during the watch.

(i) Publications required for reference and data.

(j) Proper setting of bridge clocks and course recorder. Adjust as necessary for accuracy.

(k) Status of vessel for current and anticipated weather. Precautions taken and orders in effect.

(l) Weather information on wind direction and force, sea and swell, barometric tendency, indications from weather reports.

(m) Any other information necessary to ensure a thorough understanding of the vessel status and the existing situation.

Assuming the Watch at Anchor

6. 3   Prior to assuming the watch at anchor, the relieving watch officer must ensure that his/her vision is fully adjusted to the light conditions and he/she is personally satisfied regarding:

(a) Standing orders, night orders, and any special port regulations.

(b) The position of the ship within the radius of swing and the depth or water, the times and heights of high and low waters, times the tidal current is due to change, and whether there is sufficient swinging room.

(c) The anchor(s) in use, amount of cable out, arrangements for the slip of the cable, and status of anchor windlass.

(d) The state of the main engines and their availability for emergency use.

(e) The appropriate signals or lights are properly hoisted and exhibited.

(f) The appropriate VHF channel is available for use between the ship and port authorities.

(g) Presence and movement of vessels, lights or objects in sight, and status of bearings on them.

(h) Navigation equipment in use, their operational status, and an evaluation of information obtained from them.

(i) Conditions and hazards likely to be encountered during the watch.

(j) Publications required for reference and data.

(k) Status of vessel for current and anticipated weather. Precautions taken and orders in effect.

(l) Weather information on wind direction and force, sea and swell, barometric tendency, and indications from weather reports.

7. Handing Over the Watch

7.1 The watch officer being relieved must ensure his/her relief is able and in condition to relieve, and thoroughly acquainted with the necessary facts before the OOW hands over the watch. Upon signing the change of watch checklist by both officers, the relief officer will indicate assumption of the watch duties and responsibilities by stating, "I relieve you."

7.2 If a maneuver or other action to avoid any hazard is taking place at the time the watch officer is to be relieved, *the relief of the officer should be deferred until such action has been completed.*

8. Watch Personnel

Helmsman

8.1 Watch officers are to ensure that helmsmen are sober, competent, alert, and properly dressed for duty. The helmsman station is behind the wheel to keep a constant check on the course steered and a check on the magnetic compass. Hand-steering mode will be used during the first thirty minutes of each watch, in confined waters, in restricted visibility, within five miles of other closing vessels, and when circumstances deem it prudent.

Lookouts

8.2 Lookouts are to be posted at all times between sunset and sunrise, during reduced visibility, and when in heavy or congested traffic. Lookouts are to be posted on the fo'c'sle head except when it is unsafe to do so, at which times they will be posted on the bridge.

8.3 It is the responsibility of the watch officer to ensure that the lookouts are thoroughly instructed in their duties and are alert to report all lights, signals, objects, whistles, bells, etc., and to check the condition of the running lights every half hour and ensure no unauthorized lights are showing forward. When it is necessary, due to weather, to secure the lookout forward, ensure that the telephone boxes are secured, the bullnose cover, vent covers, chain pipe covers, and watertight doors are securely dogged; lines and wires tied down, and all loose gear stowed below.

Standby

8.4 The standby is to be suitably dressed and available on call at all times. Unless otherwise engaged in other regular duties, the standby's normal station is in the sailors' mess, where contact to and from the bridge can be made by telephone. When working on deck in the daytime, the standby is to notify the watch officer where he/she may be contacted at any time. During night watches each standby shall inspect the ship at least once to ensure that decks, watertight doors, weather doors, ports, boats, tank lids, etc. are secure, safe and in order. Any unsafe or unseaworthy conditions are to be reported to the watch officer and a notation made in the log book.

9.   Watchkeeping Duties—At Sea

Proper Lookout

9.1   The watch officer must keep an efficient lookout at all times except when essential for a short period for the necessary performance of navigational duties, but should be satisfied that it is safe to do so and ensure an efficient lookout is maintained.

Hand Steering

9.2   Hand-steering mode is to be used during the first thirty minutes of each watch; in confined waters; in restricted visibility; within five miles of other closing vessels, navigation aids, obstructions, etc.; and when other circumstances deem it prudent.

Helm Orders and Monitoring of Helmsman

9.3   Helm orders must be loud and clear, and leave the helmsman no doubt as to what he is required to do. The orders must be repeated in a similar manner by the helmsman. Orders to the helmsman are to indicate direction (left or right) or port/starboard, and amount of rudder to be used. Courses are to be stated in three numerals to ensure clarity and understanding.

9.4   Orders for a change of course can be given in either of two ways:

(a) For small alterations of course in clear waters, where a desired rate of turn is not required, give the helmsman the new course to steer, but to avoid the helm being put the wrong way, order the direction the helm has to be moved, i.e., "Right/Starboard to 030°." In this case the amount of initial rudder applied and subsequent counter rudder is left to the helmsman's discretion.

(b) For alterations of course in confined waters or for collision avoidance the helmsman should be conned to, and steadied on, the new course by the watch officer, i.e., "Left 10," "Midships," "Right 5", "Midships", "Steady on course 270°."

9.5   The steering is to be monitored closely at all times to ensure helm orders are correctly repeated and executed by the helmsman, and the course being steered is correct. Close monitoring of the steering is particularly necessary in pilotage waters and it is the responsibility of the watch officer to ensure the course is maintained and helm orders correctly executed.

Automatic Steering

9.6   The watch officer must supervise changes of steering made from hand to auto and vice versa. Adjustment settings of weather and rudder must be made by the watch officer prior to engaging the auto mode. Once in the auto mode the performance of the steering must be monitored closely to see if the settings are having the desired effect, and then fine-tuned as necessary. During this period the helmsman must stand by the helm and assist with the monitoring.

9.7   When changing from auto to hand steering, the watch officer must take into account the *need to station the helmsmen and put the steering in manual control in good time* to allow any potential hazardous situation to be dealt with in a safe manner.

Monitoring of Position and Track

9.8   At all times when underway the vessel's progress must be monitored to ensure that the intended track of the vessel is maintained and the vessel is within the specified margins of safety of that track.

9.9   When coasting, the vessel's position is to be fixed on the chart every fifteen minutes, on the quarter hour. If circumstances warrant, the position should be fixed more often. In pilotage waters, regardless of the familiarity with the locale, the vessel's position must be fixed as frequently as necessary on the best scale chart of the area being transited. In addition, wherever radar conspicuous objects are available, *radar parallel indexing must be used* to monitor the vessel's position relative to the intended track.

9.10 The vessel's position must be fixed by the most reliable method available at the time. Fixing would include, but not be limited to, fixes by visual bearings, radar bearings, distances, and a line of soundings where applicable. Where other navigation systems are available, such as SATNAV, LORAN, and GPS, these also must be observed and compared against the terrestrial fix. In any event, there must be two independent means of fixing the vessel's position at any time, e.g., primary method and secondary method. The purpose of the secondary method is to periodically check the reliability of the primary system.

9.11 Where it is impossible to obtain terrestrial fixes, celestial lines of position, and SATNAV positions will be obtained on each watch and as frequently as the situation warrants. Note and plot SATNAV fixes to augment and cross check positions.

Standard Platting Symbols

9.12   Mark and identify all position lines and fixes on the chart by using the following standard plotting symbols:

Terrestrial or celestial fix _____ Dot with circle
Combination visual and electronic ____ Dot with triangle
Full electronic fix   _____ Dot with square
Satellite fix   _____ Dot with plus
Dead reckoning position _____ Dot with half circle
Celestial line of position _____ Solid line with arrows at ends
Terrestrial line of position _____ Solid line with arrow in direction of object
Transferred position lines _____ Dashed lines instead of solid lines

Periodic Checks of Navigation Equipment

9.13   Operational tests of navigational equipment should be carried out as frequently and practicable as the circumstances permit. Where appropriate, these tests should also be recorded. In particular, the watch officer must make regular checks to ensure that:

(a) The helmsman or auto pilot is steering the correct course.
(b) The gyro repeaters are synchronized with the master gyro.
(c) The magnetic and gyro compass errors are determined at least once a watch and after any alterations of course to a new heading. All details of compass errors must he entered in the compass error book.
(d) The auto pilot is tested manually at least once a watch.
(e) The navigation and signal lights and other navigational equipment are functioning properly.

Depths

9.14   One fathometer is to be run continuously when navigating in depths of less then 100 fathoms and the depths to be recorded every half hour. Depths must be taken at the time of each fix and the depth shown on the chart alongside the time of the fix for comparison with the charted depth. In addition, the shallow water alarm must be set to whatever depth is necessary to give ample warning of any danger.

Prevention of Collisions at Sea

9.15   In clear visibility the watch officer must take frequent and accurate compass bearings of approaching vessels as early detection of collision risk. Early and positive action should be taken in compliance with the applicable regulations and subsequently check that the action taken has the desired effect. Allow meeting and stand-on vessels early and wide berths.

Radar

9.16   Keep at least one radar in operation and one on standby at all times when underway. Plot all contacts to determine movements, closest point of approach, and any avoiding action if required. Ensure that the appropriate range scales are used and they are changed at sufficient intervals to ensure echoes are detected as early as possible.

10.   Watchkeeping Duties—At Anchor

10.1   Ensure that an efficient lookout is maintained.

10.2   At frequent intervals check whether the ship is remaining secured at her anchor by taking visual bearings of fixed navigational marks or readily identified shore objects.

10.3   Ensure the state of readiness of the main engines, anchor windlass, and other machinery in accordance with my instructions.

10.4   Ensure the appropriate light and shapes are exhibited.

10.5   Monitor the appropriate VHF channels for distress messages, messages from the appropriate port authority, and any other messages of relevance to the safety and operation of the vessel.

10.6   Ensure an efficient gangway watch is being maintained and inspection rounds are made periodically of the ship.

10.7   Ensure the relevant precautions for prevention of pollution of the sea are observed.

10.8   Monitor vessel traffic to ensure ample warning of the risk of collision.

10.9   Monitor weather and sea conditions to have ample warning of conditions that may affect the safety of the vessel.

11.   Procedures in Restricted Visibility

11.1 When restricted visibility is encountered or expected the watch officer is to comply with the relevant rules of the applicable regulations for preventing collisions at sea. In particular, the following action must be taken:
(a) Place main engines on standby.
(b) Commence sounding appropriate fog signal. Switch on navigation lights.
(c) Post lookout (audio and visual).
(d) Advise master and engine room.
(e) Engage hand steering.
(f) Reduce to safe speed if necessary.
(g) Maintain listening watch on VHF channel 16 unless local regulations require another listening watch channel.
(h) Commence radar plot of approaching targets.
(I) Shut specified watertight doors.

12.   Preparation for Departure

12.1 At least one hour prior to sailing, the vessel is to be prepared for departure as follows using the departure checklist, a copy of which is attached.

(a) Check on necessary calls of personnel.
(b) Set bridge clocks. Give time check to engine room. Test engine order telegraph, telephone, and console alarms.
(c) Test whistles and general alarm.
(d) Check that rudder and propeller are clear. Test steering gear on each motor and leave on last side tested.
(e) Check master gyro compass heading and synchronize all gyro repeater headings with master gyro. Compare magnetic compass headings with gyro compass heading. Place azimuth circles/alidades on bridge wing repeaters and check lighting.
(f) Energize and check for proper operation: radars and fathometer. Unlock satellite navigator and set. Check that all instrument lights are operative.
(g) Test navigation lights.
(h) Check transmission and reception on VHF channels 13 and 16. Set any third channel required to be monitored. Set all volume controls.
(i) Lay out binoculars, flashlights, and walkie-talkies. Have charts in order of use in chart table drawers, with current chart on chart table. Lay out chart instruments and necessary publications.

(j) Hoist necessary flag/light signals and lay out others that may be required.

(k) Obtain crew muster and check that ship's papers and port clearance are aboard. Confirm that tanker safety checklist is completed and signed by master.

(l) Energize bow thrusters twenty minutes before sailing.

(m)Prepare the master/pilot exchange form if using the services of a pilot.

(n) Ensure that the departure draft is obtained as soon as all cargo and trimming operations have been completed.

(o) Immediately prior to departure ensure that the steering gear compartment is manned by a licensed engineer and a qualified helmsman.

(p) As soon as possible get a stowaway report from each department head.

12.2 Record all tests and proceedings in the bell book. The bridge must not be left unattended once the gear has been tested.

13. Preparation for Arrival

13.1 At least one hour prior to arrival the vessel is to be prepared as follows using the arrival checklist, a copy of which is attached.

(a) Give the engine room one hour notice of arrival. Synchronize bridge and engine room clocks. Request power on deck. Test engine order telegraph and steering gear.

(b) Check on necessary calls of personnel for arrival duties, clearing of hawse pipes, removing anchor lashings, etc.

(c) Check that all necessary navigation equipment is working and ready for use. Have necessary charts and publications ready for use. Monitor appropriate VHF distress and calling channels. If appropriate, contact pilot station, provide ETA and confirm details of pilot embarkation.

(d) Prepare pilot embarkation gear and accommodation/pilot ladder.

(e) Hoist or prepare any necessary signal flags. Check and lay out walkie talkies.

(f) Open bow thruster vent covers and clear controls. Energize when required.

(g) Prepare pilot. Master exchange form.

13.2 Record all tests and proceedings in the bell book.

14. Bridge Logs And Records

14.1 *Bell book*—maintained by second officer and used by watch officers. Entries to be made during arrival and departure periods or when otherwise maneuvering. Enter all actions and movements of the vessel in detail as a complete record in itself of the time period covered. Extract the necessary entries for entering in the log book.

14.2 *Compass error record book*—maintained by second officer and used by watch officers. Enter details of compass errors obtained during each watch.

14.3 *Chronometer record book*—maintained by second officer and used by watch officers. Record time signals taken and details of chronometer errors. At least one time signal to be taken every twenty-four hours

14.4 *Deck log book*—maintained by second officer and used by watch officers. Entries to be made immediately after each watch.

14. 5 *Master's night order book*—specific instructions that I will require to be carried out by the watch officer when I am not on the bridge day or night. All night orders are to be read and understood and signed to that effect by watch officers prior to assuming their watch.

14.6 *Radar log*—maintained by second officer and used by watch officers. Entries to be made of targets plotted.

14.7 *VHF radio log*—maintained by second officer and used by watch officers. Enter each message transmitted and received with GMT date and time, frequency, channel, station contacted, reception, operator, and message content.

15.   Bridge Forms

15.1 *Departure, passage and arrival forms*—made up by watch officer on arrival and departure at each port. (Engine information will be provided by chief engineer.) One copy each to master and chief engineer.

15. 2 *Noon position slips*—noon position and days run information to be worked by second officer and third officer. Second officer to complete official slips. Original and four copies to be made, original for retention on bridge, copies to master, chief engineer, officers bulletin board, and crew bulletin board.

15.3 *Passage plan*—made up by second officer prior to commencing passage. Original and two copies. Original on chart table. One copy for file and one to master.

15.4 *Pilot/master information exchange form*—made up by watch officer prior to embarking pilot. Given to pilot when he boards and contents explained to him. Signed and retained by pilot. Entry must be made in bell book stating that the form has been given to the pilot.

15.5 *Navigation record log*—made up by watch officers during their watches and verified daily by the second officer's signature.

(Originally Signed)
John Merchant Mariner
Master
M/V *CAPELLA*
Dated 22 May 2008
New York

Index

A

Abandon ship, 91
Action by give-way vessel, 78
  stand-on vessel, 79
Admiral Nakhimov/P. Vasev collision,
  184–186
Admiralty Seamanship Manual,
  115–116
Anchoring, 12, 120–122. *See also* Arrivals and departures
Andrea Doria/Stockholm collision,
  167–179
Approaching, 121–122
  berth, 123–124
  pilot station, 122–123
Arrivals and departures, 127
  communication, 128
  making ready, 129
    anchoring, 129
    echo sounder, 129
    landfall, 129
    position fixing, 129
    windlass, 129
  preparations for arrival in port,
    131–133
Assuming the watch
  at anchor, 208
  at sea, 207
Automated Merchant Vessel Emergency
  Rescue (AMVER), 148
Automatic Identification System
  (AIS), 20–22,192
Automatic pilot, 23–24
Azimuthal Propulsion, 125

B

Beaufort wind scale, 107, 108–11
Binoculars, 24–25
Boarding of pilot at sea, 130
Bridge equipment, 20–38
  future, 39
Bridge organization, 127–128
Bridge simulation training, 149–150,
  164

C

"Coast-in method", 119
Calling the master, 86, 206–207
Charts and sailing directions, 130
Collision, 92
  action to avoid, 75–76
  avoidance tasks, 8
  risk of, 74–75
COLREGS, 12, 73
Commands to the helmsman, 102–103
Communication, 128
Compasses, 25
Convoys, 116–118
Course recorder, 25
Cross-index range, 52

D

Debriefing, 155–157, 163–164
Deck log. *See* Recordkeeping
Departure, 141–143
Doppler speed log, 25–26

E

Echo sounder (fathometer), 30–31. *See
  also* Arrivals and departures
Electronic chart display and Information system (ECDIS), 26–29
Emergencies, 91–99
  abandon ship, 91
  bridge control/telegraph failure, 92
  collision with navigational aid, 92
  engine failure, 94
  fire, 93
  flooding, 93
  gyro failure/compass failure, 93–94
  man overboard, 94
  steering failure, 94

stranding, 95
Engine
  failure, 94
  types, 124–125

F

Fathometer. *See* Echo sounder (fath-
    ometer)
Fire. *See* Emergencies
Flashlight, 31
Flooding. *See* Emergencies

G

Global Positioning System (GPS),
    34–37, 192
Gyro failure/compass failure.
    See Emergencies

H

Handing over the watch, 209
Heatstroke. *See* Survival
Heavy weather. *See* Weather
Helicopter evacuation checklist, 96–98
Hellenic Carrier, 179–181
Helm orders, 101–103
Hurricane evasion, 98–99
Hypothermia. *See* Survival

I

Ice navigation, 99
  tasks, 11
In-port watch, 136–141
Inter-Governmental Maritime Consul-
    tative Organization (IMCO), 73
International Marine Simulation Fo-
    rum Conference, 151
International Maritime Lecturers As-
    sociation, 222

K

Kick, 104

L

Landfall, 129
Lash Atlantico/Hellenic Carrier colli-
    sion, 169–174
Lookout, 209–210
LORAN, 211

M

M/V *Capella*, 204–217
Maneuvering printer, 31
Man Overboard, 94
Maritime Preposition Ship Squadrons,
    116
Master/pilot information exchange,
    131–133
Movement (bell) book, 71

N

Nakhimov, 184–186
National Marine Electronics Association
    (NMEA) position receivers,
    184
National Transportation Safety Board,
    151
Navigation
  coastal waters, 199–200
  navigation tasks, 8
  pilot embarked, 200
  recordkeeping, 60–72
  safety, 14–15
  tasks, 8
  tropical storm, 11, 98–99
  with pilot on board, 131
Navigation Satellite Timing and
    Ranging (NAVSTAR), 36

O

Open sea, 6–13
  change of watch (being relieved), 6
  changing watch (before relieving), 7
  collision avoidance tasks, 8
  communication tasks, 10
  heavy weather tasks, 10
  ice navigation tasks, 11
  navigation tasks, 8
  safety/casualty tasks, 10
  ship control tasks, 10

tropical storm area navigation tasks, 11

visual monitoring tasks, 7

P

Parallel indexing techniques, 47
  application, 50–57
  basic principle, 47
  echo deviation from line, 49–50
  item required, 47
  notes on use, 57–58
  technique, 47–48
Passage plan (planning), 41–47
  principles of, 45
    appraisal, 42–43
    execution, 45–46
    monitoring, 46–47
    planning, 43–45
  responsibility for, 41–42
Pilotage, 40–41
Port log, 69–70
Position Fixing, 129
Precise positioning service (PPS), 37
Preparing for and standing watch, 13
Propellers, 125–126
Propulsion considerations, 124–126

R

Racal-Decca simulator, 150
Radar (radio detection and ranging), 31–33
Radio direction bearing fix (RDF), 175
Rate of turn indicator (ROT), 33–34
Recordkeeping, 60–72
  deck log, 60
  entries, 72
  movement (bell) book, 71
  port log, 69–70
  sea log, 67–69
Restricted visibility, 83–85, 155, 200, 214
Restricted waters, 11–12
  anchoring/docking /undocking, 12
  changing watch (before and upon relief), 6–7
  collision avoidance tasks, 12
  communication tasks, 12
  navigation tasks, 12

visual monitoring tasks, 11–12
Revolution per minute (RPM), 33
Royal Majesty, 182–184
Rudder angle indicator, 34–35

S

Safety/casualty tasks, 10
Satellite navigator (SATNAV), 35–37
Sea log, 67–69
Seaman's eye, 101
Search and rescue, 100
SEASPEAK, 86–89
Securing bridge, 135
Ship control tasks, 10
Simulator training, bridge, 149–150, 164
  control station requirements, 158
  debrief, 155–156, 163–164
  gallery, 160
  general layout, 158–159
  monitor, 160–162
  using the CAORF Simulator, 150–155
Standard Positioning Service (SPS), 37
Standards of Training, Certification and Watchkeeping for Seafarers (STCW), 3–4
Steering and sailing rules, 73–82
  action by give-way vessel, 78–79
  action by stand-on vessel, 79–81
  action to avoid collision, 75–76
  crossing situation, 78
  head-on situation, 77–78
  lookout, 73–74
  restricted visibility, 83–85
  risk of collision, 74–75
Steering Failure, 94
STN Atlas, 183
Stockholm, 169–179
Stranding, 95
Survival, 95–96
  heatstroke, 95
  hypothermia, 95–96

T

Torrey Canyon, 23
Transit in pilotage, 144

Tropical storm area navigation tasks, 11
Turning circles, 103–104
  acceleration and deceleration rates, 104
  advance, 104
  drift angle, 104
  final diameter, 104
  kick, 104
  pivot point, 104
  tactical diameter, 104
  transfer, 104

U

U.S. Maritime Administration, 151
UK Department of Transport, 150
Underway replenishment, 118–120
United States Code of Federal Regulations, 15

V

Vertigo, 186–191
Very high frequency (VHF), 34–35
  procedures, 85–86
Voyage planning, 40, 43–45
  appraisal, 42–43
  execution, 45–46
  monitoring, 46–47
  pilotage, 40–41
  principles of, 42
  responsibility for, 41–42

W

watch, preparing for and standing the, 13–17
Watchkeeping, 3–4
  deck officers, 4–5
  new ABs, lifeboatman, and ordinary seaman, 5
  new mate, 5
  preparation, 15–17
  standing orders, 17
Watch officers duties in port, 136–141
watch personnel, 209
Watchstanding tasks, 5–12
Weather, 105–116

concerns for watch officer, 113–115
  heavy, 115–116
whole task training, 154–155
Windlass, 129

Z

Z-Card, 4–5
Ziemia Lodzka/Vertigo collision, 186–192

ABOUT THE AUTHOR

Robert J. Meurn, Master Mariner and Captain, U.S. Naval Reserve (Ret), received his Bachelor of Science in Nautical Science from the U.S. Merchant Marine Academy (USMMA), Kings Point NY, and his Master of Arts in Higher Education from George Washington University. He taught at Texas Maritime Academy, was Commandant of Cadets and Executive Officer of the TS Texas Clipper, and was selected as Teacher of the Year in 1978. In 1979, he began his tenure as associate professor at the U.S. Merchant Marine Academy. During 1981, he devised and implemented the first watch-standing course in the United States for cadets utilizing the CAORF simulator. Capt. Meurn also served as Dept. Head, Nautical Science Division and was honored again as Teacher of the Year in 1983 and 2003.

Capt. Meurn has authored four books: *Marine Cargo Operations* (4th edition), *Watchstanding Guide for the Merchant Officer* (3rd edition), *Survival Guide for the Mariner* (2nd edition) and *Anatomy of a Collision* (2013). He was honored by receiving the Dept. of Transportation's Bronze Medal Award and the first ever recipient of the Distinguished Service Medal for his contributions to safety in marine transportation.

He has sailed with U.S. Lines, Farrell Lines, American Export Lines, Moore McCormick Line, Grace Lines, and Military Sealift Command. A relief chief mate and master with Military Sealift Command/Atlantic, he was an active member of the U.S. Naval Reserve, where his last active duty was as a vice commodore during a convoy exercise in December 1988 in Diego Garcia.

Capt. Meurn is a member of, and has presented papers to, the International Navigation Simulator Lecturers Conference (INSLC) worldwide. He is also a member of the Marine Board, National Research Council's Committee on ship/bridge simulation training. Currently, he is a Professor Emeritus in the Department of Marine Transportation at the U.S. Merchant Marine Academy.